"You Wanna Go To Willard?"

Visit www.booksurge.com to order additional copies.

LINDA M HOLBROOK

Gerry,
Thank you for
our friendship &
guidence.
love
Lenda
M. Holbrook

"YOU WANNA GO TO WILLARD?"

2008

"You Wanna Go To Willard?"

To My Friend Anne, Who Always Knew And Understood.

Special Thanks To My Support Committee:

Heather
Jeanne
Pat

"YOU WANNA GO TO WILLARD?"

The darkness around me confuses my senses. I am moving, but my arms and legs are still. I think my eyes are open, but I can't see anything. I feel awake but incoherent. My breathing is fast and labored. People are pulling at me and taking me somewhere, but where? I want to wake up from this unsettling dream, but I can't.

BANG, WHOOSH! What was that?

WAKE UP—WAKE UP—WAKE UP! (My subconscious voice screamed at me!)

I tried to look at my surroundings. Where am I? Why is everything all white like I am in a thick fog? Is this heaven? Wait! Something just brushed by me. A shadow, now two with muffled voices, and now everything seems so bright I have to cover my closed eyes. The voices are getting louder. There are several of them coming closer to me, but I don't want to look.

Suddenly someone grabs my arms and the voice starts screaming at me saying something I don't understand. I didn't know this voice; I struggle to listen closer and the voice, now in loud hostile tone, saying **"You wanna go to Willard?"**

I open my eyes to see a stranger. He has a tight grip on my arms and is shouting at me, **"You wanna go to Willard?"**

Suddenly my thoughts are on Willard, the mental institution. It is one of "those" places where they send people that aren't "normal" and can't be around "normal" people. They put them in straight jackets and lock them in rooms like cells. Then the "normal" people caring for them don't hear their screams and cries. Some of the rooms are padded so the retards (that's what the "normal" people called them) don't hurt themselves as they slam their bodies against the walls in frustration. Why is this guy asking me about Willard? Why does he think I should be in Willard? I'm not one of those people! What's going on?

I look around and realize I am in a hospital. The guy holding my arms is dressed in a white coat with a stethoscope draped around his neck. Obviously he is a doctor, and now he is looking right into my eyes.

"What?" I asked.

He asked me again in a softer tone, "Do you want to go to Willard?"

I looked at the doctor and said quietly, "No."

"Okay." he said, "You need to calm down. What started this?"

I started to think of events from earlier in the evening. Slowly the events of the night started flooding my mind. I started telling him about the fight with my parents. I came home late and my mother was angry. She grabbed me and ripped my shirt. We were yelling at each other and she was angrier than I had ever seen her before. I wanted to get away, but she kept yelling. I couldn't do anything right. My brother told her lies about me. I was always in trouble with her. As I rambled this all into one long breath, I started sobbing again. I knew the doctor was having a hard time understanding me now, but he changed the subject by asking me more questions. How old I was, did I work, was that my boyfriend outside?

My focus changed as I answered his questions and inquired, "What boyfriend?"

"The young man standing in the hall with the older man, I presume to be your father." He replied.

I remembered the evening had unfolded with Ted, my boss' nephew, on the scene and actually the cause of this whole event. I informed the doctor he was a friend from work, not my boyfriend.

"I'm giving you a shot so you will calm down and sleep. You need some rest. You will feel better tomorrow." He said.

He left the room.

I could hear him in the hall saying, "She is stressed to the point of nearly having a nervous breakdown. I think living at home seems to be causing her problems. She said she's not allowed to leave home? Is that true?"

I could hear Dad's voice, low and muffled, but I couldn't hear what he said.

"She needs some rest." The doctor said. "I gave her a tranquilizing shot to make her sleep. Just let her sleep through it, but I suggest easing some of the pressure she is feeling. If she wants to move to her own place you need to let her so she can get on with her life. If you need anything, please call me, but I'm sure she'll be fine."

The shot started to kick in. I felt very woozy. In my blurred vision I saw my friend Ted walk into the room, I assume, to push my wheelchair to the car.

Completely exhausted, my whole body felt sore and cold. Sleep sounded good to me, but I wanted a blanket. I tried convincing myself this was all a dream. I would wake up to find it never happened. That's it…it's just a bad dream; it isn't real. I drifted off to sleep!

SAFE PLACE—NOT SAFE

It was Sunday and a beautiful spring day in rural upstate New York. I sat, on a rock next to a little creek that trickled through the pastures of my father's dairy farm. This was my favorite place and today was my birthday. I came here as often as I could to get away from the farm routine. I would just sit and listen to the sounds of Mother Nature and think about things. The creek wasn't really a creek. It was a large ditch dressed up with green grassy banks, tufts of wild flowers, weeds and big rocks scattered along it as it made its way into the swamp. I sat on the rocks often. On sunny days, it looked like a paradise to me. There were shades of green peppered with dandelions and sparkles bouncing off the rocks as the sun illuminated the tiny flat spots on their jagged surfaces. It was beautiful here. I came here to pretend, to talk to myself, and often dream of what I could be when I grew up. It was fun. I could be something different every time. Best of all, I was alone. There was no one to boss me, tease me, tattle on me or laugh at me.

I started thinking about what a perfect birthday would be like. I would have a party. It wouldn't have to be expensive. I didn't care about that, but it would be very special. Everyone would remember it and greet me with "Happy Birthday, Laura!" Maybe it would be a surprise birthday party just like the ones on TV. I'd enter the room and everyone would yell, "Surprise!" There'd be decorations, lots of people and special little presents that might be handmade or picked out just for me. Each one wrapped in colorful paper with ribbons, bows and little tiny cards. The cards would give a warm wish or funny remark. We all would laugh and dance and have a wonderful time for hours.

FACE IT, LAURA—THAT'S A DREAM. IT DOESN'T REALLY HAPPEN!

"Thank you subconscious for bursting my little dream bubble again!" I complained loud.

SORRY, I'M JUST REMINDING YOU WHAT IS REAL. YOU'RE A FARM KID. YOU'RE REALLY NOT AN ATTRACTIVE ONE

EITHER. THE KIDS AT SCHOOL ALL THINK YOU'RE WEIRD. THREE STRIKES AND YOU'RE OUT, YA KNOW.

"Look, the reason I come here is to dream. No one else knows I do it. Sometimes I just like to dream, okay? So leave me alone for a while!" I responded angrily.

YOU DREAM TOO MUCH.

I'd often thought how exciting it would be to write a book. I didn't know the first thing about how to do it, or what to write about. I'd seen people on TV who had done it. How exciting it would be if I could be on TV. Maybe the Johnny Carson show. I could hear him asking me questions like, "Laura, tell us what was the inspiration for your book?"

I could use a very sophisticated movie star voice, "Well, darling..."

I started to laugh out loud as I rolled my head up toward the sky, distracting me with its beauty. The sky was a collage of huge white billowy clouds floating in an ocean of shimmering deep sapphire blue. The brilliant sun was shining on my face. Peaceful, serene, safe, but suddenly a mental message zaps through my head like a leopard after a kill. *The sun is low, it must be chore time.*

DON'T BE LATE OR YOU'LL BE IN TROUBLE!

I lowered my head from the brilliant sky. I sensed something. An uneasy feeling, like someone was watching me or standing behind me. I didn't know what it could be. I was suddenly scared. Slowly I looked down at the grass-covered ground to jump off the rock. There, to the left of my foot, a **snake**. I screamed and jumped. I landed in front of two more.

DON'T LOOK DOWN! DON'T LOOK AT THE GROUND AND YOU WON'T SEE THEM. LOOK TOWARD THE HOUSE AND RUN AS FAST AS YOU CAN!

I did as I was told. I looked at the house that now appeared to be miles away. I was running as fast as I could. It felt like I was running in slow motion. I wanted to be back to the house, but couldn't get there fast enough.

"Please, please dear God; help me get away from here." I prayed.

The time seemed long until I finally reached the yard behind the house. I stopped to catch my breath. I looked back at the little creek. I felt sad. I knew I could never go back to the little creek again. The snakes were there now.

*THEY HAVE ALWAYS BEEN THERE, STUPID. YOU JUST
NEVER SAW THEM BEFORE!*

"That may be true, but I saw them today. I don't want to see
them again. I'll never be able to go back there, never." I declared with
disappointment.

Chore time came and passed only to be followed by supper, as usual.
I had forgotten about my birthday after the shock of the snakes. Everyone
came in from the barn and we took our usual spots at the table. Suddenly
I noticed all my favorite foods: mashed potatoes, meat loaf, lima beans,
warm rolls, and applesauce. This is great! Then I realized. It was still my
birthday! Mom always made our favorite meal for our birthday supper.

While we ate supper, Dad talked about farm events they finished
today, what was left to do tomorrow and the things that need to be done
before it rained. Not that it was going to rain, mind ya, but Dad always
covered everything just in case. My Dad was a typical Dutchman: not
very tall, about 5' 8 or 9" with a husky middle, sandy brown hair, a
round face that he shaved about once a week, and a deep tan year-round
from his eyebrows down. He had the whitest forehead I'd ever seen. He
always, always wore a hat. I don't think his forehead ever absorbed a ray
of sunlight! His bib overalls, tied at his shoe tops with baling twine kept
the field dirt, barn sawdust and hay chaff from getting into his shoes.
They were his trademark.

My two older brothers listened to Dad's every word. They were as
different as night as day or day and night. Lyle had a lot of physical
similarities to Dad except the grown up parts. His facial hair was only
peach fuzz and he doesn't fit in dad's bibs yet. Lyle's hair was darker, but
he had the same square Dutch face (without that white forehead). Dick,
two years younger, was thinner, lighter-haired and often broke the rules
of expected behavior. There were horror stories about Dick misbehaving
and everyone always laughed. I always wondered why he didn't get
punished for those shenanigans.

Dad finished discussing the work schedule with the boys, while my
little sister, being her usual self, shined up to Dad like she always did.
Sometimes she could be a real brat, even at seven years old. Mom got up
from the table and went to the stove for something. She came back with
my birthday cake and placed it in front of me.

There weren't any candles, but that was normal. I knew it was banana nut, because that was my favorite. I cut the first hearty piece for myself.

"Happy Birthday" Mom said.

"Thank you" I replied happily.

Mom wasn't quite as tall as Dad and had darker hair, blue eyes and with English and Irish ancestry. She was strong built for a woman, but then she did farm work as a child and wife and mother.

I shoveled the fork full of cake into my mouth. Dad tried to be funny by asking "birthday questions." "How old are you now? Are we going to be seeing the boys hanging around? We'd better keep an eye on that, don't you think?" I just looked up at him and smiled. My face glowed red with embarrassment as I felt the hurt deep down in my gut. I knew he was teasing, but he should have known that boys hanging around wouldn't happen because I was too dumb and ugly for that to be possible. Nobody, especially boys, looked at farm girls. Not even ones with tits, which I got for last year's birthday!

Mom finished cutting and serving the cake to everyone, and left the kitchen. She returned almost immediately with a huge box. It was just a plain box, but it seemed giant to me. It must have been a foot and a half wide and three feet tall. I couldn't begin to imagine what might be inside. Things on the farm were so busy this time of the year that I knew Mom had not been shopping. I wondered what she could have gotten for me that would fit in a box this big. My excitement grew in leaps and bounds. The top of the box was just folded shut. I quickly opened it. I looked inside to see wadded newspaper. I frantically pulled it out only to find more. Then, down in the corner, I saw one of my Dad's cigars. When I picked it up I felt a rubber band around the cigar. I quickly examine the cigar and found it wrapped with paper money of some kind. I frantically removed the rubber band to unfold a ten-dollar bill. I was in shock...$10.00, WOW! I felt immediately rich. I'd never had a $10.00 bill of my very own before. This was a great present! Everyone was laughing at my excitement over this simple $10.00 bill. It was wonderful. I said "thank you" a dozen times. I gave the cigar to Dad. What a great surprise! What a great birthday!

NOW THAT YOU ARE RICH, MAYBE YOU SHOULD WORK ON BECOMING FAMOUS AND BEAUTIFUL!

I was so pleased with the ten dollar bill that I put it away for safe keeping. I carefully tucked it in my jewelry box I made in 4-H.

TRIXIE'S BIRTHDAY SURPRISE—MINE TOO

It was the day before my sister's eighth birthday. Dad and I were filling milk cans with water in the back of the truck for the heifers at the other farm. For some reason we were talking about Trixie, who had always been Dad's favorite. Of course she was. She was the baby and she was so cute with her very curly blonde (almost white) hair, deep blue eyes and smiles that seem to get inside everyone. She really was a cute little kid, but it hurt because I always felt so ugly. Maybe it was because she being four years younger than me gave her puppy syndrome. Puppies are cute, but dogs are ugly. Even though relatives said we looked alike, I didn't feel that was true.

Dad was rattling on about what to give Trixie for her birthday. He asked me what I thought she might like. I gave him suggestions, but I could tell they weren't the ones he wanted to hear. Finally, he asked if I thought she might like a baby calf. I was speechless. For a moment all I felt was the flood of emotion fill my body like a Tsunami. I tried talking just to hold back the tears. I told him she would probably love the calf. I continued explaining why. I thought the calf was a good idea because she would be old enough by next summer to show at the fairs in 4-H classes (the qualifying age to show was 9). I thought she would be really excited about it. I felt a gut wrenching pain from the idea. Dad was visibly pleased with my response. It was very apparent he wanted to give her the calf for her birthday. I had just gotten my first calf in April and I had been old enough to show for 3 years!

I helped him finish filling the cans and he went to the barn. I walked to the edge of the yard where I could look at my little creek. I had not gone there since I saw the snakes. I swore I wouldn't go back, but I wished I could go there now to cry. My Dad never seemed to have any time for me except when there were chores to get done. I was hurt that he could concentrate on Trixie so much. Dad obviously thought about her more than I ever imagined. Suddenly I felt like a hired man more than ever.

I stood and stared at the creek a long time before I decided I would not go there. I went into the loft of the barn instead. It was half-full of hay, but no people. I just want to be alone for a while. I went into the hay mow and sat on a bale of hay in front of the big doors that opened to the west. I could see the rocks by the creek. There was no subconscious, no people. I felt alone, sad, and really hurt. I just needed to cry.

I thought about Mom, Dad, Trixie and the boys. It seemed like everybody had time for Trixie and the boys, but I was just chore help. I tried to think of things I had done to make them not like me. I had always done exactly what they asked and worked really hard to get everything they wanted done. I didn't talk back or show disrespect in any way. I didn't even disagree with any of them. I didn't feel like I was being treated equally. I often thought maybe I was retarded. I wasn't sure what made you retarded, but I knew people treated retards different from regular people. They usually laugh at them behind their backs and make fun of them. That is exactly what my family does to me. I didn't understand. I could only conclude that somehow I was different; retarded. I just couldn't figure out how I got that way.

My mind raced. Thoughts flew back to painful events of my past. Maybe if I could relive some of those events I would be able to make sense of everything.

The first event I remembered was a time in kindergarten. It was spring. Dick and I had been outside trying to play baseball. He would practice batting by hitting the ball onto the chicken house roof. When the ball rolled off the roof, I would get it and take it back to him so he could hit it again. While I waited for the hit, I walked on some boards Dad had just bought for some calf pens. As Dick swung the bat it slammed into my head, hitting me just above my left eye and instantly knocked me to the ground.

As I slowly picked myself up, I could see shocked expression on Dick's face. I reached up with my left hand to touch my forehead where I felt a stinging sensation. I remembered feeling a lump that filled my hand, but there wasn't any blood. I thought I was okay. Dick took me by the hand and walked over to our brother, Lyle, who was mowing the lawn.

Lyle was always our leader, and when Dick showed him the lump, he asked, "Do you think we have to tell Mom?"

Lyle, also with a shocked expression, confirmed we had to tell Mom. All three of us marched into the house. Lyle did the explaining, like he usually did, and Mom told the boys to go back outside. She put a cold cloth on my head and told me to hold it while she called the doctor. When she got off the phone she told me I didn't have to see him as long as I felt okay (which I did), but Mom put clean clothes on me anyway and told me to lie on the couch for a while with a fresh cold cloth.

This incident didn't seem like such a big deal until a few days later when I had to go to school with the worst pair of black eyes I had ever seen. I couldn't look in the mirror for a while because it was just too scary. The kids on the bus and at school would stare at me, make fun of my face and call me "raccoon." It seemed like it took forever for my eyes to look normal again. I didn't play baseball with Dick any more.

My mind continued playing flashbacks. I remembered the time in second grade when the school nurse told our teacher that we would be getting our eye exams that day. I didn't think too much about it because I could see just fine. One by one we went out in the hall and stood with our backs against one side of the hall and read the chart the nurse was holding on the other side. We had to hold a card over one eye and point in the direction the "E" was facing on the chart and then change the card to the other eye and do the same thing.

My turn came and out to the hall I went. I got the cards from the nurse and she told me to start pointing. I covered my right eye and read the whole chart with my left eye and did it perfectly with ease. Then I covered my left eye and realized I couldn't even see the chart, so I decided to point in a direction I hoped was right. Then thought about it and changed my mind. I remember pointing in all four directions, thinking I must have gotten at least one right. The nurse stopped the test and told me to go back to class. I thought I must have done really well because I was done quicker than the other kids.

I went back to class. After a while the teacher received a call on her intercom phone. She looked right at me during her conversation. When she hung up, she came over to me and told me my mother was there to pick me up to go home. Suddenly I was terrified. I didn't understand why my mother had to pick me up from school. I thought I must have been in some really bad trouble, but I couldn't figure out what I had done to get there. I went to the office and left school with Mom. In the car, she told me she had gotten a call from the nurse about my eye exam. She was taking me to the eye doctor right then. The nurse told her she thought I was blind in my right eye. I didn't understand—I could see just fine as long as I looked with both eyes.

We got to the eye doctor's office. He did a thorough examination. He determined I had a lazy eye. Typically, kids with a lazy eye had to wear a patch over one eye until the eye got better, but my doctor said he didn't like doing that. He treated lazy eye differently. I got to pick out new glasses. I was getting glasses. That would make me special.

The day came for me to pick up my glasses. When I put them on for the first time I thought they looked great. The doctor then put clear nail polish on the lens of my good (left) eye and put them back on my face. I could hardly see anything! Everything was so blurry I had to be hold onto things to walk. The doctor told Mom to watch me very carefully because I would be very unsure of my footing and visual judgment. He went on to say I would have to do exercises with my eyes every day. He would see me every week to check my progress. Now I was scared.

I went to school the next day and soon found out I wasn't as special as I thought. The kids were asking me what was wrong with my new glasses. Soon the curious questions turned into name calling. With the assistance of my brother, Dick, I was now called "four eyes" and it wouldn't stop. He always laughed after saying it, which really bothered me more than the name calling. I just had to take it for a while. Finally, I told Mom what he was doing and she told him to stop. He only stopped when she might hear him. It took a couple of years before it finally came to an end.

Now I cried in the hay mow. After taking some time to catch my breath, I went down to the main barn and began putting grain in the mangers. It was almost milking time. I didn't stop for the coffee (snack) break with everyone else; I just started chores. No one noticed.

***

Time passed and so did the hurt. I carried the scar, as my life continued. (I tried to understand what I was to do with my life.) But I felt some decisions were out of my hands. Fate would eventually guide me in the right direction to my destiny. I thought I'd endured the worst pain of my life at this point. Little did I know what lay ahead.

PLAY IT AGAIN!

School time was almost here. Show day at the state fair was over. I pondered school and the pressures I would again face…not the homework or bus riding or finding my new classrooms, but the kids. Classmates that would say mean things or treat me like I was a vagrant's kid. I just didn't seem to fit in anywhere—not at home, not at school, not anywhere. I knew the comments would start up again. They always did.

Comments like, "Oh, Laura, you have cow shit on your sneakers!"

It didn't matter if it was true or not or how much I washed my sneakers, they would still say those mean things and giggle. I didn't know why I wanted these kids to like me, but I did. It seemed like, in their eyes, I couldn't do anything right.

PUT YOUR HEAD BACK ON AND THINK OF SOMETHING ELSE. THERE IS MORE TO GOING BACK TO SCHOOL THAN THOSE KIDS' COMMENTS. THINK ABOUT WHAT YOU ARE GOING TO WEAR THE FIRST FEW DAYS OF SCHOOL. YOU NEED TO GO SHOPPING DON'T 'YA?

Yes, I did need to go shopping. I had my fair money and some baby-sitting money. I went to look at my $10.00 bill. I wondered if I should use it now? There were times I had thought of spending it, but always talked myself out of it. I thought I would save that $10.00 for my whole life, but it was nice to know I had extra if I decided to buy something.

I raised the top of my jewelry box and my heart sank. I stood in shock, paralyzed in horror. It was gone. My $10.00 bill was gone. I ransacked the jewelry box, then my dresser, the bed, under the bed, the closet, behind the furniture, and the little chest of drawers. I checked every spot in that tiny room. I finally sat on the edge of my bed and held my face in my hands trying to hold back tears. I struggled to rationalize what I could have done with the money.

I was alone and felt like I had just committed murder. I lost my $10.00. How could I have done that? Where would I have put it? I didn't remember moving it to another place. Could someone have stolen it. Maybe Randy took it. He was a high school kid that worked at the farm for the summer. I couldn't ask anyone about it because then I would have to admit it was gone. Everyone would think I was careless and just lost it. No one would ever believe me if I told them it had been stolen. They would say I was lying or I just forgot I spent it.

I thought about the time Mom accused me of stealing money. There was a small silver barrel coin bank with a slot in the top that allowed coins to go in, but wouldn't let them come out. There was a keyhole in the bottom so it could be emptied. I remember it was just about full of coins. My mother put it in the top drawer of my dresser for safe keeping. There were a lot of things in that drawer that were my Mom's things. I never could figure out what that funny funnel shaped glass thing with the rubber squeeze ball on the end was. (It was a breast pump). I just knew I wasn't to mess with the things in that top drawer because they belonged to Mom. So I didn't.

One day I was looking for something. When I opened the top drawer I saw the silver barrel with the top slot ripped away from the sides, all twisted and bent, and it was empty. I was horrified! Who stole the money? When did they take it? I was too scared to go to Mom and tell her. After all, it was in my room. Of course, she would think I stole the money. So, I just closed the drawer and pretended I never saw it.

It was a few months later when Mom was putting clothes away upstairs when she called for me. I went immediately upstairs and I could hear she was in my room. When I walked into the room I saw her standing in front of my dresser. The top drawer was open and the silver bank was in her hand. She had a very serious look on her face. She asked me if I broke the bank or knew anything about who did. I told her I didn't know anything about it except that I had found it a while ago and it was broken then. She asked again and I told her with all the genuine sincerity in my body that I had not. She then called for my sister to come into my bedroom and asked her the same questions. Trixie stood there looking so innocent. She said she had not done it, but suggested maybe one of the boys had. We knew Mom was mad, but she didn't punish us. She told us the bank was very special to her. She looked at me the whole time and told me, if I had done it, the best thing would be to tell the truth and admit what I had done. I told her again I didn't do it. She took it away and I never saw it again.

***

Five years later

It seemed like I had waited for this birthday, forever. I always wanted to be 17 years old. Now, tomorrow, I would finally to be 17! It felt great! I wanted to shout, squeal, scream I was so excited.

NOBODY HEARS YOU, 'YA KNOW. THIS ISN'T A BIG IMPORTANT EVENT. MOST KIDS ARE CELEBRATING AT 18, NOT 17. YOU'RE A STRANGE ONE.

Well, I didn't care that other people thought I was strange or weird, at least not today. I was delighted to be 17.

"Leave me alone, today!" I protested.

GOT IT, ALREADY! NOW IF YOU DON'T GET MOVING, YOU'LL MISS THE BUS.

"All right, all right already."

I finished getting ready for school.

It was 7:30 AM when the bus rolled into the driveway. I flew out of the house. I found my friend, Barbara, and sat down, exhaling a sigh of relief that I made it on time. Barbara waited till I settled myself and my books before she started teasing me.

"Are you going to make it today or what?" She picks.

I smiled and assured her I would, but told her I wasn't an organizational expert and she would have to be patient. We laughed and she started telling me about a phone call she got from a guy asking her for a date. As she spoke my mind drifted. I thought about dates and guys. I analyzed every possible angle. I had a good figure, really. My measurements rolled out at 36-26-36. I fit into everything nicely. I was athletic and able to handle myself pretty well in all the girls' sports. I had very blonde hair almost too blonde. In the summer it was so light it looked white. My eyes were very blue. I had good teeth without braces. Yet, I didn't seem to fit in. Suddenly a voice breaks my concentration.

"Hey, are you getting off the bus or what?" Barbara remarks.

I guess she had been talking to me all the way to school. I was so engrossed in my thoughts that I didn't hear a word she said. I passed it off as something about her boyfriends that I didn't need to hear anyway. Although, I thought it would be nice if I could have a decent boyfriend.

But I was a farm girl and farm girls were only good for farm boys. Which I was not interested in. Farm boys were in the same group as me. They were considered to be dumb, not well dressed, and worked in smelly places. That's probably why all the town kids put me down. My clothes, for the most part, were hand-me downs. I didn't wear enough make-up. My life was different. I just wished I could have been more like them so I could be their friend.

FORGET IT, LAURA. GET YOUR BUTT TO CLASS. YOU THINK TOO MUCH!

***

Fourth Period Gym Class

I changed into my red gym suit quickly, like always. The "quick changers" could shoot baskets or play some one-on-one basketball before class. Mrs. Noffe, the gym teacher, came out of her office a little earlier than usual. She saw me on the floor and walked toward me. I looked and waited for the sound of her whistle signaling lineup to begin warm up exercises. Instead, she motioned to me.

I walked over. She asked, "Laura, could I speak with you in my office a moment?"

Panic hit my body like a runaway freight train.

MAYBE SHE WANTS YOU TO LEAD THE EXERCISES TODAY. SHE'S DONE THAT BEFORE, RIGHT?

Never in the privacy of her office though.

My mind raced to find an answer. Was it about softball tournaments? No, it couldn't be, it was too late in the year. Maybe...We reached her office while I struggled for an explanation. Her office was located under the gym bleachers. I always thought that to be an odd place to have an office, especially for a teacher. Her steps slowed as we entered the office. She turned to face me as she closed the door. My fear was strangling the life out of me.

"I wanted to talk to you about something personal," she said.

Now, I was absolutely horrified and really confused. Nobody ever talked about personal stuff with anybody and never with a teacher.

"I wanted to ask you if you used deodorant."

I was frozen. I could feel the blood rush to my face. I had to think... I had to respond. I was so embarrassed. I just wanted to evaporate. She stared at me, looking right into my eyes!

QUICK, ANSWER!

I responded the only way I could, "Ah...well...yes..." My voice stuttered.

I was lying. She knew I was lying. I had to lie. I couldn't say no. It just wouldn't come out.

"What kind is it?" she persisted.

"Oh, dear God, please give me an answer, please!" I silently pleaded.

Silence consumed me for a moment. I was unable to speak. I felt my face pulsating red.

"Ah...ah...I think it's Ladies Old Spice. My mom bought it," I squeaked out.

"Well, some mention has been made that you have an odor problem. Maybe you should try another brand, perhaps a stronger one. Be sure to bring one to class with you to freshen up after," She said with soft concern.

She knew I was lying about using deodorant, but she didn't let on. I could feel her empathy for me, but I felt the worst embarrassment of my life. My face was on fire, which meant it was glowing like a red hot poker. This was absolutely the worst day of my life! Nothing, past or present, could ever be worse than this moment.

"God, she's letting me off easy," I thought. I didn't realize I had B.O. in school! I didn't know. Why didn't I know? Why didn't I do something before this? Why didn't someone else tell me a long time ago? How am I going to get through class and the rest of the day? I STINK!!! God, this is horrible.

ALL RIGHT, ALL RIGHT—GET A GRIP—YOU CAN'T STAND HERE FROZEN IN THIS TEACHERS OFFICE. YOU HAVE TO LEAVE NOW! THINK OF SOMETHING NICE TO SAY AND GET OUT OF HERE!

"Sure. I ah, I didn't realize, I will buy some tonight." I finally responded.

She interrupted, "That's okay. I just wanted to mention it to you."

"Thanks," I replied as I turned to leave.

I wanted to say more, but I couldn't. I walked out onto the gym floor as she followed me and blew that whistle, calling the class to order. Barbara didn't get a chance to ask me what the teacher wanted and by the end of class she must have forgotten about it, unless she already knew. Why hadn't Barbara told me? She was my friend. She would have known.

I got through class with my arms glued to my ribs the rest of the day. I didn't say much to anyone, even Barbara. I thought about it every minute. I knew I had to get to the store as soon as possible—tonight!

"God, please tell me, is this why everyone has been so distant?"

I was a dumb, <u>stinky</u>, farm kid. God, I hated myself. Why didn't Mom ever tell me? I felt like dirt. Why didn't I know? Why couldn't I smell it?

Eight PM—Chores were done. I changed quickly, and went to the store.

BE CAREFUL WHAT YOU IMPLY...

Barbara and I planned to go "cruising" to celebrate my 17th birthday. I could now drive past 9 PM, and we wanted to look for guys to pick up.

DO YOU KNOW WHAT TO DO WITH THEM AFTER YOU PICK THEM UP?

I picked her up around 8 PM. We went to get something to eat at Freddie's Drive-In Restaurant, the place where they serve you while you sit in your car. Dad would to take us there during hay season when Lyle, Dick and I would spend the day in the hay mow stacking bales of hay in temperatures of 100 degrees or more. All of us would get banana splits for supper. Tonight Barbara and I were on our own. We were getting banana splits and kicking up our heels a little too—by trying to pick up some guys.

Barbara was a pretty girl. Maybe not gorgeous, but she always had the latest looks in makeup, even though Mom said she used way too much face paint. She had black hair, but it was thin. She always wore it teased up on top so it looked really high, but I could see through the high mound. I felt tall compared to her, but I think she was only an inch or two shorter than me. We were a pair. Her parents had a farm, but farming was a hobby, as her dad now worked for the state on the road crew. We lived close to each other and our families had been friends for years. Barbara had really nice parents. They were soft spoken, loving people with a great sense of humor. Often times we would spend time laughing and telling stories when I went there to visit. I enjoyed going there.

We were off to town with my parent's car. It was a silver 1964 4-door Plymouth Fury that had one of those push-button automatic transmissions. Pretty classy for a farm kid, but I'd be passing myself off as a town kid tonight. We drove to Freddie's and parked in the center of the parking area. There were always kids hanging out and this night was no exception. We ordered our banana splits and they were soon delivered. We ate, making snide comments about the kids hanging out. We noticed another car pulled up on the right. It was full of guys. A couple of them got out and started talking to others. They eyed us several times. Barbara and I verbally size them up. Barbara was really good at creating detailed rating systems for guys. We both agree that these guys are attractive— not prom kings, but not dogs either. They looked to be in sports of some kind, because they had this "cool" body motion, which mean one or two things. One, they were real hip with the times and smoked marijuana; or two, they watched some really cool guys and tried to act like them, but didn't have a clue what they were doing. They waited until we finished our ice cream before they approached the car.

"Hi, I'm Jerry." He announced.

"Hi, I'm Laura." I replied.

WHAT ARE YOU DOING? HE ONLY CAME OVER TO TALK TO YOU BECAUSE YOU ARE THE DRIVER OF A NEARLY NEW CAR, STUPID!

I dismissed the comment. I didn't care why. I just wanted to be noticed for whatever reason. The boys asked if we had plans. Barbara and I looked at each other. I wanted Barbara to answer, seeing as she had more practice at this than I did. She quickly turned to Greg (the other guy) and said we were just cruising around town tonight. The guys ask if they could go along with us. Barbara and I softly laughed and said "sure."

Barbara quickly got into the back with Glen. The guys were very quick to tell us they knew a great place we could go. We drove around town for a while, but soon found ourselves on a road that seemed more like a path. My mind raced.

THIS PATH IS TRAVELLED LESS THAN THE ONE THE COWS USE GETTING TO THE BACK PASTURE!

Quietly I thought to myself, you're right—I'm not **that** stupid.

We drove to a point where we couldn't go any further. The guys suggested we park for a while.

LAURA, WHAT ARE YOU DOING? GET OUT OF HERE AND GET RID OF THESE TWO SEX MOOCHERS. THEY JUST WANT TO GET LAID—CAN'T YOU SEE THAT?

I knew my subconscious was right, but I had Barbara to consider too. What if she wanted to stay? Jerry was now kissing me tenderly and making moves with his hands. I could barely hear Barbara in the back seat. I thought she was trying to discourage Glen. I waited…

Things began to get more intense. I was ready to tell this guy to go find himself a whore and get it over with.

"I'm not your free piece of ass tonight." I whispered in his ear.

"No, no…I'm not that kind of guy. I just wanted to be close to you and…" he rebounded.

OH, YES HE IS…GET OUT OF HERE. GET OUT OF HERE NOW!

I thought my subconscious yelled so loud that Barbara heard it.

She suddenly piped up from the back, "We need to get out of here."

She opened the door and climbed out of the back seat. She opened the passenger door of the front seat and told Jerry to get in the back. He followed orders as Barbara climbed in saying, "Let's go."

We proceeded to leave this dark, secluded area. Barbara asked the guys where they wanted to be dropped off. They hemmed and hawed. We thought maybe they were adjusting their pants to accommodate their erections. They mentioned a party of a friend. But when we tried to find it, there was no party.

Suddenly, they blurted out, "Oh, we can get out right here."

I pulled to the curb and they got out. As we drove away we laughed about what asses they were. We didn't need to look for guys any more! Barbara turned to retrieve our purses from the back where we left them. She quickly realized the guys had robbed us. We're furious. We didn't have much money and these two scums weren't going to get away with what little we had.

Barbara suggests, "Let's go back and try to pick them up again. We'll tell them we changed our minds and that we really do want to be with them tonight."

"What do we have to lose?" I replied.

"Our money if we don't do this." Barb retorted.

So we went back to where we dropped them off. They hadn't gotten very far as we pulled up along side them. Barbara was very convincing…

"Hey, guys! You don't look like you have a party to go to and we are having second thoughts. We were just playing hard to get. Do you want to start over?"

The guys stood there for only a second when they scrambled for the car. Barbara stayed in the front. As soon as they piled in the back and shut the doors, I started driving like we are going to a fire. Barbara reeled around to confront the two. She hit the door locks and hung over the front seat close enough to spit in their faces as she yelled.

"You assholes took our money and we want it back. We are not as stupid as you think! Unload your pockets and give us our money or we'll take you to the police. Driving like this, it shouldn't take long to get their attention!" Barb spewed.

The guys turned white with fear. They gave Barbara dollars, change, and even my silver dollar. We kept them in the car as we raced through the streets. Barbara was still screaming at them when I got hung up behind cars at a red light. I cut into a parking lot. I soon realized there was no other exit. We were stuck. Jerry and Glen violently grabbed at the door locks. Their grips made contact after a couple of tries and missed passes, while ducking Barbara's attacks. Finally they opened both back doors and ran across the parking lot like they were running for their lives. Barbara and I just watched them run and in a few seconds they were gone. We looked at each other and started laughing uncontrollably.

My subconscious was now quiet, but I had a feeling it was smiling. We regained our composure and got out to close the rear doors. It was then I notice something hanging out of the door. It is my knitting yarn that I had from my Home Economics knitting class. It had been rolled up in a ball and was in the back seat. The guys must have kicked it out of the car during their escape. The yarn had rolled almost the entire distance of the parking lot like a trail for us to follow.

"Hey, look, my yarn!" I called to Barbara.

Off in the distant end of the parking lot sat this lone ball of Navy yarn. We just about wet our pants laughing. It took a few minutes to compose ourselves again as I rolled up the yarn. Our sides were aching from laughing so hard. We got back in the car when I noticed something across the street.

"Look." I said.

"What?"

"The building across the street…"

"Oh my God, it's the Police Station!" Barbara said with astonishment. "No wonder those guys ran so fast. They were probably crapping their pants!"

We broke down laughing once again.

We cruised around town for a little while and soon went home. We decided we didn't need to "pick up" guys ever again.

My birthday present turned out to be a lesson in life. Happy Birthday to me!

***

The close of the school year would bring the normal summer routine very quickly. The Brown Swiss Canton Show was first and the county fairs would immediately follow. Dick and I were the main workers to get things together for the shows. I had a good chance to win some classes with my cow, Brenda. She was looking real good this year. Brenda was a little smaller in size than other cows in her 2-year-old class, but she had a very dairy top line, a tight fore udder, a full balanced rear udder, nice teat placement, good legs and a very dairy head and neck. In translation: her backbone was really straight, she was a little boney and pointed at her shoulder, her full-bodied boobs didn't sag, she had nice nipples, she stood up straight, she didn't have a turkey neck, and was blessed with nice facial bone structure.

The Brown Swiss Canton Show was a show only for Brown Swiss cows. Throughout the state they were separated for competition by regions. It was usually held at a large farm or fairgrounds in various locations within the region. Professional photographers took pictures of the winners of each class at each regional show. The regional winners would compete (via photographs) with other region winners to later be awarded state honors by the state association board of directors. The state winners were given the prestigious title of New York State Bellringers (this meant the animals were the best Brown Swiss for each class in the state.) There were advantages for the farmer earning these awards. It would generate sales of the offspring or the animals themselves selling for higher prices. Usually these awards went to the larger, more elaborate farms, but sometimes, others would get lucky.

The show would last only one day because there weren't many registered Brown Swiss cows in each region. Regardless, it was still hard work. The animals would have to be loaded onto the truck, driven to the show, settled, fed and then prepped for the show which entailed spot washing them, brushing them, combing tails, putting show halters on them and praying they would lead properly in the show ring. That also meant wearing "whites" (the leadsman must wear white pants and shirts to present the animal in the ring). 4-H animals were shown at the same time as the adult classes and the awards were the usual trophies, rosette ribbons or banners. I didn't think too much about winning, but I did think about what had to be done. Dick and Dad would usually bag the cows for show (which meant they would figure how many hours of milk should be in their udders to look their best at the time their class or age group would show). The rest of the work would need to be done that day.

Dick and I did the showing—actually in that order. We always showed our own 4-H animals. Dick was the "pro" in a sense. He always had the best cows to show and I only got to show the one that was not likely to beat his if we had two in the same class.

The day, as always, would go by fast. Soon, it was time for me to show Brenda in the Showmanship Class. This class was usually first. It was critical for you and your animal to be in total control, the cleanest, neatest, and most poised. The animals' body types were not considered in this class, just the preparation and handling of the animal by the showman.

All the 4-H kids showed in this class. They were in two groups: juniors, nine to thirteen years old, and seniors, fourteen to eighteen. Typically the older showman had more experience and more practice with the animal which gave them a definite advantage, but one step out of place or bad move and it could be all over. I walked Brenda into the makeshift ring in the pasture. I walked backwards (as protocol required), so I could watch Brenda, checking her body moves, and watch the judge. When the judge motioned to you he expected you to respond immediately. I always feared missing a signal and losing position.

The ring had a sharp incline at one end which put the animals at a disadvantage for positioning. For the animals to look their best, their front legs should be together and elevated if possible. They were to have their rear feet placed so the leg facing the judge would be slightly ahead of the other leg, giving a glimpse of the rear udder. The judge asked us to stop walking the cows and place them.

I was at the wrong end of the ring to position Brenda correctly, I had to go against the norm and face her up the hill, which was counter clockwise to the rest of the showmen. I had never seen this done before, but I knew she would not look her best if I didn't. So I took her out of line and faced her up the incline. I placed her as quickly as I could (facing the wrong way) while glancing at the judge. I could feel my face turning red with embarrassment.

I waited for the judge's signal. He walked around looking at all the cows. He glanced back at me a couple of times. Brenda was perfect. She stood just like I placed her. The judge motioned for us to continue circling. I turned Brenda around and continued. He watched each of the animals move around again. We all waited for another motion.

There it was—he motioned me for first place. I was really nervous now. I led Brenda in to form a line in the center of this make-shift ring. He motioned for others to line up next to me. I was sweating. It was hot, but I didn't let my guard down for a second. We stayed lined up while the judge walked around us again. Brenda stayed poised. She was chewing her cud and I think she was enjoying this, but I was a wreck. As the judge strolled in front of me, I turned to face him (just as my brother, Dick had taught me) and then turned back when he passed, still checking Brenda's feet—perfect. The judge walked to the microphone. It was over. I had won!

OH, MY GOD, OH MY GOD—YOU DID IT!

Oh, my God! I won! The judge gave reasons for his placements. The one that did it for me was turning Brenda around so she was placed in a better position up the hill. I just won the Senior Showmanship Trophy. This was the first trophy I had ever won. It was better than my ten dollar bill. Dick couldn't take credit for this. I quietly congratulated Brenda, getting her a drink and a fresh slab of hay.

I had to stay calm because there was more to come. At this point of the show, things moved very fast. Brenda had the 2-year-old class to show yet. She would need to look her very best for that one. It would be like preparing for a swimsuit competition (she would have to show off all her great parts)! The judge called the class to enter the ring (this class was somewhat smaller, but tough competition). Around the ring we went again: placing feet, eyes on the judge, head poised and ears perked, doing anything that would get the judges attention. Stop. Go. Around we went, waiting for the motion. It seemed like it was taking him forever to make this decision. We kept walking and waiting. Finally the motion:

THERE IT IS—IT'S TO YOU, FIRST PLACE, GO, GO.

As I placed Brenda in the front of the lineup he motioned the rest of the class into line then went for the microphone. He liked all of Brenda's parts. I was delighted.

The day was far from over. We had more cows to show in the older cow groups and then there would be the Grand Champion to decide. All the first place cows two to five years old would have to face off for that, along with the Junior Champion (the best animal from the calf and heifer groups ranging in age from six months up to two years old, without giving birth). Usually, the older cows won this because of size and maturity. It was very rare for a two-year-old to win Grand Champion. But by the end of the day Brenda was awarded Reserve Grand Champion of the adult classes and Grand Champion of the 4-H group. This day would end with more surprises than I ever could have dreamed.

The fairs followed the Canton Show and the routine was the same except we had a week of work at the fairs. Sometimes the field work, necessary at fair time, left no one at home to milk, except me. I didn't really mind, but it was tiring and very hot. Cows sweat too. Milking while sandwiched between cows, well, gets sticky to say the least.

Most of the time, there were about seventy cows to milk at home during the summer. I wouldn't get home from the fair at the usual milking time, so I didn't get finished until 9:00 at night. This was our life. Morning would start pretty much like it ended. Dad would wake me up between 4:30 and 5:00 AM to milk again. He would have coffee while I dragged myself out of bed. Then I would have coffee with him and talk about the day. It was a quiet time with just the two of us, even though the talk was all about chores. Sometimes I felt taken advantage of, but I never said anything. In reality we all worked. It just seemed like Dick had a management roll, while I was a worker bee. Out of the nine weeks of summer, we usually went to about five shows. The rest of the time we harvested crops. Summer vacation was not a vacation. It was almost a relief to go back to school in September, in spite of my troubles with school.

SENIOR YEAR

The New York State Fair was over. The results of the summer shows were good. I earned more money than I ever had and Brenda had done well, taking first place in her class at each show and being awarded the New York State Bellringer Award for the two-year-old class. For that, she got her picture in the Brown Swiss Bulletin and a certificate. I had a Bellringer! Cool!

The first event of the school agenda was the senior class magazine sales. I dreaded the very thought of this, but we all had to do it. A few weeks after school started we got all the information and books for the magazine sales. There were prizes involved for the top sales people. This was news to me, and I thought it was cool. I especially liked the tape recorder for second place and for some reason, I thought I could do that, so I took my books and order forms and started out to sell some magazines. I asked everyone I knew and some I didn't know. From somewhere I found the courage to go door to door. Knocking on doors of people I didn't know. I tried to be friendly and polite but was unprepared for their questions asking what school district I was selling for. I would get the responses like, "Oh, sorry, I don't buy magazines from that school district." I didn't realize just how much rivalry there was between schools. Luckily for me, it didn't matter to some of them. I would talk myself into continuing, and I sold magazines. At the end of the contest I had gotten second place in sales. It was like something major had just happened in my life. I counted for something. I did something better than all the town kids. First place went to a country girl, but not a farm girl.

My life started to feel different. I was able to talk to more of the kids and do some of the "forbidden" things, like fool around in class just a little. I found out that life goes on even if you don't obey the rules exactly.

One day I had been caught throwing lifesavers (in defense) during office practice class, and that silly lifesaver I threw landed on edge and rolled and rolled across that wood floor for what seemed like ten minutes.

The classroom was so quiet that the rolling sound seemed enormous. Barbara and I got laughing, which triggered everyone else in class until we were so out of control laughing we were told to put our heads down on the desks. The teacher waited for our silence and said, "That will be enough candy for today." She was glaring at me with obvious anger, but I didn't die! I always thought if you disobeyed any teachers or broke the rules you were severely punished or tortured or something. But that wasn't the case and the class continued. I even lived to tell about it on my way to the next class. Barbara, a few other classmates and I laughed about that lifesaver. It was fun actually and I felt like I fit in with the crowd that day. The problem was the teacher treated me with contempt there after. Some kids still appeared to have the old opinion of me as the dumb farm kid with shitty sneakers.

One of those old opinions was from Paul. He was a cocky, arrogant guy, about 6' 3", blonde, very short hair (not a brush cut, but close) and long skinny legs. He was a rebel of sorts and hung around the popular kids and I wasn't sure why. Maybe it was because he was the class "hippie" and he carried his "fight the establishment" attitude inside an arrogant container that got lots of attention. He had ocean blue eyes that would look right through you and a smirk on his face like he was doing something against the rules and getting away with it. Rumor had it that he was smoking pot and I believed that. He just had a different way about him. One day Paul asked Barbara if he could hitch a ride home from school with her. She told him that she had ridden to school with me, but she suggested he ask me for a ride. He just looked at her and said, "Thanks, but no thanks." At the end of the day, Barbara asked me if I talked to Paul and I told her I had not. She told me what Paul had said and that hurt more than I expected. I hadn't done anything to him to generate that kind of comment. Just when I felt like I could fit in and someone like him comes along and kills it. Now I hated his arrogant smirk and strut even more. I saw him at the end of the day as I was leaving to go home. As we passed in the hall, he just stared and smirked and never uttered a word. I decided to give him one of his smirks back as I greeted him. "Paul…" is all I said.

YOU ARE SUCH AN ASS! (Subconscious opinion which I shared)

***

The school year was flying by and all the senior events along with it. There was the senior ball, which for me was pretty eventless. I went with Neil (one of my Father's hired men), but it was fun. There were midterm exams and the last of the sports events—volleyball, basketball then softball. I had done basketball, volleyball, and just finished softball. By now all of the seniors had to go to the guidance office to finalize our four years of study and decide what to do after graduation, or so I thought. I had not given this much thought because I was a farm kid and worked on the farm. When it came my turn to go see Mr. Woodsen, I was totally unprepared for what would take place in his office.

Each year we met and he wrote down the subjects he thought I should take. There wasn't usually much discussion about it except the one time I told him I thought I wanted to take French. He told me in a soft, pleasant voice that he felt that I would have difficulty with that class and probably wouldn't pass. The subject was dropped, and I felt that retarded thing again. We would finish the list, he would finalize it and I would leave. This time there would be no class agenda to discuss. I wasn't quite sure what we would talk about.

I walked in and sat down in front of his desk. He seemed a little nervous. He asked me what I thought I would like to do after graduation. I didn't have an answer and responded with an "I don't know". I had always thought the guidance counselor decided that for you. He started discussing options with me. Those options suggested going to work as a secretary because I had taken some business courses, or becoming an airline stewardess, or maybe a hair dresser. I asked if I could do something like be a gym teacher? I thought I would be good at that, but he told me I did not have a high enough grade average to get into any college. I needed to maintain a "B" average throughout the four years of high school. This was news to me! I had no idea school was a preparation for college. In my world, the boys prepared for college and the girls got married, but I didn't want to get married. I didn't know what I was supposed to do. I was stunned and didn't say anything.

YOU ARE PANICKING AGAIN! LOOK AT YOURSELF! PICK YOUR HEAD UP! DON'T LET HIM KNOW THAT YOU'RE ABOUT TO CRY. PULL YOURSELF TOGETHER AND TELL HIM SOMETHING. YOU KNOW HE'S CONVINCED YOU ARE STUPID

*AND BORDERLINE RETARDED. TELL HIM YOU WILL GET A
JOB AND LEAVE IT AT THAT.*

I told him I would probably get a job and left it at that. He said
okay and that I was dismissed. All kinds of things went through my
mind that day. My grade point average wasn't high enough to go to
college. Why didn't someone tell me about college and grade averages?
I did my schoolwork, but the farm work always came first. If I got my
homework done, fine, if not, I got a lower grade. It really didn't matter as
long as I passed. That's all any farm girl had to do was pass and graduate
without being pregnant. I <u>could</u> have done a lot more; I just didn't know
why I was supposed to. Besides it didn't appear to be important to anyone
(teachers, parents, etc.) what grades I got. They always treated me as if
I were stupid and if I did anything it was an accomplishment. I had
thoughts in the past of being retarded. I always talked myself out of it,
but now I felt that maybe the retarded thing was real.

I went home from school that day feeling confused and depressed.
I decided I had to talk to someone about it. I tried talking to Mom, but
she just seemed too busy to enter into a conversation with me. When
Dad came in for coffee at 4:30, I asked if I could talk to him. He agreed,
after he finished his coffee. I had never talked to Dad about this kind of
stuff, but I didn't know what else to do. He and Mom talked quietly as I
went into the other room. I heard them, but didn't pay attention to what
they were saying. I was thinking about what I would say to Dad when he
came in to talk to me.

Thirty minutes later he came into the TV room where I was sitting.
I didn't figure out a good opening line, so I just started talking. I told
him what the guidance counselor had told me, and asked him if I could
work on the farm like Dick was going to do when he returned from
college in June. The look on his face was one I had never seen before.

He looked at the floor. His somber, soft voice uttered, "No".

WHAT?

My heart sank. I couldn't believe he said no. My mind raced. Flashing
replays from the past. I couldn't blurt out my lines of defense fast enough.
All of us kids were to work on the farm. What about the time I had tried
to get a job when I turned 16. Barbara wanted me to work with her at
the Thruway Restaurant. Dad told me I couldn't because I had to work
on the farm. When did this change and why didn't they tell me? I was
upset, spewing questions as fast as I could.

"Why can't I work at home? Why can't I help make this farm like the ones on the covers of the farm magazines? Why? I do a lot of work here, how do I just quit? Why?" I screamed hysterically.

Dad was almost trembling. I knew he was holding back his emotion. I felt like my insides were out of control. We both started crying. He told me the farm would never be like the ones on the magazine covers. I demanded it could. I did not understand. I knew the farm could be more than it was and I knew I could help make it happen, but he acted like he did not want me on the farm anymore. I was confused and the hurt was excruciating.

During the conversation I noticed Mom walking back and forth in the kitchen. She would pass in front of the doorway making it look like she was cleaning off the table. It really looked as if she was trying to hear what we were saying, yet she never came in to give any suggestions, solutions or advice, which was odd. She usually gave her ideas whether anyone wanted to hear them or not. Our conversation had been tidal waved with emotion. Dad broke the silence and said he had to go to the barn. He left me there alone without saying anything about doing chores. I wondered why this was happening like this. I now had to make a decision by myself. What was I going to do after graduation?

YOU ALREADY HAVE THE ANSWER. I TOLD YOU EARLIER TODAY.

I guess I did have my answer after all. I'll find a job.

***

A month had passed and the shock and pain did too. I told Dad that I would get a job, but I wanted to spend my last summer at the fairs. He said that would be okay and he would appreciate the help. Mom never said a word. I knew she knew, but for some reason, she chose never to discuss it with me.

Graduation was just around the corner and I was almost ready. Sometimes I would find myself thinking what it would be like to not go to school anymore. It was hard to think of replacing it with work because I didn't know what a regular job would be like. My thoughts about the future didn't last very long. I couldn't focus on something I didn't know anything about.

Preparations began for graduation with the fitting and ordering of the caps and gowns. The school colors were red and white and the caps and gowns were bright red. Red was always a good color for me. Our class was the first one graduating from the new auditorium and it was a very special time with decorations throughout the school building. Graduates were feeling the end of something coming, and it was the anticipation of the unknown that made it so thrilling. It was a sad, frightening and exciting all at the same time. We had never been here before, and we shared thoughts, ideas, plans, old stories and good times, right to the last day.

***

Graduation Day

Everything was all set to go. I had my dress, the party prepared, the cake bought, relatives invited and I was ready.

The ceremony was to start at 7 PM, and I arrived at the school by 6 PM. It felt wonderful to be the first graduating class. Everyone was excited, but we had lots to do before the march down the aisles of the auditorium. We posed in front of the school for our group graduation picture. We practiced being arranged on the staging platforms exactly as we would be on the auditorium stage. There was this feeling of closeness with all of us. The past was gone on this day. We were all friends just the way I always wanted it to be. The picture was done with military precision, and now it was time to hide away in the dressing rooms for the last touch ups of hair and make-up, waiting for all the parents and guests to be seated.

Soon we had to line up for our grand entrance. Alphabetically in two rows we would walk down the center aisles of the auditorium then off to the side into our pre-assigned seats. The band started to play the traditional graduation march. Suddenly I felt strange, like I was in a dream and everything seemed to be happening in slow motion. I wasn't light-headed or dizzy, but more like I was walking into a clouded sky where everything was visible yet somehow distorted. My jitters were at peace.

YOU'RE SUPPOSED TO REMEMBER THIS!

I walked smiling and said to myself, "I will always remember this day".

The announcements, congratulations, speeches and awarding of the scholarships and diplomas went just as rehearsed, and soon it was over.

We marched off the stage the same as we marched on, and this time it was for the last time. We all felt the end of something knowing we might never see each other again, but some of us wanted to think this ceremony would not be so final. We could never really know.

Almost everyone in the class was having a party after the ceremony. I lived in the country, so the kids would not be coming to my party. When I arrived home there were relatives and neighbors in almost every room of the house. There were presents in a pile on the table of the TV room. There was food galore and the cake, a huge store-bought cake decorated with red flowers and white frosting with a little statue of a graduate holding a little scroll to look like a diploma. It said "Congratulations, Laura." It was a great looking cake. As I greeted my guests and started the food line, I felt closeness to these people that had been rare in the past. Not even the family reunions were this good. They were all there to celebrate with me! God, that was special. My sister was there, but not in my spotlight this time. Everything was going well until my Aunt Irene arrived.

Trixie was going to be a freshman in the fall and we were still very much alike, physically. I guess more than I admitted. My Aunt Irene walked into the kitchen and stepped up to Trixie, who was standing an arm reach away from me, and said, "Congratulations, Laura" and handed my gift to her. Trixie enjoyed this quite a lot, and after a minute, corrected her and gave me the gift. Aunt Irene was my father's sister. We had visits from them fairly often. It wasn't like a long lost relative that just walked through the door! I was quite surprised by her actions and very hurt by the laughter generated from family members. I tried to let it go like it didn't bother me, but that was hard.

Soon the crowd started to thin. I teamed up with another couple of country classmates who made a surprise visit to my party. Joe and his girlfriend, Mary, came to see if we could all go out together to other parties. We took my parents car and started seeking out parties. Joe was more of a town kid and was quite popular in the class. He knew all the great places to go. Mary would be graduating next year and also lived on a dairy farm. Our families knew each other through farm business. For hours we drove and stopped to wish everyone good luck in their future and toasted with a few beers. We found out there was a breakfast planned at Kellie's. Her dad was an attorney and they lived in the grandest house in Manchester.

When we arrived at Kellie's house, it was packed with people. Everyone sat around banquet tables on the huge back porch. The teachers were telling stories and graduates were giving admissions of guilt and laughing like kindergartners. Everyone was pretty drunk from beer, but when the breakfast came the beer was replaced with orange juice.

We ate a breakfast fit for kings. People were clustered into smaller groups and did some private reminiscing. I met up with Mitch and we started talking about the past. I didn't tell him that I had the wildest crush on him all through school, but I bet he already knew. He and Paul were best friends. I never really understood that because they seemed so different. Mitch had a warm personality and always had a positive, friendly outlook. As we spoke, our conversation came around to Paul and I just qualified my responses by explaining that I didn't know him very well. Mitch went on to defend my "poor farm kid" title with some similar information about Paul in a somewhat teasing fashion.

It seems Paul had worked a few summers for my brother's girlfriend's father. Obviously he kept his farm work pretty much contained when interacting with other town kids. Mitch was laughing while telling me the stories. He reiterated that Paul liked being mysterious and mischievous, striving to be secretive and different, and that he was. I must admit I didn't feel a "farming bond" for Paul after this conversation with Mitch, but it was just a good time to talk to an old time classmate in a way we never had.

I returned home around 7 AM. It was too early for chores to be finished, but Mom was up fixing coffee for the guys and tea for herself. We talked about the night and how much fun it was while we ate leftover cake. There was never a curfew on graduation night. It was always understood that we came home at any time, and that was a real privilege. After an hour or so of talking, I decided I had to get some sleep, which came quickly and soundly.

THE LAST SHOW

The summer fair routine began almost immediately after graduation with the selection of cattle and shows to attend. This would be my last year in 4-H. It was really my turn to win the Showmanship Class at the local county fair. My brothers had won this in previous years, and I really felt I could win with Brenda. Soon I would find out, but right now I had to help with the leading of the various calves (under one year old), heifers (under 2 years old) and cows (over 2 years old that had calves) that would have to walk properly around the show ring to look their best to win and qualify for the show at the New York State Fair at the end of summer. Brenda was my prize cow. This summer she would be in the 3-year-old class, and I must admit, she had started showing signs of her age quicker than I wanted, but that is life's process. I could only hope she would be good enough to win, but it didn't look as promising as last year. My only real chance to win would be in the Showmanship Class.

We moved cattle into the county fair grounds. It was always a hectic day and a long one. I would stay at the fair grounds to help Dick with the chores. Usually we took at least 20 head of cattle and we literally had to baby sit them every minute, which included bathing, feeding, milking, watering and maintaining totally clean bedding. Totally clean bedding means, every time the animal poops or pees, it needs to be picked up and replaced with fresh straw each time for each animal. That was almost a full time job in itself. Each day leading up to show day would start very early and end very late.

Most of the work at the fairs was manual—no motorized carts, augers, or milking stations. Even the manure was taken away in a wheel barrel and dumped in a pile at the end of the tent. It was like camping with 20 large 4-legged babies. Most of the older animals were pretty well-behaved, but the newcomers could be very nervous about being out of the barn and around all this commotion of tents, people, kids and dogs. We weren't the only ones there for the show. There were other types of animals, some of which they had never seen before, and every group had specified areas, but there were noises and smells that would be foreign to the first-timers.

It was finally here and I had been up most of the night helping Dick feed, bag and bed the cows. The Showmanship class was the first class in the morning, so cows going into that class would have to be washed early enough to get dry. Brenda was in the wash rack by 6 AM. I gave her the bath of her life and then the rest of the primping began. Clean ear wax out of her ears, linseed oil her body to make it shiny, brush her tail switch (don't let her lie down in case she lies in something). She would need special feed to fill out her body—but not too much so she looked too full or "round" in the belly. The meal would consist of beet pulp and grain called fitting ration. The beet pulp is shredded dehydrated beet to which water is added and it soaks it up and expands as it softens. The fitting ration is a mixture of tasty grains with a touch of molasses, and the cows really liked it.

It was getting close to show time. I had to change into my pressed white jeans and shirt with a belt. I had to fix my hair and makeup and then attend to the final details of Brenda. She would need oil on her hooves, fly spray, a final brushing, a show halter put on, a walk around to calm the butterflies (hers and mine). My brother Dick was giving me direct orders. Walk her slow and watch the judge every minute you can. Keep her head up all the time, but not so high that it looks awkward. Make sure she doesn't lie down in the ring and don't let wood shavings from the floor of the ring stick to her legs, knees or belly. If she does get shavings on herself, be sure to take them off, even it you have to walk around her to do it. I was nervous, but I wanted to win this class. Brenda and I headed for the show ring.

We walked around outside the building where the show ring was for a few minutes to try to relax. Brenda seemed a bit uptight, so I let her kick up her heels and jump around a little. She jumped and kicked and threw her head around. It didn't seem like just jitters. She was unhappy about something. But now it was time—show time! There were five exhibitors in this class, all younger than me with less experience, but wanting that trophy as badly as I did. We walked our animals around the ring, once and then a second time. Brenda was not relaxed. Suddenly she tried to lie down. My subconscious went wild.

NO, NO, DON'T LET HER GO DOWN. GET HER UP, GET HER UP! QUICK, QUICK!

I scrambled to react, pulling on Brenda's halter, pinching her under her neck, and quietly coaxing her, "Come on Brenda, get up, come on Brenda, please get up." She rose from her kneeling position on her front legs and stood up. I quickly repositioned her. Head up, left rear foot forward, I was watching the judge in split second flashes. He had seen Brenda go down on her knees, but now he was watching me to see how quick I could recover and put her back to a poised position.

It didn't take long, less than a minute I would guess, but Brenda was still very unhappy and restless making it hard to keep her under control. The judge stopped the group and then walked around each animal individually. When he came to Brenda and me, we were like statues standing perfectly and as he walked up in front of us, I turned to face him. He looked and walked. Brenda held on. Then he walked away to the center of the ring. He looked the group over one more time and motioned for us to start walking again.

Brenda and I got half way around the ring when he motioned me to come into first place. We walked toward the center of the ring; Brenda tossed her head like she had had enough, but she settled back down. The judge motioned the rest of the exhibitors into line. He looked over the lineup of animals one last time and during that last look, Brenda decided she was finished and it was time to leave. She threw that head of hers up, twisted her body around and her 1400 pounds took me out of first place and headed for the exit door. Spectators helped grab us and I walked her back into the ring. I watched the judge and he motioned for me to go to the end of the line. I was crushed. Brenda was still dancing around as the judge gave explanation for his placement. He started explaining why he had picked Brenda and me for first place by saying he was impressed with my recovery of her lay down, but further explained he could not leave us in first with her becoming uncontrollable at the end. I knew it too, but it was a crushing defeat.

Brenda and I exited the ring at the "dead last" end of the other exhibitors and took the long way back to the barn. I wanted to cry, but knew I couldn't (being in public and all). I knew I had just missed my last chance to accomplish what every 4-H kid ahead of me had in their last year of 4-H. I had done a good job, but Brenda was just not in the mood today. It just wasn't meant to be and there would never be another chance.

When I got back to the barn Dick was waiting. He had watched the show, and I think he knew how I felt, but we didn't talk about it. I just tied Brenda back to the fence in the barn and started preparing for the next classes. The rest of the day would be consumed with preparations and the showing of other animals for different classes. It was over and I didn't win.

There was another class for Brenda and me and that was the 4-H 3-year-old class. The competition wasn't as strict as the showmanship class, but by the time this class was ready to show, the day had grown long and tiring. I wasn't excited. I was tired and dirty, but this judge was not taking a long time to make decisions, so we would be done soon. Brenda had had a nap and was chewing her cud and appeared very contented.

SURE, WHEN YOU DON'T NEED HER CONTENTED, SHE IS. WHERE WAS HER CONTENTMENT THIS MORNING? COWS ARE FINICKY.

We did the usual waltz through the show ring. The judge made his decision very quickly and placed Brenda in first place. She would have to return to the ring for 4-H Grand Champion. I wasn't thinking much about it because generally it goes to the older cows. The rest of the cow classes had finished. The announcement had been made to bring the winners back to the ring.

The first place animals in the 2-year-old, 3-year-old, 4-year-old, and the aged cow (5 years and over) classes and the Junior Champion all came back to the ring. I was disciplined by my brother to pay attention to the judge every second possible, but this was difficult. I was tired and definitely slowing down, but I noticed the judge watching Brenda intently. He had made short work of his decisions in the later classes, and it appeared this would also be the case. I was starting to perk up a little when he made the motion to the ribbon girl to bring him the 4-H Senior and Grand Champion Ribbons. He then motioned to me to bring Brenda into the center of the ring, which I did gladly. In his explanation he said he really liked just about everything about her and felt she was the deserving 4-H Senior and Grand Champion Cow of the show.

I was thrilled, tired, happy and grateful all at the same time. This was my last Grand Championship for all my years of showing cows at the fair. I would now have a pass for the New York State Fair competitions in September and a trophy to hold all the memories. This fair was over with three more to go.

The Job Offer

It was Sunday morning when I got a phone call from Cyndy, a girl my brother Lyle had dated. She was calling to ask if I would be interested in a job working at the car dealership where she worked. She went on to explain some of the details of the work. She said if I were interested I could come in and talk to her boss on Friday, because he was out of town till then. We talked about the fairs, and I thought I might be able to sacrifice the rest of them except the state fair. She said the boss was a real nice guy to work for and he might agree to some kind of arrangement. I agreed to come in on Friday at 9 AM.

When I hung up I felt like I had butterflies in my whole body. I was excited, yet frightened. I started to think about what to do next. I decided to find my Dad to tell him about the call. As I was looking, I was thinking of the things that getting a job would affect. Dick would have to do all the fair chores, but that just meant he would have to work a little more and supervise less. I would probably have to help with chores at home after work, but I felt this opportunity was one I needed to check out. I had never looked for a job before. Now a job was looking for me. It also meant I already knew someone there and I wouldn't be among strangers to start work. All these things were going through my mind as I searched for Dad.

I found him in the shop fixing a broken part from the baler. I wasn't sure what he would say, but I had to talk to him about this first. I told him about my conversation with Cyndy while he kept working. I watched his expression, and it was very close to the one I saw back in April when he told me I could not work on the farm.

"How do you feel about it?" he said, with calm voice.

"I don't know" I said, "I guess I should go talk to the boss first and see if he will hire me. How about the fairs? Everybody will be shorthanded if I'm not there."

"Well, we'll get by somehow" he said, "Trixie will be able to help at the fairs and you will be able to help with night chores, but let's wait till Friday to see what happens."

"Okay." I agreed.

I left the shop feeling like I was leaving home in some way. I wasn't sure exactly why or how. Maybe because Dad said they would get by somehow at the fairs without me. I knew how much work I did, but it didn't sound like Dad knew. I walked back to the house to find Mom still reading the paper. I interrupted her and told her about Cyndy's phone call. She thought it was a good opportunity for me and that I should take the job. I told her I would have to see how the boss felt about me taking time off for the State Fair.

She shot back with, "Well I think the job would be more important than the fair. It isn't like it's your first fair, and you may not get another opportunity like this one."

"Yea, I guess."

What she didn't understand was that it was my last fair. I wanted desperately to get out of this conversation because I knew she would continue trying to convince me to take the job even before the interview. I was struggling for something to say to get out of this room.

YOU HAVE TO GO CLEAN THE BARN.

"Well, I have to clean the barn. I'll see how it goes on Friday." I replied.

Mom obviously wanted me to take this job, no matter what. She had a way of convincing me that her ideas were always best. Everybody should take her advice because she knows what is best for everyone. I never doubted or questioned her in the past, but this time I wondered if she knew how I felt. I always felt that my feelings weren't visible to anyone else, yet I was taught to be considerate of others feelings. Why didn't anyone have to consider my feelings?

She continued to read her paper as I left for the barn.

As I started working things came to me that I had not yet thought about with this job. What would I wear? How would I get there every day? Use mom's car? I don't know anything about what happens at a job. How will I know where to go or what to do?

DON'T PANIC! CYNDY IS THERE TO HELP YOU AND YOU KNOW WHERE TO GO. WALK IN THE FRONT DOOR AND LOOK FOR CYNDY. JUST DON'T PANIC!

I'll just force myself to think about what I have to wear for the interview. Mom won't have a problem with me taking the car because she wants me to take this job regardless. I continued cleaning the barn, but thinking of all the things that would be affected if I got a job.

**

It's Friday. I am all dressed for my interview (that is such a strange word to me). I was trying to think of it as a chat with Cyndy's boss. I have no idea what to say or what he will ask. I am only going on the suggestion of my subconscious to just go and find Cyndy. She will take care of the rest.

I drove Mom's car, the "Silver Slave," to the car dealership and parked in front of the glass window showroom. The trip was only seven miles, so I didn't get a lot of time to think about the unknown of the interview. I just had to get there and walk in the front door. As I did, I could see Cyndy sitting in a room just off the back side of the showroom. She obviously had been watching for me because she came right out to greet me.

"Hi, are you nervous?" She asked,

"Of course I'm nervous, what do you think?"

She laughed and said, "Don't worry, Rusty is a real nice guy, and you will like him. Wait here, I'll tell him you're here."

I felt conspicuous just standing there as people were coming and going. It was only a minute when Cyndy motioned for me to come into the corner office. I took a deep breath and walked over to her. I walked into the office and standing behind a large desk was a man about my parents' age, maybe a little younger, dressed in a dark suit with a crisp white shirt and red tie. He wasn't real tall, about my Dad's height, but slightly thinner. He had dark thinning hair and a round friendly face. Cyndy did the introduction and went back to her office, shutting the door behind her.

Rusty offered me a chair and started talking about school and graduation. Cyndy was right; he was easy to talk to and he had a terrific sense of humor, which helped ease my jitters. We talked about the courses I had taken in high school and what kind of work he wanted me to do. He said Cyndy would help show me how to do everything. I asked when the job would start and he said as soon as possible. I told him about the State Fair problem and offered up my services starting Monday if I could have a few days off to show at the State Fair. He said he didn't have a problem with that and he would appreciate my starting that soon. He said I would start at $1.50 per hour and the hours were 8 AM to 5 PM with a one hour lunch, Monday through Friday. Another plus was that I would get my gas at cost and could use the shop evenings and weekends to wash my car if I wanted to. After six months I would get a raise if things were going well. I heard what he said, but I was in a bit of in a blur.

YOU HAVE A JOB! AND YOU ARE GETTING PAID BY THE HOUR. CAN YOU BELIEVE THAT? THE PAY IS TWICE WHAT YOU MAKE BABYSITTING!

It was like having conversation with two people at the same time. I was trying to keep my composure in front of my new boss and struggled to respond at the same time. I was feeling the contagious excitement from my subconscious, but I was not totally sure why. I finally responded to Rusty with a thank you and confirmed that I would be at work on Monday, with a hand shake. We walked back to Cyndy's office. He asked her to show me through the shop, introduce me to the rest of the employees and show me where I could park.

After our tour Cyndy and I walked back to the front and I told her I would see her on Monday and thanked her for her help. The drive home was with mixed feelings and numerous thoughts of what was to come in the next few days. How would I get to work every day? Dick's college graduation was without a party, but he got a new car from the farm. I guess Mom and Dad thought he would need his own transportation. When I got home, Mom was in the kitchen and she immediately asked how the interview went. I told her that I was to start work on Monday. She seemed very pleased. I asked her how I would get to work indicating I needed to use the car. She said if they needed the car they would just take me to work and pick me up. Suddenly I was thinking about <u>not</u> having mom's car. I wondered why they couldn't use Dick's car to get parts or whatever they needed. Plus they had the truck. I guess I thought I would have the use of the car to go to work. After all, it was what mom wanted.

I told Dad when he came in for lunch. He sounded glad for me, but I thought maybe he was not really glad. He appeared glad because Mom was. I thought maybe they were surprised I got the job. Maybe they felt it would take me longer to find a job because I was so stupid. I wondered if Mr. Woodsen had told them that I wasn't capable of doing much. I didn't know. I didn't know what to expect on Monday, either, but I did know that I would soon find out. I felt sure this weekend would pass very quickly.

The weekend passed in a flash. Dad and I talked about the fairs and the fact that I was going to take time off to go to the State Fair only. I would be able to come home after work at 5 and milk. I didn't think much about that reality, until later. I was working two jobs and getting paid for one!

I was still Dick's back up and he was still the "authority". He liked being the tallest one in the family, figuratively speaking, but Dick looked like Mom's side of the family. He was tall and lanky like Grandpa, sandy brown hair with one of those deep receding hairlines. He was the only one with brown eyes. He was the defiant one while growing up. Mom told stories of Dick as a baby that appeared to be funny, after the fact. He didn't talk for the longest time because Lyle would get the things he wanted without having to ask for them. Mom put a stop to that. He wouldn't potty train either and he refused to use the toilet. He would go in other places, like the coal pail and one time he peed in Dad's dress shoe and then put it back in the closet. No one knew about it until Dad had to dress up for a wedding and found this shoe shriveled up and moldy. All of us knew who had done it, but I didn't ever remember him being punished.

Monday came and went faster than I ever expected. Cyndy showed me how to take care of customers and run the cash register. I learned how to do the books and stuff the billing. Cyndy did the posting to the accounts. There was another employee in the office with us and that was Slim. He was an older gentleman and he hardly ever spoke. He did the payroll and other book work. He was a giant of a man; with short dark hair on the sides and a bald spot that shown the whole top of his head. He smoked the biggest cigars I had ever seen. He had a very deep voice that almost growled when he talked. He would joke about things with such a dry sense of humor that I had to get used to listening and think about what he said before I could laugh about it. Slim had asked me for my social security number on Monday. I didn't have a clue what he was talking about. He was very kind about it and told me to go to the Post Office to fill out the form to get one. I couldn't get paid without it. I went to the post office during my first lunch and filled out the paperwork. I did want to get paid.

The week passed as fast as Monday did and I found myself not knowing how to be as friendly as Cyndy with the customers. They came to the window to pay their bills and I would be so shy that I barely spoke. It was hard for me to talk to strangers. I didn't know how to be friendly to someone I had never met before and I struggled with it. Friday came and I still had not gotten my social security number, but Slim said it was okay as long as it was coming. They paid everyone in cash in these little gold envelopes. Slim would go to the bank about 11 AM and then break down the money, stuff the envelopes and hand them out after lunch. I got mine about 3 PM and I didn't dare to look at it. I was busy at the time so I just put it in my purse and waited till I got home.

At 5 o'clock it was time to head for home. I had to do chores and I had to look at my pay. I drove Mom's car home as fast as I could (keeping it close to legal). After I parked the car and went inside, I dug through my purse to find my pay envelope. I ripped it open and took out the folded dollars. As I unfolded them I fanned them in my hand and started counting.

Oh my God, there are five ten dollar bills here. I have fifty one dollars and change. This is so great! I yelled.

I KNOW YOU ARE EXCITED, BUT DID YOU FORGET ABOUT CHORES? YOU HAD BETTER GET YOUR CLOTHES CHANGED SO YOU CAN GET AT THE MILKING. DAD WILL BE LOOKING FOR YOU ANY MINUTE.

I tucked the money into my wallet and took my purse upstairs to change. I was so excited about the money. I thought to myself, I get the same amount next Friday. This is so fantastic.

I changed my clothes and went to the barn to start milking. I thought I would not tell anyone how much I got unless they asked me. I didn't want to have to pay cash for stuff at home. After all I was there to do the milking every night.

The routine continued. I went to work, came home and milked cows. Things were going great. I bought some new clothes and kept some of the money in my wallet. I even bought lunch once in a while. Sharing the car didn't seem too bad, but I thought I should think about getting a car. When Mom needed the car she would take me to work after lunch and pick me up at five. No one at home ever said anything about getting a car. Then the day came when the reality of having my own car hit me right between the eyes.

It was State Fair week. Dick had gone with the cows and I decided I didn't want to sacrifice any more money than necessary, so I was going up for the 4-H show later. One day Mom needed the car to take food and clothes to the fair. So she took me to work in the morning and said someone would be back at five to pick me up. I had lunch with Cyndy. It was about five minutes to five when I heard a loud truck pull up out front of the dealership. I looked in horror and I saw my Dad with the cattle truck parked right at the front door. I wanted to die.

"It looks like your ride is here" Cyndy teased, and we both laughed, but I was horrified.

Those five minutes lasted for what seemed like an hour. People were looking and asking about the guy sitting in the truck out front.

Finally Cyndy declared, "Well, time to go. I'll see you in a couple of days, right?"

"Yea," I said, "I'll be back on Friday, after the show."

She wished me good luck at the show on our way out and I thanked her as I exited the front door. I got to the truck, reached for the door handle and as I was opening the door, I realized I had on a skirt and I would have to quickly get into this thing with my skirt hiked up very high. I pulled up my skirt and stepped into the cab of the truck in a split second. The look on my face had to have shown my feelings about getting picked up in the truck.

"All set?" Dad asked.

"Yup" I sheepishly replied.

As we drove home the conversation with Dad was about the fair and the plan for the next few days. I thought he talked like nothing was wrong. He didn't even notice that my face had turned beet red from embarrassment climbing into the truck. It just didn't bother him. I just listened and agreed to the plan and tried to put the whole incident out of my mind.

While I was milking I thought a lot about getting a car. I wondered if I could afford one, even though I felt somewhat rich at the time. I worked in a car dealership, what a great place to work when you are looking for a car. My Dad had always bought his cars from a car and implement dealer in town. He was their best customer and whenever we needed a new car he would just go and get one.

I remember Mom telling about the day Dad bought a new car when he went to pick up some parts. It seems the old car heaved its last breath when Dad drove it into the dealership. It literally died while he was there. So he decided to buy another car right then. The salesman and Dad picked a new car from the lot, did some paperwork and sent him on his way with his parts and the new car. When Dad got home, Mom asked him what he had done with the other car and he explained about the breakdown of the old car. She stated the old car had not been cleaned. There was always "stuff" in the car. Lots of stuff like papers, tools, parts, almost anything could be found in there. Dad told her the salesman would clean everything out of the car and Dad could pick up the stuff at his next visit. Well, a couple of days had gone by when the salesman stopped in at the farm with the bag of "stuff" from the old car.

The salesman, named "Dutch," was a good friend and had a real devilish sense of humor, as did most of the guys at the dealership. Dutch was delighted to tell her what the guys found when they cleaned out the old car. Mom's girdle was under the front seat. Mom was horrified, but everyone was laughing so much that she had to laugh too.

As the story goes, Mom and Dad had been to the State Fair as visitors one day and Mom wore a dress for the occasion. After several hours in the crowded fair grounds on a classic hot, humid summer day, Mom decided she had to take off her girdle, so she removed it in the car and put it under the seat. Now she didn't wear a dress that often so it had slipped her mind that she had left it in the car. Dutch suggested she be prepared for questions the next time she was at the dealership. After that she didn't stuff things under the seats anymore!

I thought maybe I could ask Dutch about a car too. I really knew him better than my boss, but either way I had to get a car. I had always remembered Dad buying our new cars so I thought I would do that too. I would talk to Cyndy about it when I went back to work on Friday. She had her own car. My brothers Dick and Lyle had their own cars. I should too.

The next couple of days were busy. I would go to the fair very early the next morning. There were the usual preparations for the show, and this was my last one, ever. I wanted it to be fun and successful. I didn't have time to think about the car now. Brenda's 4-H class for 3 year olds went pretty well. She placed first in her class and was eligible for the open class show for 3 year olds. She didn't do as well there, placing 5th, but I was pleased overall. I even entered in a state milking contest and placed in the top ten. I wasn't sure what that would do for my future, but I got a framed certificate for the gesture.

I was tired and it was very late when I got home Thursday night. Now I had to go to work the next morning. I thought about my pay. It would be short this week, but I made up some of it with my winnings. I fell asleep the minute my head hit the pillow. My days of showing cows were over, and I was too tired to think much about it.

The Car

Cyndy was there when I arrived at work. She asked about the shows and how I did. I told her about my winnings and the milking contest, and she thought that was pretty cool. When I felt it was an opportune time, I asked her what she thought about me buying a car. We talked about new cars and used cars. I told her I was thinking about a new one. I wanted to order one just like my brothers did. She suggested I talk to Bob about it. Bob was one of the salesmen and had been selling cars there for a long time. He was a funny kind of a round jolly guy with a balding brush cut and a fat bottom lip. He had one of those contagious laughs that could start you laughing even if you didn't hear the story behind the laugh. I decided to talk to Bob even though I was shy and reluctant at first because he was still a stranger to me.

When I mustered up enough courage to ask Bob about a car and he said, "When you're ready, I'll talk to you about what we have." He seemed like he didn't have time to talk about it or didn't want to. I was so shy I didn't know how to push the issue. I decided I would go see Dutch and see what he had to say. It was September and I really wanted a car.

The next day I went to see Dutch. We talked and he said he was going to a car show in the city (Rochester) to see the new cars for 1967. He asked if I wanted to ride along. I said sure. We left the dealership mid-afternoon. We went to a couple of large dealerships in the city, and I saw a lot of cars. The one that caught my eye was the new model of the one my brother Dick had gotten for graduation. He had a 1966 Plymouth Satellite. The 1967 models had subtle differences, but I liked them. Dutch told me to look over the brochures and get back to him. He would see what he could do to get me one as soon as possible and I agreed to call him later in the week.

I went home that night and though of nothing else but that car. I looked through the brochure for hours. I talked to Dad about the trip with Dutch and that I figured I could afford a new car like the boys. I told him I could not continue using Mom's car and that I had to have my own; after all the boys had cars. Dick had a free one—brand new! He didn't say much (I thought because there was no possible way to argue). I didn't go into a lot of details about the financing and he didn't ask. I figured I would let him tell Mom about the car.

Monday came and I went back to work. I told Cyndy about the car and my trip on Saturday. She could tell how excited I was. I told her of my plans to go back to my dad's dealer tonight to talk about the deal. She went to Bob and told him that I was trying to buy a new car from another dealer and that he had better start talking to me about a car or I would buy somewhere else. Well, the wheeling and dealing began. I worked at a Chevrolet dealer and the comparable model to the Plymouth Satellite was the Malibu. Bob said he had a used one and I said I wanted new. He just didn't seem to take me seriously. It almost seemed like he thought I was a dumb, poor farm kid. He just didn't seem to get it, but he wrote me a deal on a new Malibu with all the features I wanted. He gave me the price and I told him I was going to compare it to the other dealer's offer.

Monday night after work I went to talk to Dutch. I explained my situation. He didn't realize that I worked at a Chevrolet dealer and I showed him the deal they had quoted me. He wrote up a new Satellite with comparable equipment. The prices were close, very close. I told Dutch I had to go with the lowest price no matter what and I had to get around the co-signer requirement. I had learned a little about contracts and financing since I had been working, and I was able to tell them what I was looking for in terms they understood. I found myself getting caught up in something I found to be very exciting. I was making decisions and I was putting pressure on other people to give me what I wanted and they were responding. It gave me a sense of power I had never known before, and it was fun!

When I went to work the next morning I had two car deals in my pocket. I told Bob about the other deal and that the bottom lines were very close and we needed to talk about it. After I had been at work about an hour, Bob asked if he and Rusty could talk to me in Rusty's office. I said okay and proceeded to follow Bob into Rusty's office. When I walked inside, Bob shut the door and I suddenly felt scared. I didn't know what they were going to talk to me about and at this point, I didn't think I wanted to know. Rusty, being the friendly guy that he was, started talking almost immediately. I think he sensed my terror.

"So I hear you want to buy a new car," he said with a hint of question in his voice.

"Yes." I said.

"You were checking on prices elsewhere?" Bob questioned.

"Yes."

"Do you have their offer and are we close?" He continued.

"Yes."

Rusty asked, "Can I see the write up on that deal?"

"Yes," I said, and took the paper out of my pocket.

He and Bob looked over the paper for a few minutes. I sat quiet, almost afraid to say anything. They got out Bob's papers for the deal and started comparing. They looked at the papers with surprise and some bewilderment on their faces.

Rusty finally broke the silence with, "These deals are very close in price."

"Yes, they are." I said.

"These guys can't be making a hundred dollars on this deal." Rusty said,

"Well, forty-nine dollars as a matter of fact," I said, "My father is their best customer and has been for a long time. I'm sure that influenced the deal."

"I can't beat this deal," Rusty exclaimed, "but I can throw in floor mats and prep for you."

I thought about it for a minute. I wasn't sure how to tell him that I didn't care about the floor mats and prep. I was worried about the co-signer and said, "Do I have to have my parents co-sign the loan?"

I could tell by the look on his face that I had just asked a question he did not want to hear. He bowed his head and looked at the papers again.

Slowly answering, "Yes, I will have to have their signature as co-signers for the loan."

I asked, "Are you sure? I don't have to at the other place."

Rusty was puzzled and asked, "How can they do that? You're only 18."

I responded with, "I believe the salesman is co-signing for me. I just cannot have my parents on this car loan, and if that is something you can't get around, then I guess I have my decision as to which car I am buying."

There was a silence and long pause. I almost felt sorry for Rusty; I think he was lost for a moment. I'm sure he was thinking about me being an 18-year-old kid with a new car loan. He didn't really know me or my family well, and it left him with the only decision he could make. After all he was one of the "city" people and I was a farmer. This was just a safe business decision. But he was my boss. He should know where the payments would be coming from as long as I stayed working for him.

Rusty apologized that he could not compete with the co-sign stipulation and said he hoped there would be no hard feelings. I said I sincerely hoped that because I planned to continue working for him. I liked my job and the people I worked with and I didn't want that to change. I just needed a car with the best deal. We kind of laughed about it as I left the office. I know he and Bob talked about it after and were convinced it was the right decision to let the other dealership take the risk.

After work that night I went to see Dutch. He got out my order and we finalized the deal. He said he would try to expedite the order, but it would probably take 6 to 8 weeks at best. I told him to do what he could and let me know when he heard anything. He said he would.

I went home and told Dad about the car and the deals that day. We didn't discuss the co-signer thing, I think he thought I would get stiffed when I went to pick up the car and that I would have to ask them to co-sign. I never did.

The news spread at work by the next morning and everybody was teasing me about being a traitor. I think they knew I had some relationship with the other dealership that made this deal go down the way it did. Rusty probably would have done the same thing for his best customers' kids and that was the only difference. But I must admit it was fun getting the attention from everybody.

Four weeks later I got a call from Dutch. The car had been shipped and was scheduled to arrive sometime the next day. I was so excited; I couldn't believe it was almost here. I didn't feel comfortable saying anything to anybody at work just yet, except Cyndy. I told her I was going over to see if it had come in that night. Work couldn't end fast enough. I wanted my new car.

When I arrived at the dealership, I looked for my car. I didn't see it. I went inside to find Dutch, and in the process he found me.

"Well, is it here?" I asked.

"Follow me!" Dutch replied.

He took me down stairs where they usually park the implements when they came in for repair. There it was, brand new and beautiful. It was being cleaned up and waiting for a quick inspection by me. It was exciting to see, and even more exciting to sit in. This was mine! This brand new 1967 Plymouth Satellite with a 383 cubic inch engine, 4 speed floor Hurst shift, white bucket seats, and gold metallic paint with the silver strip on the rocker panels. There were only three miles on it. It was beautiful. I started it up, tuned the radio and just sat there thinking this is mine. This dumb farm kid just got this great car. I almost couldn't imagine what it would be like to have my very own car to come and go as I please. I could see my friends, cruise through towns and show off just a little. No, show off as much as I wanted. This was a new life for me.

Dutch told me they had to finish prepping the car before I could pick it up, but they would have it done by Friday. I thought that would be perfect! We went upstairs to talk about the money, how much they needed down and registration costs. I told him I would be there to pick it up right after work. He said that would be good because he only worked until 6 on Friday. It was set; Friday I would have a brand new set of wheels that were mine and only mine.

I went home and told Dad that my car came in and that I was to pick it up Friday night. He didn't say much about it. He was unusually quiet about it and I didn't know why. I was excited enough for both of us, so I didn't really care. I saw Mom a little later and told her that I could pick up my car tomorrow. She said she knew it had come in. Someone had gone for parts and was at the dealership when it was unloaded. She seemed a little quiet about it too, but I didn't care. My car was here.

DON'T GET TOO EXCITED ABOUT PICKING UP THIS CAR. DID YOU FORGET YOU HAVE TO BABYSIT TOMORROW NIGHT?

Oh, crap! I did forget I promised to baby sit for Betsy, our neighbor. I wouldn't let Betsy down. My car would still there when I got home.

Friday came and I struggled to get through the day. I got home and Mom drove us to town, first to the bank and then to the dealership. As we pulled into the dealership, there it was sitting right out front. The parking lot was small and there was a steep slope at the far end of the lot. It was parked at the top in the sun glowing like it was in a spotlight, on stage showing off. It was the most beautiful car I had ever seen. Mom dropped me off and left. She didn't even ask me anything about the car, insurance, financing or anything. She and Dad probably talked to Dutch about this and just never said anything to me. I guess they thought I would have to do this on my own, but it was very different from when the boys got their cars. Mom and Dad were both there through the whole process and there was almost a party when they brought the cars home. I didn't understand why this was different, but I was so excited I didn't care.

I walked up to the car and looked inside. It was perfect. Dutch came out and asked if it looked okay.

"Are you kidding," I said, "it is perfect! How soon can I drive this away?"

"Just as soon as you sign your name in a couple of places on the paperwork and give me some money," he replied laughing.

"Deal" I said, and we proceeded into the show room.

The papers were all laid out on his desk and the signing only took a couple of minutes. I gave him a $500.00 cash down payment and a hand shake. I noticed on my copy of the finance contract that his name was signed on the co-signer line. I felt like a new person and now I owned a new car. We walked back out to the car and he gave me the keys. I got in and started looking at the dash and the necessary equipment I would have to use to drive this beauty home. Dutch went back into the showroom. I put the key in the ignition and almost started the car before I noticed the gas gauge was on empty. I quickly got out of the car and headed back to the showroom. Dutch met me halfway and asked what was wrong. I told him it didn't have any gas in it and asked if I could get a couple of dollars at their pumps. Suddenly his attention was on something behind me.

"Quick…your car!" he said, with sheer panic in his voice.

Here was my brand new car rolling down the hill headed for those gas pumps I had asked to use. I ran to the car without thinking. I'm chasing it down the hill with Dutch running after me. Luckily I had left the driver's door open and I was able to jump inside without opening the door to catch it. I slammed my foot on the brake just before it rolled into the gas pumps. Dutch caught up with me and asked if I was all right. I said I was while catching my breath.

"What were you asking me up the hill?" Dutch remembered.

I looked up at him feeling very foolish and said, "There is no gas in the car. Could I get a couple of dollars from these pumps?" By this time I was almost laughing while breathing a huge sigh of relief.

Dutch tipped his head down and started laughing too. "No, these pumps have been shut off. Its 6 o'clock and everyone has gone home."

He reached into his pocket and pulled out $2.00 and said, "Here's a couple of bucks to get some down the street, but be careful, okay?"

We both laughed and I promised I would be a lot more careful driving home. He patted me on the shoulder and said, "Okay".

He walked away from the car. I shut the door, started it up, shifted into first gear, drove into the street, and shifted into second without skipping a beat. I don't think Dutch thought I would get home with this car in one piece. I got some gas and proceeded to drive like the car and I were one.

THE ULTIMATUM

The car had been a positive and negative addition to my life. My brother Dick appeared to be very jealous. I'm not sure if it was because the car was newer than his or because I had more time to have fun with it than he could, but I was free to come and go as I pleased just about every night. I still helped on the farm, but after the fairs were over the work load got much lighter for me. I did the milking through October until Dick got back from the Eastern States show in Harrisburg, Pa. At that time, I was milking before and after work. That was an exhausting three weeks, plus I had to mow the lawn every Saturday. But after that I was able to meet up with some new friends I had met through work and we would cruise through towns trying to meet up with other friends. Most of the time it would be in Canandaigua, but one night it was in Newark.

It was December and the eve of Mom and Dad's anniversary. Dick had asked me to get them something for their anniversary, but he didn't ask me to do that until about 8 PM and the stores were only open until 9 PM, so I had to scramble. I picked up my friend Lois and we were off. We exchanged gift ideas and stores to buy them along the way. The traffic in town was terrible.

It was a couple of weeks before Christmas and everyone was out Christmas shopping. Driving through this traffic with a short deadline became a little frustrating for me, so I started to "bend" the traffic laws. I coasted through stop signs and drove 40 MPH in a 30 MPH zone. I got to one traffic light with a car in front of me that was obviously waiting for Santa to appear because she was turning left at a four corner intersection with a traffic light and it was still green, but I knew she would not go until it turned yellow for me. I was running out of time and parking spaces were sparse. She started to turn, and I thought, "Oh, good I'm going to make it." Then she stopped (she appeared to be waiting for a car coming from the next town!). The light turned yellow and she turned. By this time I was so frustrated I didn't consider waiting for the next light; I just drove right through the yellow light that changed to red (It wasn't like other people didn't do that). It was a holiday and I had to get to this flower shop before it closed. I thought I was safe because the car behind me did the same thing.

I had to turn down another block so I could park behind the flower shop and in the process of going around that block I realized the guy followed me through the light because he was a police officer. We found that out when he turned on his lights and siren to pull me over.

Panic set in along with the fear that goes with the whole "police" thing. He came up to the side of the car and asked if I knew I had gone through a red light. I told him that when I last looked at it, it was yellow and I was in a huge hurry because I had to get flowers for my parent's anniversary and the store was closing and the traffic was horrible. I assured him I didn't mean to break the law. I rattled off a lot more explanation than he needed and I don't think he wanted to hear all of it to begin with. He finally interrupted me and asked which flower shop. I pointed to the one kitty corner across the street.

"Okay," He said, "get your flowers and please don't go through any more red lights, all right? You might not be so lucky next time when someone could be driving through the light the same way and crash into you."

I promised I would drive properly. He left the side of my car and went back to his patrol car as I drove to the flower shop to park.

Somehow Dick was able to get information about my whereabouts with the car, or so I thought. He told Dad that he heard from some people that I was racing through town and squealing the tires on my car, outrunning the police, and being disorderly with my new car till the police told me to stay out of town. The major problem with that was I was doing some of that stuff, but not in that town. I could only guess that maybe Dutch, from the car dealership, knew the cop or had coffee with him. Maybe he told Dutch this funny story about this scatterbrained girl in a new car with his dealership sticker on it to see if he knew who it might be. In turn Dutch could have told Dick about it when he was in for parts. Or it was just a coincidence. Either way, Dad was mad and he believed every word Dick told him. He told me about what he heard and said I was grounded for two weeks. I wasn't to go anywhere except to work and then I had to come straight back home. I respected my Dad and I obeyed his order, but at the end of two weeks I had a heart to heart talk with him.

He was in the milk house alone when I asked if I could talk to him. "Yes" He answered, with a puzzled look on his face.

I said, "Dad, this is the last day of the two weeks you grounded me. I just want to explain something. I was grounded for misbehaving with my car. The story was that I was running red lights and pissing off the cops in town until they asked me to leave. I did drive through a yellow light that turned red and I happened to do it with a cop behind me. He did pull me over. But, if I were violating the laws so badly don't you think he would have given me a ticket? The cop never mentioned anything about not coming back into town. I bet that was an added feature Dick put into the story. Did you talk to any of the police about this?"

I looked at him with demanding eyes; I could feel them glaring at him. I felt his discomfort radiating out of him. I didn't like doing that to him, but I wanted him to realize that Dick was causing trouble. I wanted to tell him he should not be so quick to judge considering his only line of information was coming from Dick. He looked down at the floor. His expression was that of humility. I waited for a response.

After a minute, Dad said, "You're right. You should have gotten a ticket if you were breaking the law."

I interrupted him, "Dad, I haven't gotten ANY tickets. None! You get my mail before I do. Have you seen anything from the police? Why didn't you ask me about what you heard?"

"No I haven't seen anything and yes, I should have asked you…"

I interrupted again, "I just wanted you to understand what is happening here. Dick is being nasty to me for some reason and I think it's the car. You should have asked me about it. I don't know what Dick is thinking and I don't care, but I am not going to sit down and take punishment again for something he made up."

"You're right, you're right."

I looked at him with anger racing through my body. I said bitterly and sarcastically, "Thank you," and turned away, leaving the milk house feeling like I just beat him up somehow. I didn't feel I was disrespectful, just honest, but it looked like it hurt him. For some reason I felt righteous and guilty. I hadn't done that before and I didn't like feeling I had just hurt my father when Dick was the one that created this situation. Dick had always enjoyed being "the power" and I was fed up with that and his games.

I remembered one time a couple of years ago when Dick was giving out his usual orders to me in the barn and I was in no mood to listen to it that day. He followed me down the manger just spewing his discontent about something I had or had not done. I was fed up with his mouth and turned around swinging my fist and it connected with his nose. I was as shocked as he was, but he reacted instantly. He grabbed my arm and twisted it around behind me and proceeded to bleed on my arm like he was marking me in some way. After he left I cleaned up with paper towels from the milk house and continued with my chores, but I was chuckling the rest of the night thinking, is that all he could do—bleed on me!

The discontent and jealousy continued and so did the stories, but Dad never grounded me again. By spring things had gotten so tense I found myself coming home later and later. On weekends it would be between 2 and 4 AM. I contemplated moving into an apartment, but every time I hinted at that, Mom and Dad would discourage the thought.

One Saturday night I just couldn't deal with it any longer. I was depressed and my mood was righteous again. I got in my car and drove to the corner store and bought a 6-pack of beer. I put it in my car to have in case I needed it. I didn't drink much beer, but it just seemed like the thing to do at the time. I stopped at the car wash, washed my car and drank a beer in the process. Then I just started driving. I went to Canandaigua and drove around for a while. I met up with Ted, my boss' nephew, and we went cruising together. We parked my car in the park by the lake, drank a couple more beers and talked for hours about what was bothering me. I didn't know he had an 11 PM curfew until it was about 3 AM. He was in trouble and felt he could not go home. By this time I wanted to get rid of him because I was in enough trouble already and I didn't need any more.

For some reason we decided to go back to my house so he could call his mother. I don't know what I was thinking—obviously I wasn't because as we drove in my driveway I could see the kitchen light was on and my mother was standing in front of the picture window. I knew I was dead. We went inside and Dad came into the kitchen. Mom started yelling at me at such a rate I could hardly understand what she was saying. It seems Ted's mom had called looking for him and went into a fit, yelling over the phone. She got my parents all riled up and it went down hill from there. I went to leave again just to get away from the whole wretched scene and everyone followed me out the door screaming and yelling. I was forbidden to go and that triggered something inside me that made me listen even less. I didn't have to listen any more.

My mother was grabbing at me. Pulling me by my shirt and ripping it. She was yelling and screaming at me to do as I was told and my mind started wandering away. It was taking me to a dark place I remember screaming back at her, but the voices were becoming muffled. I just kept screaming louder and louder, "Get her away from me, get her away from me," but I could not scream loud enough to turn off this movie.

I was losing control of myself, my mind and my awareness of surroundings. I couldn't stop screaming and shook uncontrollably. I collapsed to the ground. I didn't know what was happening to me. I thought maybe I was dying. I was scared. It was like I couldn't get my brain under control.

Dad finally intervened and got Mom away from me. He told her to get in the house. He and Ted tried to settle me down, but it wasn't working. I could hear them, but they were far away and seemed insignificant. All I could hear was my mother's voice yelling at me, telling me to straighten up, behave, and stop my yelling and screaming. Dad and Ted decided to take me to the hospital.

***

When I woke up from my shot at the emergency room, I found myself on my brother's hideaway bed that he stored in the front living room of my parents' house. I tried to see what time it was, but there were no clocks in the room. The house was quiet and it was gray outside, like it was morning, but also dark like it was about to storm. I tried to sit up and found myself short on strength. I just propped myself up against the back of the couch and sat there for a few minutes. I felt like I'd been hit by a truck. I looked at my shirt. It was ripped. Then I realized the incidents of the night before were not a dream.

Suddenly the whole incident was vivid and the horror of that night was flooding my mind. I wanted to die. I truly wanted to die. These horrible thoughts were passing through my head. I was lost in a place in time that I could not change. Last night was real and today people would think I should be in Willard. How could I face any of them? I considered not leaving the room, but knew I had to. I didn't want to speak to anyone. I just wanted to die.

The silence in the house was deafening. It brought my mind into focus to go out to the kitchen to see what time it was. I quietly got up and walked into the kitchen. Mom was standing at the sink pealing potatoes. I looked at the clock. It said 1:30 PM.

Oh, my God, it's Saturday afternoon. I must have really been out. I thought to myself.

Mom asked, "Do you want something to eat?"

I paused for a moment, trying to figure what to do. Do I bring up last night? Do I pretend it didn't happen? Do I tell her I'm not hungry? Fix something myself?

JUST ANSWER THE QUESTION—ARE YOU HUNGRY?

"A little." I said

Mom responded with, "I have some cold cuts. Do you want a sandwich?"

"Yeah, that'd be okay."

She put down her paring knife and started fixing me a sandwich. I was going to make it, but she started and I decided to let her continue. I got a glass of milk and sat at the kitchen table. Mom finished making the sandwich and brought it to me. She went back to peeling potatoes. We didn't talk about last night, and I was glad about that. After I finished my sandwich, I thought I should lie down again for a little while. I returned to the front living room. Sleep was fast coming and I slept soundly. I didn't wake up again until 7 PM. I still wanted to be alone so I just stayed in that room the rest of the night thinking about what to do. I decided to not say anything about that night unless it was brought up.

The next morning I got up like I normally did. Dad was in from the barn for breakfast and Mom was hanging out the wash. At first he didn't talk about Friday night, but his tone and expression changed and I knew it was coming. Dad told me I was asleep long before we got home from the hospital. Ted's mother came and picked him up. He told me the doctor recommended that I be allowed to make my own decisions in my life, which included getting my own place if I wanted.

The conversation was somber and it simply ended with Dad saying, "If you want to move out you can, but you don't have to if you don't want to, okay?"

I just said, "Okay, I'll think about it and let you know."

We didn't go into any details and the conversation was over as Mom came into the kitchen from the clothesline.

The next day I went to work and I knew this was going to be tough because Ted's mother was Rusty's sister. Everybody would know what transpired Friday night by now.

As I walked through the shop to get to my office everybody said "Good Morning" just like they always did, but when I got to the show room I ran smack into Rusty, face-to-face, at the doorway.

I said, "Good Morning, Rusty," but the uncertainty in my voice gave away the fear that was flooding my body at that moment.

"Good Morning, Laura," Rusty said, "I wasn't sure we would see you today."

"You heard about Friday, huh?" I said sheepishly.

"Yes," He said softly, "my sister was pretty mad at Ted."

I smiled back with my thoughts saying "Thank you" so loud Rusty must have heard them.

"I'm sure she was!" I replied.

Rusty continued on his way, but I knew he understood and in his own way let me know it was okay and it was over. I kept myself very busy that day and soon the incident was beginning to fade. Quitting time came and I went home feeling better. It was over.

When I got home, I changed my clothes and fixed myself something to eat. I needed to think about what I was going to do. Dad made me feel like I didn't have to go. I got the impression he really did not want me to go. I didn't want to hurt him, but I didn't know what Mom was thinking. We never talked about that night. I had no intention to bring up the subject for further discussion in fear of a repeat performance. I was lost in my thoughts while eating my supper when Dick came in from the barn. He stopped at the table where I was sitting and asked what was going on.

I looked up at him and said, "Not much, why?"

"Well," He said, "I think it would be a good idea if you got out of here. You can get your things and leave or you can pick them up in the road by Saturday. Do I make myself clear?"

"Ah, yeah." I said, with great hesitation.

He then turned and walked out the back door to go back to the barn.

I was in shock. I started to panic. I had six days to get out. So much for deciding what to do; it looks like Dick just did that for me. I had to find someplace to live, in a hurry. I guess that set my plans for the next few days. My mind raced. How do I find a place in only six days? I had become afraid of Dick because of the power he had over Mom and Dad. I didn't want to make him mad again by staying and I didn't want to know what he would do to me if I disobeyed his order.

I remembered Emmitt. He was a friend of Neil's, who I had met recently. Neil and I dated when he worked for my father. Emmitt and his wife, Carol, had an apartment they were in the process of remodeling. They talked about renting it, but I didn't think they had. It was in the country just outside Canandaigua. Emmitt was a part time farmer who worked for the county. The house was between the city of Canandaigua and my work making it close to all the places I worked and played. I had never lived in town and I wasn't sure if I could do that. I thought this would be a place to start. I needed something cheap, small and fast.

I decided to finish my supper and go see Emmitt and Carol.

When I arrived at Emmitt's house, he was just walking out of the barn. He was a friendly person with a chubby cheek smile. He had very large teeth and a red face, a bit like my Dad, but in all other aspects he was average.

I parked the car and he walked up to my door.

"Hi," I said, "do you remember me?"

He smiled and said, "Yes, I think I do. You were a friend of Neil's when you were here once."

"That's right," I laughed, "and I'm still a friend of Neil's. I wanted to stop by and ask if you ever rented that upstairs apartment."

"No we haven't finished downstairs so we can move our bedroom out of the apartment. Why do you ask?"

"Well, I'm looking for an apartment and was wondering if your upstairs apartment was available."

"Ya know we could go inside and talk to my wife about this and maybe we can come to a decision. It may help spur us to finish all this remodeling." he suggested.

"Okay," I said, as we proceeded inside.

Carol had remembered me the same way Emmitt had and we all laughed about it. We got right to the point of the conversation. They said it would be a little while before they would be able to move their bedroom downstairs, but maybe we could share the upstairs. They would use the one bedroom and I could use the kitchen, living room and bathroom. I said I wouldn't have a problem doing that. I didn't have any furniture at this point. I would probably get a sofa with a hideaway bed. We all agreed this was workable and after I explained my short time frame they thought I could move in on Saturday. They suggested they might need to do some touch ups after I got moved in, but we all felt good about the arrangement. They would be getting some income, and I would have a place to stay.

When I got home it was about 8:30. Dad was just coming out of the barn, heading toward the shop, as I drove in. I stopped him in the driveway and told him I was moving on Saturday. He seemed quite surprised. I think he thought I was going to stay. I knew he did not know of Dick's threat and I did not feel I could tell him. I wasn't sure he would believe me anyway. For some reason I was sure this was better left unsaid. I didn't need to stir up any more trouble. His only reply was, "Okay, if that's what you decided."

IT WAS DECLARED NOT DECIDED!

He went on his way and I went into the house. Mom was doing laundry. I joined her there and told her I found an apartment. I would be moving out on Saturday. She also acted very surprised. That confirmed my suspicions that Dick had not told anyone else what he had said. I didn't feel like telling her either, because it would boil down to who would believe who and I wasn't up for that kind of battle. Dick always won.

The Apartment

I couldn't stop thinking about the move. It was exciting. Who would have thought this would feel so good? I thought it would put an end to the whole story telling by Dick and I would be on my own and out of his grip. I just wanted to get my things together and move as quickly as I could. Every night I sorted and packed. I was replaying memories of the previous years. I found yearbooks, prom dresses, homework papers, report cards, award ribbons, trophies, records and pictures. All these things flooded my mind. What do I take? What do I leave? I'll be back to pick up stuff I can't pack this week. I'll just take the important stuff. It helped erase the memories of last week.

There were few conversations of the move the rest of the week. I asked at one point what would happen to Brenda and my other 4-H animals. Mom said I could sell them back to the farm and they would let me know how much they were worth. She said they could not afford to give me any money right now. I told her I didn't care because I had enough to get started. I opened a charge account with a catalog store to get things I needed like dishes, silverware, towels and cookware for a small monthly payment. I had a phone installed, but I would have to be careful about calling home because it was long distance. As the week sped by, I was getting more and more excited about the move.

Trixie seemed like she was a little unsure about the move at first, but we talked about the apartment and after I explained the positive points, she seemed to share my excitement. We talked about getting together at my place and that sounded like fun. It seemed we were getting close, just as I was getting ready to leave. She was helping Dick at the fairs now and he had reregistered all of the best show cows in her name. She could show the best cows in every class and take home the 4H money from all the wins. I thought how nice it would have been if I could have had that option, but I didn't. It didn't matter now anyway. I was out of it and I had a new life to live.

Saturday came and I borrowed a truck from Rusty to move the couch. Ted helped with the couch and a new dresser I bought from a small general store just down the road from my apartment. Ted took the truck back while I got the second load of my belongings in the car. It was about 4 o'clock when I was ready to leave. I walked through the kitchen; Dad, Dick and the summer help were sitting around the kitchen table having coffee. I asked Dad if I could take a couple of packages of meat from the freezer so I didn't have to get food tonight. He told me to go help myself. It almost felt like I was stealing as Dick watched me go to the freezer. I got the meat, a steak and a couple of packages of hamburger and went back to the kitchen. I wanted to make sure Dick saw the <u>three</u> packages of meat in my hands.

I walked toward my Dad. He was looking down at the floor. No one was talking. The kitchen was excruciatingly quiet. I felt like I was standing in the eye of a F6 tornado. The velocity of tension whirling around me was out of control yet there was not a sound.

I looked at Dad and said, "Thanks for the meat."

He didn't look up. He solemnly uttered, "You're welcome".

I hurried out the door and into my car. I could still see them sitting there not saying anything. They acted like they were frozen in time. No one said anything. Not a goodbye, good luck or offer to call. Nothing! *IT'S OVER—JUST LEAVE. GO NOW!*

In leaving, I felt like I was a stranger that just walked through someone else's house. Trixie wasn't there, but we had said our goodbyes and promised to call each other often. I truly believed we would. I thought we had become friends as well as sisters and that made this whole thing sad. We had spent fifteen years together and we had just gotten around to realizing that we liked each other. We probably loved each other, but we didn't say it. Love to me was a word for married couples. The reason people get married is because they love each other, but I never thought of love for my brothers and sister. Love for them was just being in the same home. Love was a word, it wasn't an emotion. If I were to say I love my parents, it only meant that I had respect for them as parents. I was positive I hadn't experienced what I thought love was supposed to be. I didn't feel any love as I walked to my car. It was like I hadn't been there at all.

As I drove down the driveway, I looked back to see if anyone was watching out the picture window. No one was. I pulled onto the road and I could feel the tears running down my face. This was so painful, but I knew I had to do it this way (Dick said!).

Once in my apartment I realized life was different. Actually, it was fun. I was poor, but I didn't care. There was a hamburger stand on the lake called Dandy's. They had hamburgers, fries and milk shakes for $.25 each. Usually I would eat there at night. It was cheap and right in the heart of the action in town. People I knew would stop and hang out. They were mostly guys with cars similar to mine. They had seen my car literally racing through town enough times to want to find out who drove that new Satellite. Most of the guys had either the Malibu or the Dodge R/T's. Gold metallic was the new color for the year and there were a few around. The Dodge and Plymouth were near identical in body shape and paints. I knew a couple of guys with the gold Dodge R/T and it was hard for me to tell them apart sometimes, but we would beep and wave to each other or talk sometimes at the hamburger stand.

Part of the entertainment for young folk like us was street racing. We would pull up at stop lights and wait for the green light. When it changed, we'd pop the clutch and hit the gas as fast as we could. The object was to leave the light like we were driving in the Drag Racing National Championships, final round! I had more fun because I was the only girl doing it and the guys that didn't know me would pull up alongside, look over and smile while waiting for a light. Then they'd turn their head to their buddy in the passenger seat, and I just knew they were saying, "Oh, a girl in her brother's car!" Then they would laugh, the light would change and I could, as they say, "lay rubber" in all four gears while they sat there with their mouths gapping. That was quite fun actually. By the time they caught on, I was long gone, but I always caught the look on their faces in my rearview mirror.

***

It had been about a year since I moved to my apartment and my life was my own. I had new friends and very little communication with my family with the exception of my sister. We had become very close and my phone bill proved it. She told me of the things Dick was still saying. He had told Dad that I was sleeping with any guy that came to my apartment. I had turned into a whore. That hurt, but I knew I couldn't change or stop Dick from doing what he did, so I didn't try. I could tell by their actions, when I did see them, that Dad and Mom thought the stories were true. I didn't ever take anyone I dated over to the house to meet them, because they would be scum in their eyes no matter who it was or what they did. I never talked about the guys I dated with anyone except my sister. My life went on and the empty space where I once had a family was a haunting memory that didn't go away. I didn't go to the county fair that year even though it was only two miles from my apartment. It was like going back to the little creek with the snakes. Sometimes you just have to walk away and never look or go back.

In late August a new twist came into my life. I was cruising around town one night and saw the gold Dodge R/T that I thought belonged to Doug and Gill, but I soon found it wasn't, after I tooted and waved. It was another guy that I didn't know. He turned around and followed me.

I pulled into Dandy's and he pulled up alongside. I smiled and waved to both guys inside and I knew only the driver by face, not name. He got out of the car, came over and started talking. His name was Daryl. He was a large man about six feet tall with a husky build. He wore glasses, had mousy brown hair and was somewhat attractive, but not what I would call "cute". The conversation was very nice and we talked quite a while. It was getting late and I finally said I had to go home as we said our goodbyes.

I left first. It was very dark as I left town and thought a car might be following me. When I saw the four-way flashers come on, I instinctively pulled to the side of the road. I wasn't sure if it was a cop or what, but Daryl got out of his car and walked up to the side of my car. He said "Hi" again and asked if I would join him for dinner on Saturday with his friend, Andy, and his girlfriend. I thought this was a real date offer. I had never been to a real restaurant for dinner. I said I would be able to do that and told him to follow me to see where I lived. I gave him my phone number and asked him to call me later—like tomorrow during daylight hours! He said okay and we continued on our way. It was less than a mile from my apartment and Daryl just turned around in the driveway and left with a quick toot of his horn as he drove back to town.

I went to bed thinking that I had a real date on Saturday. We were going to a real restaurant for a real dinner. I was going to have steak cooked by someone else for a change. I dropped off to sleep thinking of steak!

After work the next day I got a call from Daryl. We talked about Saturday and I asked him what I should wear. He said it was a jacket and tie kind of place so I might want to dress up a little. I acknowledged I could do that and I would see him on Saturday around 7.

Daryl arrived promptly at 7 on Saturday in sport jacket, white shirt and tie. I was wearing a marine blue chemise dress with long puffy sleeves and a deep "v" back with a dangling tie. It always looked nice on me. That night, for the first time in a very long time, I felt very special, maybe even pretty. Daryl commented on how nice I looked, and we proceeded on our way to pick up Andy and his girlfriend.

We went to a well-known restaurant about fifteen miles outside of Canandaigua. Actually, I had never been to a restaurant where you had to dress up, and I was excited. It wasn't until we were seated at the table that the terror set in. I hadn't done this before and there were all those forks and spoons and knives. I looked at the menu and saw the prices of the food and nearly dropped the menu. I was trying to keep my classy composure and praying that my terror was not showing on my face. What would I order? I'll just get what Daryl gets.

WHAT IF YOU DON'T LIKE WHAT HE ORDERS? YOU DON'T KNOW WHAT PRIME RIB IS AND BESIDES YOU WANTED STEAK, RIGHT? THEN GET STEAK!

Well, that suggestion didn't help much. There were Porterhouse, Delmonico, New York Strip and Prime Rib (under the steak column). I was reading all the choices, quickly and over and over. Then the waitress came back to take our orders. She looked straight at me to give her my order. Panic set in and I just picked the cheapest steak entry there was. I said I would have the Prime Rib. I thought—wheeeu I got through that one okay.

Then the waitress said, "How would you like that cooked?"

I thought to my self, what? What the hell does that mean?

JUST SAY MEDIUM-RARE, THAT'S HOW PEOPLE ON TV ORDER IT!

So I did, but the questions didn't stop there. What kind of potato, salad dressing, and beverage? It felt like an interrogation. Before she got through with me and went on to someone else, I was sweating and feeling like my face would explode with my embarrassing red glow. Thank God it was dark in the room. No one else seemed to notice. Or at least they didn't say anything.

We had drinks and comfortable, casual conversation while we ate our salads. I was beginning to feel more relaxed and was actually having a good time with my new friends. Then our main course came and I got the reddest piece of meat I had ever seen. I had seen some pretty red meat in my day, but even the meat juice was bright red! I kept my calm and decided I would eat it no matter what.

"Is that cooked enough for you?" Daryl asked.

"Yes, this is just the way I like it."

"It looks a little rare; do you want to send it back?"

I was even more horrified. I thought, send it back? You don't ever send anything back! You take it the way you asked for it and like it. I could never send it back even if it came to me still alive!

I thought I would take a bite just to show Daryl that I liked it raw. I cut a small piece and put it into my mouth. It was warm and definitely raw in the middle, but it was very tasty. I thought this won't be the torture that I originally thought it might be. The rest of the meal was as good and we all seemed to enjoy each other's company. As the evening rolled on the jitters left me and I found myself feeling like I had known these people for years.

It was about midnight when we arrived back at my apartment. Daryl walked me up the outside stairs and we stood on the landing and talked and talked—for hours, actually. I invited him in, but he said he did not feel comfortable coming in so late, so we just stood on the landing and continued talking. We finally realized how late it was when we heard Emmitt come out his back door and leave for work—it was 6 AM! Daryl now realized he had to go too.

I knew he wanted to kiss me good night, but he didn't. He said he would call me later that day, but he had to work until 4 PM. I said I would be home when he called and he left, waving as he drove away.

I couldn't help thinking what a gentleman he was and how nice it was to go out with someone that wasn't groping me or taking me to a pizza joint or hamburger stand for a date. This was really nice and we found out in our long conversation that we had quite a lot in common. His father was a salesman for farm equipment with an implement dealer that my father had done some business with in the past. We both liked drag racing, watching it and playing around in the streets with it. He was an only child, but had very close ties with all of his family members. He was twenty-four years old and I was nineteen. I was impressed with him. I liked being treated with respect for a change.

Daryl called me Sunday afternoon. He asked if he could stop by after work and maybe we could get something to eat. He suggested stopping at his house so I could meet his parents. I didn't see any harm in that and I told him so. I didn't even feel nervous about it. I almost felt I knew them already.

Daryl arrived at 4:30 and I met him at the bottom of the stairs. He opened the car door for me and soon we were on our way. He asked if I would mind meeting his parents before we got something to eat. I told him I didn't mind. He still lived at home, but I didn't think that was too odd, after all he didn't have a brother to throw him out like I did. When we arrived I saw a two-story house very similar to my grandparent's house near my Dad's farm. It had a large lot with blacktop drive and a two-car garage at the end. It was well cared for with mature trees, shrubs and flowers. Inside, the rooms were small, but very neat. It was decorated a lot like my grandparents house, with old style wallpaper, knickknacks and collectibles. His Mom and Dad were in the living room watching TV and came to greet us in the dining room.

The introductions were made and Daryl's father asked if I were Marvin Vandermae's daughter. I confirmed that I was and he said he knew my Dad and had done business with him in the past. Daryl's father, Daryl, Sr. was a very tall man, about 6 feet two or three. He had a laugh that came from his diaphragm and seemed like a very friendly person with a mischievous sense of humor.

Daryl's mom, Jeanette, was different in that she was a bit reserved, but friendly, about my height, and dark brown hair that had been done at a beauty parlor. After the immediate introductions we were invited to sit, but Daryl said we were going out to get something to eat. After a little more conversation we said our good byes and Daryl's father gave me a hug and a kiss. His mother gave me a hug. I was surprised and unsure of proper behavior here, so I just went along. I never had any touching like this by a parent before and it felt wrong, uncomfortable, actually. I just didn't know what I should feel about this. It was brand new.

OBVIOUSLY THIS FAMILY DOES THAT KIND OF THING!

Daryl and I left, but the touching thing stayed with me. I actually got a kiss from his father before I got one from him. That seemed weird.

From that point on we saw each other every day. I really liked being around Daryl and his family. They always treated me like I belonged in the family even from the very beginning. I met some of his other relatives and they were of the same nature. He had cousins that had gone through divorces and some of the kids lived with their grandparents. This too was new to me, but the families seemed strong and supportive. It was very evident they loved their kids no matter what they had done. I liked that. Most of the aunts and uncles were huggers, too. Someone was always around to put a hand on my shoulder or arm around me, and I got used to feeling very welcome. It was a nice feeling and I was enjoying this family.

It was September 7, and Daryl was coming over after work. We had been seeing each other every day for two weeks. I felt content and happy and I didn't want that to change. When Daryl got to my apartment, he was acting a little funny, actually silly. He was trying to hide something he had in his hand, but wanted me to see it at the same time.

I asked him, "What's going on?"

"Oh nothing," he just said, and then laughed a little.

It didn't take long to find out why he was so giddy. He asked me to look at something he was holding in his hand. When I looked I saw a diamond ring. I almost fell on the floor.

I looked up at him and he said, "Will you marry me? I know this is quick, but I really love you and want very much for us to be together."

I was breathless for a second. I was trying to think fast. I had to give him an answer. I really did like Daryl. Maybe I even loved him, but I didn't know. I was never really sure what love was anyway. He and his family treated me better than my own did and at that moment I thought spending a lifetime like the last two weeks would be wonderful. If we got married, we could be together all the time. I didn't see that as a bad thing.

I looked at Daryl, "Yes, I will marry you."

He slipped the ring on my finger, kissed me, and held me tight while we exchanged our feelings of love. I was convinced our love was true. We were both very happy. This must be what love feels like. The thought of a lifetime like the past two weeks was something I wanted to keep. We went to get ice cream to celebrate.

The next day we decided to show the ring to the family. We went to the store where Daryl's mom worked.

When I showed her the ring, she took my hand in hers, looked at the ring very closely, looked up at me and said, "What? Not another one?" then walked away.

I looked at Daryl with question and he said he would tell me the story later about another diamond ring. We caught up with Jeanette and told her that we really felt our relationship was strong enough for marriage. We were very happy and loved each other and didn't feel we were children. We both had jobs. I had an apartment and thought of myself as responsible. She apologized for her actions and said she would be happy for me to join their family. She seemed to have more history about Daryl's past relationships than I knew about. I wasn't sure if I wanted to know. I suspected I would hear them at some point.

I hadn't thought of a wedding date at this point. I was just trying to get over the idea of being engaged, when the thought came to me that I had to tell **my** family. Who would I tell first? Trixie would be first. She would be happy and excited for me. Mom would be next and I would let her tell Dad. I couldn't think of anyone else that I needed to tell. The word would get around fast enough anyway. I knew no matter what my husband did or who he was; he would never be accepted by my family, but at this point I didn't care.

I called Trixie and told her the news. She was excited and I was glad about that. Then I talked to Mom and told her that I had met someone and we had just become engaged. She talked to me very calmly. She actually spoke to me like I was an adult. She said she just wanted me to be sure this was the man for the rest of my life. I told her I was sure, even though we had not been together long. I didn't tell her it had only been a couple of weeks, but I was sure this was the right decision. I really felt Daryl and I were meant to be together.

It didn't take too many days before Daryl started asking about a wedding date. I was a little surprised, but didn't see any reason why not to set a date. Daryl gave me three dates he thought would be good with his work schedule. He had chosen one Saturday in October, November and December. I almost didn't know how to react. October was only a couple of weeks away. But I was in love and being together was all that was important to me now. I told him it would take a little time to put a wedding together so we went with the December date. My thoughts were that we could be married before Christmas. A family Christmas would be wonderful. My last Christmas was much less than the ones I enjoyed as a child and changing that would be good. The wedding date was officially set for December 2, 1967.

THE WEDDING

It was the day before my wedding. The last two and a half months had been filled with arrangements almost every day. There was so much to do and very little time to make it all happen. Daryl and I had gone to pre-nuptial counseling at his church where we would be married. I had bought a lovely gown and had five bridesmaids. The arrangements were coming together better than I expected. Mom was taking the event seriously and decided to make the food for the reception. Daryl's family had invited 300 guests and I had about 100 invited from my family. I had five showers, mostly given by Daryl's family and friends. My girlfriends, Alice and Mary, from high school had given me one. We had talked to Emmitt and Carol about the apartment and they had gotten enough of the downstairs remodeling done so we could have the whole upstairs of my apartment.

Daryl suggested I sell my car because he had bought a new one last month and we didn't need two car payments. We felt we were close enough to our jobs to share one vehicle. I felt a little uneasy about selling my car, but Daryl thought it was the best thing to do. I didn't challenge him. We sold my car to a guy Daryl worked with and we were supposed to drop it off tonight. It felt like the hurt I experienced when I left my cows on the farm. I had a tendency to hang onto material things. It did hold a lot of memories and those I would have forever.

Tomorrow at 2 PM I would walk down the aisle with my dad and he would give me away to the man I loved. My sister would be my Maid of Honor, and rightfully so. I had asked my brother Lyle to be an usher because we were so much alike. He too felt trauma on the farm. He had been driving a trailer truck for about seven years now. I guess I wanted at least three of my family members to be a part of my wedding. I was thinking of all the things that had happened and questioned if my decision was absolutely the right one. I knew everyone got last minute jitters and I guess I was feeling a little that way. Then, I thought how I truly loved Daryl. My life felt complete with him in it. All the arrangements were made and all we had to do was go to the rehearsal tonight and arrive at the church on time tomorrow.

Daryl picked me up after work so we could drop off my car to its new owner. Then we went to the rehearsal at the church. Daryl and I were both nervous, but that was to be expected. We walked through the routine with everyone in the wedding party present except my brother Lyle. He was stuck with the truck in Buffalo. He told mom to tell me not to worry because he had been in a few weddings and knew the routine and would be there Saturday. The party at Daryl's parents' house went well, but it sure was crowded. That little house was not meant to have that many people in it at one time. It soon came time for everyone to go home and Daryl's cousin, April, gave Trixie and me a ride back to my apartment.

We spent the late hours talking about the wedding and practicing my new name. We laughed about possible mishaps and finally decided to get some sleep. We had to be at the hairdressers by 9 AM and I was sure we would be awake long before then. As I was trying to drop off to sleep, I was replaying the events of the past few months. One came to mind immediately.

It was the night of the shower given by Daryl's cousins, April and Ellen. The party was a lot of fun and when it came to a close I offered to give April a ride home. It was late, probably around midnight or so, and we thought we would cruise through town one last time before going home. We were laughing and having a great time when we saw Daryl cruising down the other side of Main Street. We decided to play a game with him. We left town and went to the used car lot, just down the street from my apartment. We backed in between a couple of cars in the front row and could see my apartment driveway perfectly. April told me that Daryl had a jealous streak in him a mile wide, so we decided to test it.

We waited in the car to see if he came to the apartment looking for us. Well it didn't take long before he showed up. He pulled into the driveway at my apartment, turned around and left. After about a half an hour or so, he came back and did it again. We just sat there in the car and watched. By the third time, we decided we better go back to the apartment. But we wanted it to look like we had been there the whole time. We barely got upstairs and he pulled in. We sat in the kitchen with the lights off just to see what he would do. Well, he parked his car and came upstairs. By this time it was after 2 AM. He was not a happy man. His anger radiated in his face and actions. It was a side of him I had not seen. He was trying to control his anger, but was not doing it very well. He made insinuations that we were out looking for guys. That was the kicker. April was married to Cory, who was in the Navy and out to sea for six months. She was the most trustworthy person I knew. I would have thought he felt that way too. After all she was <u>his</u> cousin.

We got into our first fight and I remember feeling like he didn't trust me. Honesty and trust were huge issues with me, and the old adage, "lie and be lied to," stuck in my mind. Why wouldn't he believe me? I had not done anything dishonest, prankish maybe, but not enough to imply I was running around on him. I had been brought up to <u>always,</u> <u>always</u> tell the truth or God would punish me severely. After all, I had been with his family. April injected her opinion into our heated conversation and it helped a lot. After some defensive rebounding from April and me, Daryl calmed down and we came to terms with the problem. We kissed and made up. Daryl offered to take April home. I wondered now if he took her home so we wouldn't be out on the street together. Just a thought.

The first fight always stays in your mind a while anyway and I just thought that was the reason this situation flashed back into my mind now. I wanted to think I wouldn't see any of that kind of behavior ever again. I wanted everything to be perfect. I wondered if my rapport with Daryl's parents would be consistent too. The day we showed Jeanette my engagement ring was another flash. I will always remember her words, "What, not another one?" Daryl had told me the whole story a few days later.

It seems Daryl had tried to get married before. When his Mother came out with that statement, he almost had to tell me all of his history. Daryl had four previous relationships, which had appeared to be serious, that involved a diamond ring. To demonstrate his love he would give them an engagement ring early on in the courtship. I think he fell in love fast, or fell into what he thought was love. Over the past six years, he had given out four engagement rings before mine, all of which were given back at the breakup.

IT'S A LITTLE LATE TO THINK OF THAT STUFF NOW. DON'T THINK ABOUT IT.

I dozed off to sleep thinking how lucky I was and that I was a very happy person. In my dreams, everyone was smiling and laughing. I couldn't think of anything I would want to change.

It was about 7 AM. The sun was streaming in the kitchen window. It was December 2nd, my wedding day. Sunshine wasn't a daily commodity this time of the year, so it made it an especially beautiful day. It was unseasonably warm and a little balmy. I thought this was a good omen. I had been up for a while when Trixie came into the kitchen. I asked her if she wanted some breakfast. She said not right now. She asked if I had been up long. I told her I didn't know exactly what time I got up, but I had to finish packing my suitcase for our honeymoon. It was going to be a short one because we wanted to go to Florida for two weeks at the end of January with Daryl's parents. We didn't know exactly where we were going to stay the first night. We thought we would drive till we found a motel somewhere. That seemed appropriate for our lifestyles. It protected us from the pranksters in the family so they wouldn't sabotage our luggage or the car in some way.

We chatted about the schedule for the day. I felt excited and not real nervous. I was in dream land and I just knew nothing would go wrong today. Everything seemed so right.

After our hair appointments, April took us back to the apartment where we got some lunch and put together the last minute things. Everyone was calling to make sure we were on schedule. Everything was, until the call from mom around noon. She told me she had gotten a call from Lyle and he was still stuck in Buffalo. He was not going to get here in time for the wedding. I panicked. I was trying to think of what to do when she suggested that I have my cousin Wade stand in for him. Lyle and Wade were close to the same size and they were planning to be at the wedding anyway. I took her suggestion and called Wade. He was a little shocked, but understood the situation and agreed to stand in. I told him to call mom to find out how to get Lyle's tux. I suggested he be at the church a little early to get any "new" instructions. In a flash, a perfect day became chaotic, but the solution came just as quick. We were still on schedule in spite of the hang up with Lyle.

We left for the church around 1 PM. All the bridesmaids were congregated at the church and were as excited as I was. Relatives and the photographer were popping in to see me as the time grew closer.

It was a frenzy of activities and more exciting than anything I had ever experienced in my life. Suddenly, it was time. Dad appeared at the door with the photographer right behind him. All the bridesmaids filed out of the room and started down the aisle of the church. As Dad and I walked into the hall I was thinking how pretty I felt. I didn't feel like the ugly duckling and I was dressed in the most beautiful white satin and lace gown, I had ever seen and it was mine. It had a spectacular train that fell from my shoulders and spread into a breathtaking cascade several feet behind me. It was the gown I never thought I would be able to have, but I did. This was truly a wonderful day for me.

I looked at Dad. He was so handsome. I rarely remember him being dressed up. Now here, today in front of me in a tuxedo, he looked like a movie star and he was waiting for me.

"Are you ready?" he asked.

I smiled, staring into his eyes, noticing his happy expression. He had a bit of sparkle dancing around in those eyes. I knew he hated getting dressed up, but today he had a glowing aura. He appeared to be really happy for me. I was feeling very proud to be standing next to him at this moment.

I hoped he knew my eyes were saying, "Thank you and I love you" to him, while my mouth said, "Yes, I'm ready. I'm not turning back now!" We both chuckled as we started down the aisle.

Cameras were flashing and people were standing and smiling. They were just a blur of faces to me. I couldn't seem to recognize any of them, but as I walked and my eyes passed down the aisle and to the altar, I saw Daryl. He looked very handsome too. He was smiling and all the ushers were there, including my cousin Wade.

As Dad and I arrived at the altar, we paused and stood like we were in need of catching our breath. There was the pause while everyone in the church sat down and then the Minister asked the question, "Who gives this bride to enter this marriage?"

Dad responded, just as he was supposed to, "Her Mother and I do."

He gave my hand to Daryl, backed away from the altar and joined my Mother in the first pew. I wasn't thinking of anything else but how wonderful this day had turned out and how lucky I was to be doing this. I looked at Daryl thinking, I really do love this man and I'm sure he loves me. As the ceremony continued, my knees got shakier and my confirmation of love got stronger. When we got to the part where we pledge our love to each other, I did it without hesitation while I stared into Daryl's eyes and with all the feeling I had swelling inside, I made those promises and meant them. Daryl recited his back to me and he looked like he was feeling exactly the same, but I could see the jitters hovering in the back ground. The moment was here as the minister announced, "I now pronounce you man and wife. You may kiss the bride."

After the receiving line came the pictures. Pictures of my parents and his parents felt awkward to me. It was like putting a cow in the kitchen! It was two elements together that didn't seem to belong together, and yet we did it anyway. Everything happened just the way it was supposed to with moms and dads smiling and laughing through it all. Everyone seemed to be having a great time and they all seemed happy for us. Finally it was time to go to the reception. There were still a lot of people at the church when we finally got ready to leave. Mom and Dad left just ahead of us so Mom could make sure the food was ready. The wedding party of fourteen people piled into cars and we drove the traditional horn-blowing routes through town.

We arrived at the reception quite late. Mom was busy setting food on the tables because people had gotten tired of waiting for us, so she started serving. I didn't mind, at that point I just wanted everybody to be happy. As we mingled through the crowd to the head table, my brother Lyle intercepted us. He apologized for the problems and told us that he had gotten two speeding tickets trying to get home. I told him that everything worked out fine and that I was very glad he was here. We preceded with the traditional routine the best we could.

It was close to 7 PM and people had been at this wedding a long time. Lots of people were at the bar, but it was getting time for us to go.

We said our goodbyes to folks and families and Daryl's best man, Nick, took us back to Daryl's parent's house to change and pick up Daryl's car. We thanked Nick for all his help and got into the car. As Daryl reached for the shift lever we noticed something. There, on the end of the shifting arm, was a condom. It looked like it once had air in it, but was now hanging there quite deflated. Daryl grabbed it and stuffed it into his pocket as we laughed and left for our honeymoon.

About 10:30 PM, Daryl pulled into a motel that seemed to be in the middle of nowhere. It was perched up on a hill and overlooked a valley with a small town below. The room was small and clean with a TV, phone and double bed. I turned on the TV out of habit, and Daryl said he would get our luggage. He returned after a few minutes and I took my bag and proceeded to the bathroom to put on my negligee. It was a two-piece white (of course) gown with matching robe trimmed in lace and embroidered flowers. I wasn't a real feminine kind of girl, but when I saw my image in the mirror, I felt beautiful.

When I emerged from the bathroom, Daryl was laying on the bed in pajamas. We both felt as awkward as two people could get. I think Daryl and I were feeling the pressure of our upbringing. Daryl's parents were very strict about Daryl's behavior, especially with women. He was told numerous times by his father that if he ever got a girl pregnant that he would immediately be disowned by the family. I too had pressure from my family about sexual activity with boys. So there had not been much desire for either of us to pursue that frontier. But now it was expected of us. We were married, and on your honeymoon, you do it. To me it still seemed like it all boiled down to: "Yesterday—sin, God will strike you dead; today—okey dokey fine." It just felt like a contradiction to me.

As I stood there looking at Daryl smiling and seeing in his expression that he was trying to cover up sheer terror, he bashfully uttered in a quiet voice, "You look very pretty." The nice part about that was, I felt very pretty, but nervous! I walked over to the other side of the bed and lay down beside him propped up with pillows so we could watch TV. After a pause, he turned to me and said, "I know we are supposed to do this tonight, but it is late and you must be tired. I love you and we have our whole lives ahead of us and lots of time." I felt the same way. I was delighted to hear him say it.

We watched TV for about an hour and just curled up together in bed. When we kissed each other good night, we fell asleep almost immediately.

The next morning we woke up in each others arms and lovingly kissed each other good morning. We talked about what we might do for the day. We got up around 9 AM, showered and dressed—separately. We packed up our night clothes and checked out of the motel. The comfortable thing to do was to get into the car and just drive, just like we had always done. So from town to town we drove, stopped for breakfast and talked along the way. At about 4 PM, we decided it would be fine if we just went home, to our apartment. Daryl had taken a few days off work, but it would be fun just to settle into our home together. With Christmas just around the corner, the money was short, lots of things to figure out and we both knew now that there were things we didn't know about each other.

The next few days were busy. We had to open all the wedding gifts and move Daryl's clothes and personal belongings. We had fun getting to know each other and even the trip to the grocery store picking out food together was enjoyable. We felt good about us and comfortable enough to consummate the marriage. Somehow it seemed right to get to know each other intimately in our own home.

The week passed very quickly and soon it was time to go back to work. Daryl worked a "D" shift which meant that every two days he would work a different shift. It seemed to take a lot of time away from us being together, with my working 8 to 5. Daryl thought he could make enough money so I wouldn't have to work at all. I thought that being a full-time housewife with his schedule would be okay, but I felt unsure about leaving my job that I liked so much. Daryl talked to me about quitting during almost every conversation we had that first week.

On Friday Daryl asked me to tell my boss that I could not return to work anymore because of his work schedule. I felt bad about doing that because Rusty had been very good to me. I thought I should at least give him some notice to get someone else to cover my position. Daryl insisted, however, so I told Rusty that Friday would be my last day of work. He took it well and I told him I would try to help out if he got into a jam. He felt better about that and wished me well even though I could sense that he felt Daryl was being a little controlling. I guess I thought that too.

I passed off the guilt of leaving my job and substituted it with the scurry of Christmas. There were presents to buy and wrap and Daryl's company Christmas party to go to. We also had to prepare for our trip to Florida. I had never been to Florida and I was really excited about going.

In a flash it was Christmas Eve. Daryl got out of work and we went to his parents' house for dinner. We had all the festivities of the holidays spent with friends and more than double the relatives. After dinner we opened presents. There seemed to be a lot of them for just the four of us, but most of them were for Daryl and me. Jeanette had bought me several clothing items, some of which I would be able to take to Florida. She worked at a W. T. Grant store, so she had access to a lot of things first hand. There were a couple of things for the apartment too. It was a very special time.

We went home around 11 PM and set our tree aglow. We sat in front of it and commented on how pretty it was. It seemed just like a page out of a storybook to me. There were presents under the tree in colorful papers with Santa Claus faces and candy canes. The room had a reddish glow from the tree, and we opened a bottle of wine, we had been given, to celebrate our first Christmas together. Daryl suggested we open our presents. It just seemed like the moment was right and I agreed. We opened presents and sipped wine. I was really enjoying this Christmas Eve. I was happier than I could remember and I didn't want it to end. But soon we became tired and decided to retire and give each other one last gift.

The next morning I woke and went to the kitchen to make coffee. As I walked through the living room, I looked at our Christmas tree. It was a sunny morning and the sunshine came through the kitchen window and shone on the tree. It looked different from last night. As I walked by it, I was thinking, this is Christmas morning. I had never opened presents before Christmas morning and this morning felt empty. There weren't the normal things that Mom always had for Christmas morning. Like the huge fruit basket with oranges, tangerines, bananas, grapes and nuts to crack. The plate of fresh baked cinnamon rolls was missing. And the tree didn't look like the one we enjoyed last night. I thought it looked very commercial with its new red, green and blue glass balls and aluminum garland and tinsel. For a moment, it didn't feel like Christmas morning. I suddenly felt like I knew why we were never supposed to see or open gifts until Christmas morning. It was the only day to celebrate Christmas.

I cast these thoughts aside and prepared the coffee. I tried to think of what we had to do today. We were to go to Daryl's folks' house for dinner and we had to go to my folks' house later in the afternoon to exchange gifts.

Daryl soon joined me in the kitchen and wished me a Merry Christmas with a tender kiss and a warm hug. I could tell he was really happy to be with me for this Christmas. It was different for me, but I loved being with him and this was **our** first Christmas. I shouldn't expect it to be like the ones my parents had created because this was the one we created. When I thought of it that way, it made the old memories from home take a back seat. I started preparing our Christmas breakfast.

THE HONEYMOON

It was 5:30 AM. Daryl and I were just leaving the apartment to meet his parents at their house to leave for Florida. We were both very excited. We would ride down to Tampa, Florida with them and after two weeks Daryl and I would fly back. Nick would pick us up at the airport. This was double excitement for me. I had never been to Florida and I had never been on an airplane.

Daryl had been to Florida many times before because his father's stepfather and mother lived there six months of the year. They always talked about them with forced respect because they had a lot of money. I got the impression that was the primary reason they appeared to like them so much. I met them before we were married and they were at the wedding, but they didn't look like the kind of people that you would pick to be wealthy. I didn't think much about it usually because wealth wasn't that important to me. It was pretty evident that Daryl's family thought differently about wealth. Everybody talked quite a lot about how much money people had or how much they thought they had. Daryl's grandparents were just people who talked pleasantly to me and comfortably included me in the family gatherings. I enjoyed seeing and being with them.

By 6 AM we were loaded and on the road. Daryl Sr. drove the whole time with the plan for our first stop to be in South Carolina to spend the night. We would arrive in Tampa about mid afternoon the next day.

We checked into a motel early evening. We got settled into our room and then went out for supper to the restaurant at the end of the motel. It had been a fairly long day even though we just rode in the car. The sightseeing was somewhat restricted because it had been raining most of the way down, but the temperature was much warmer and that was a treat. It felt odd to have temperatures of mid 60's in January.

After supper we retired to our rooms. We would have another early start in the morning. I crashed on the bed to watch TV for a little while and Daryl was fiddling with stuff in the bathroom. As he was doing so, he started talking like he wanted me to hear without actually speaking to me. I was listening, but still watched TV. He was suggesting that maybe he should grow a mustache. I was quite surprised and somewhat displeased with the suggestion. I now focused my attention totally on his loud mumbling.

After a minute or so he said, "What do you think?"

I think he already knew I wasn't thrilled with the idea and I couldn't understand what brought this subject up to begin with.

"I don't think that is a great idea. I like you the way you are." I replied.

He was beginning to tease and push the issue and I was still wondering why when he said, "Well, if you don't want me to grow a mustache, stop taking your birth control pills and I won't."

I was shocked with his suggestion, and not comfortable with the idea. Actually it had not dawned on me that he was thinking of having a baby this soon. I didn't want to go against his wishes, but I wasn't sure I was ready for a baby yet. I started to panic a little and tried to side-stepped the conversation as quickly as I could.

The next morning we got up and Daryl started shaving. I remembered his offer of last night and thought I would pretend it never came up. But when Daryl emerged from the bathroom he had not shaved his mustache. I was disappointed and feeling pressured again. I didn't know how to say no to him about this, but the facial hair was not only unattractive on him, being sparse and scratchy, but unpleasant for kissing too. We didn't mention it in front of his parents, but he seized every opportunity to mention it that he could.

Finally by January 31st, I gave in to the pressure. I thought I could do this for him if he really wanted a baby. The only real problem I had having a baby was that I would have liked to be in a house of our own first. I was taught to take orders and believed when you marry the man makes the decisions. I stopped taking my birth control pills that day. The mustache came off the next morning. Our sexual encounters became very frequent at that point. I just felt it was my duty as his wife. We had been married long enough to prove we didn't <u>have</u> to get married just for the benefit of all my family members who were saying we did.

The remainder of the vacation was a lot of fun. We went to Busch Gardens, Tarpon Springs, St. Petersburg, and lots of other places I had never seen. I got to walk in the Gulf of Mexico. We walked sandy beaches picking up sea shells. Some I had never seen before. Daryl's grandfather took us to a beach he said would have lots of great sea shells. He told us to watch for sea creatures.

We arrived and headed immediately to the beach. His grandfather was telling us to watch where we stepped because of the jellyfish that wash ashore. He was right! They were nearly transparent and very hard to distinguish on the sand. We proceeded with caution and found the beach to be loaded with jellyfish, starfish and unusual shells. Daryl found a large shell of a deep burnt orange and picked it up. As he turned it over to look at it, legs came wiggling out and he dropped it like it was a burning ember.

His grandfather started laughing, "I forgot to tell you that the shells here would be inhabited."

"Thanks, Gramp," scoffed Daryl with a chuckle.

We decided maybe we would just go buy some uninhabited shells from the tourist shop. We left the beach as soon as we could walk back to the car. Daryl's grandfather got quite a chuckle watching us dance on the beach, tiptoeing around the jellyfish, back to the car. I think Gramp enjoyed our visit just so he could get a good laugh.

Too soon the vacation came to an end. It was time for us to return home. We went to the Tampa airport giving thanks and goodbyes to his parents and grandparents and boarded our plane. The flight was a direct flight into Rochester, NY and would take about three hours.

I was more excited about flying than scared so I hadn't thought about how I usually get motion sickness. I didn't have a window seat, but wished I did. The view was incredible. My stomach was doing some summersaults during the take off, but soon settled down. It wasn't until the descent that I knew I wouldn't make it. The closer we got to the ground the closer I was to throwing up. Just before the plane touched down I started dry heaving (thank God) with horrible regurgitating sounds coming from my throat and mouth. The stewardess appeared with a barf bag which I quickly placed over my mouth to, at the very least, muffle the sound. By the time I stopped dry heaving and regained my composure, the plane was at the gate. People around me were desperately trying to get off the plane as fast as possible. I couldn't blame them.

The weather leaving Tampa was 70 degrees and beautiful. In Rochester it was 7 degrees. I didn't realize how different that would feel after being in the warmer climate for two weeks. I soon found out. I don't think I ever felt that cold in my life. Nick was there to pick us up and we were soon home with fond memories of a lovely vacation.

I didn't think about the "baby thing" much. We got home and continued our life together. I just knew it would take several months to find out about it anyway, so I put it out of my mind.

By April I had noticed some changes in my physical self, and the "baby thing" seemed to be the probable cause. I had not gotten my period, but that wasn't unusual. I only had it four times a year until I went on the birth control pills, but Daryl insisted I go to a doctor to find out. The doctor confirmed my reluctant suspicions. I was pregnant and Daryl was delighted. I didn't know how I felt about it. I just thought it was my duty as his wife to provide him with children when he wanted them. So I guess I was happy that I could make him happy.

Now, we had to tell the parents that they would be grandparents. I was excited for his parents, but terrified to tell mine. The announcements went well and the responses were just about as I expected. His parents were thrilled and very excited. My parents were less than excited. The rumors from my family had the baby delivering in May. More than likely it was Dick that started them.

It was the last Sunday in April. Daryl had to work 8 to 4. He suggested I spend the day with his parents, instead of home alone. He said he would call his Dad to pick me up and suggest we have dinner together. I agreed and went to get ready.

Soon the phone rang and it was Daryl's father. He said Daryl called and he could pick me up in about 15 minutes. I said that would be fine, I would be ready. It was a nice sunny day and quite warm for that time of the year. I just put on a casual long sleeve A-line dress and waited for Daryl Sr. to arrive. Promptly, 15 minutes later, he drove up our driveway. I was ready to go and looked out the kitchen window to see where he parked. I wanted to be downstairs before he got out of the car, but it was too late. He had already gotten out of the car and started up the back steps of our apartment. I met him at the door, but he stepped inside asking if I had the coffee on. I was surprised he asked for coffee. I told him I had just turned it off, but that it should still be hot. We proceeded into the kitchen.

I poured us each a cup and we started conversation about the weather and stuff. He was telling me about his plans for the day to start digging up the flower beds to prepare for the spring planting. I agreed the day was nice enough to do that. The conversation dwindled and soon our coffee was just about gone. I suggested we better get going. He agreed, but suggested I get a sweater or jacket because it was still chilly outside. Even though it didn't look that chilly to me, I went into the living room to get my jacket from the closet. He followed me and when I turned around after getting my jacket from the closet, he was standing right behind me. I was startled and before I could ask what he was doing he proceeded to wrap his arms around me.

"You know you have never shown me your bedroom." He said.

I responded with hesitation and curious fear in my voice, "Yes, you have seen our bedroom. You bought the bedroom suit and helped us set it up."

"No, I have never seen your bedroom. I want to see it. You can show it to me right now."

While he was talking and holding me, he was pressing his body against mine. I could feel his penis, hard and rubbing against my stomach. He was moving as if in some kind of mating dance. Up, down, side to side so he could feel his penis rub my stomach. He was enjoying my panic. I didn't know what to do. All I could think was that this was not happening. Things like this just don't happen to people around here. It happens in big cities and to the prostitutes that live there, but not to me. I didn't do anything to provoke this behavior. I was trying to get a grip on my mental state and keep him from dragging me to the bedroom. He was pulling me toward the bedroom. I wasn't going to let him take me there. I knew what he was planning. That was evident by the actions of his thrusting body and hard penis. As he pulled me away from the closet and around our living room chair, I had a chance to break out of his grip. I ran for the back door. I ran down the stairs and stood in front of his car.

The reality of what just happened was smothering me, but I heard….

WHAT ARE YOU GOING TO DO NOW? ARE YOU GOING WITH HIM? WHAT HAPPENS WHEN YOU GET INTO THAT CAR? DO YOU THINK HE WILL TAKE YOU TO HIS HOUSE?

My mind was racing. I was trying to answer the questions my subconscious had asked me, but didn't dare. I didn't want to hear the answers. I didn't know what I was going to do. While I stood there thinking, almost shaking, I heard the back door of the apartment close. At the same time the downstairs door banged. Daryl Sr. was coming out of our apartment and Emmitt was exiting the downstairs apartment.

"Hi," Emmitt said, "How's the pregnancy going so far?" as I saw Daryl Sr. coming down the stairs.

"Hi," quickly responding to Emmitt, "I'm doing fine, thanks. I'm going to spend the day with my in-laws while Daryl works."

"Well, it looks like a nice day. Have a good time!"

"Thanks."

By now Daryl Sr. had reached the bottom of the stairs as Emmitt greeted him with "Hi, how are ya?"

Daryl returned the greeting and proceeded to get into the car. I reluctantly eased in the passenger seat. I was scared to death. I didn't know what was going to happen. I wanted to believe this whole thing didn't happen. I was searching my mind for a dark hole to put this incident into and seal it up.

IT DID HAPPEN! DON'T LET HIM CONVINCE YOU THAT IT DID NOT! HE WANTED TO HAVE SEX WITH YOU PLAIN AND SIMPLE. YOU KNOW YOU FELT HIS ERECT PENIS. HE TRIED TO PULL YOU INTO THE BEDROOM! WHAT DO YOU THINK WOULD HAVE HAPPENED IF HE HAD GOTTEN YOU THERE?

I didn't want to think about it. I wished this day had never happened. Daryl Sr. started the car and drove away. He started asking me what kind of music I wanted to listen to on the radio. He was making conversation like nothing ever happened. For now I would play along, but I prepared myself to jump out of the car if I needed to. We drove into town and back to their house. I quickly got out of the car and went inside to find Jeanette. I was still terrified. What do I do now? All I could think was that I would tell Daryl as soon as he got out of work, but that was a whole day away. I would have to pretend nothing was wrong all day.

Jeanette and I were inseparable as the day passed. I helped her in every room she went into. I helped with flowers, crossword puzzles, dinner, anything I could so I would be away from Daryl's father. He just acted like nothing happened.

Finally it was 4:15 PM and Daryl pulled into the driveway. I went immediately out to see him, but his father was already talking to him. I could see I wouldn't be able to tell Daryl what happened until sometime later. After dinner I suggested we go home and that I was very tired. We I left by 8:30.

I tried to think of how I would tell Daryl. There wasn't a proper way. But then this wasn't a proper situation. How would he react? I didn't know, but I knew I had to tell him or the attacks might continue. They might anyway, but I thought it would be less likely if I told Daryl about it. Daryl would protect me. He would believe me. He would fix this horrible situation.

We got home and I went in the bedroom. I sat on the bed wondering how to tell Daryl what I had to tell him. He soon came into the room and asked what the matter was. I told him I had to tell him something, but I didn't know how. It was horrible, unfathomable and would hurt our relationship with his parents severely. He was confused and asked me to be more specific. He demanded I tell him what I was talking about. (He sat next to me now trying to comfort me as I started to cry.) I looked into his eyes and began telling him what happened. The further into the story, the more emotional I was. By the end of the story, I was almost out of control crying. Daryl was hopping mad. He left the bedroom and went directly to the telephone.

He called his parents' house and evidently his mother answered the telephone.

"Let me talk to my father!" Daryl demanded aggressively.

His father came to the telephone and Daryl started explaining about how upset I was over an incident that had taken place that morning in our apartment. He fired questions, like projectiles. "What were you thinking? What did you have in mind? Why would you do such a thing?" He was spewing so fast there wasn't time for answers in response.

The telephone conversation only lasted a few minutes when he hung up. He came back into the bedroom and said that his folks were coming right over. I was horrified.

I asked, "Why? Why are they doing that?'

Daryl said they wanted to talk to me about what happen. They felt that I obviously misunderstood Daryl's father's closeness to me. He had denied anything happened.

When Daryl Sr. and Jeanette arrived, I stayed in the bedroom. I could hear them talking about what I had said. Daryl Sr. was denying the entire incident and said that he had just kissed me hello when he had arrived. He solemnly stated to Daryl that he would never do anything like that to anyone. My God, he was married and was his father. How could I even say such a thing? It was so ridiculous. That never could have happened. I must have thought he was going to do something when he kissed me "hello".

Daryl asked if I could come out of the bedroom and talk to his parents. I said, "No." I didn't want to talk to them or see them. They were telling Daryl I was a liar. It looked like Daryl believed them. That horrified me. How could we continue this relationship with these feelings? What do I do now?

After some time, his parents left. Daryl returned to the bedroom and I asked him, "Do you believe me?"

"I don't know." He sighed, "God, he's my father!"

"Why would I make such a thing up? What would I accomplish by making this up? What would I gain? I know what he tried to do. I didn't understand why he was doing it either. I was scared, but I did not misinterpret his actions! What do we do now?"

"I don't know."

I knew he wanted to believe me, but that meant he had to put me in front of his parents. He had only known me a few months and now he was faced with making a choice between his wife and his parents. He couldn't make that choice. He wouldn't make that choice.

"From now on," Daryl said, "my father won't give you anymore hugs and kisses if it bothers you that much. He said he didn't realize you were so sensitive."

I couldn't believe my ears. He didn't believe me. He was saying his father didn't do anything wrong. I was frozen in disbelief. The subject was closed. I had just misinterpreted his actions. We would not confront them again about this and it was never discussed again. I felt betrayed. This new family I had just acquired was not what they appeared to be a few months ago. I was angry, angry that he said he couldn't believe that his father could or would do such a thing. That said it all. We lost something that day. I lost something that I would never get back. I lost some of my naiveté that I had been carrying my whole life. I just expected everyone to be as honest as I was. I thought everyone that lived away from the city was decent and honest. We were better people for living away from the corruption of the big city.

Now I had to go on like it never happened. I would have to pretend we were one happy family. I had to eliminate that day from my memory. I didn't know how to do that. I loved Daryl, but if I wanted to keep him as my husband I would have to do this. He couldn't accuse his father of such actions. It just couldn't happen. It just didn't happen. For my husband I would do as he asked. I didn't want to live with this lie, but I would have to find a way.

By June I was wearing maternity clothes for the first time in my life. I felt enormously fat even though I really wasn't. I was barely six months pregnant for Dick's wedding. I was there in the thinnest maternity dress I could make. To that point I had been lucky gaining only a few pounds. The doctor set my due date for October 27. I remember feeling uncomfortable, stimulated by guilt, because I was pregnant. I had no reason to feel guilty, but I did. I knew Dick would believe only what he wanted to believe no matter how much proof I could provide. He wanted everyone to see proof that I was a slut like he had been saying.

July passed as did August, September, and now it was October. My mother's birthday was the 28th and my Dad was scheduled to go on a hunting trip to Montana at the end of the month. Dad and I talked about my having this baby before he left, but we both knew it was out of our hands. This was their second grandchild, but really it was the first one. Lyle had a baby daughter with his first wife, but the marriage only lasted a few weeks. She found out she was pregnant after they split.

I was afraid the relationship with my parents and my baby would be similar, but Dad would talk about the baby with me and I always felt he was excited about it. Mom and I were able to talk about the pregnancy more comfortably than I expected, but her excitement was controlled. As the month passed I thought about the things that went along with taking care of a baby almost constantly. I had a couple of baby showers and had gotten most of the necessary equipment. I wondered about why God made the process so difficult, especially at the end. When the egg and sperm come together, the result is so tiny it can't be seen by the naked eye. Then God waits until it grows so much that you have to go through this painful process to get it out of the womb. I remembered seeing and assisting cows with deliveries most of my childhood. For a long time I thought the process for humans was different somehow, but when I realized it was the same, I was shocked. What do they do with that sack thing? I vividly remember seeing that huge mass of stuff coming out of a cow and I was grossed out with the thought that I had to deliver one of those with this baby, too!

Daryl's mother was more than excited. By now she had the market cornered on knowledge of babies and was telling me what I had to do on an hourly basis. The closer it got, the more annoyed I got. She usually made reference to the baby as <u>her</u> baby. One day I couldn't take it any more so I told her, bluntly, bordering on hostile, that she needed to stop making that reference. She quit saying it, but I could tell she wasn't pleased with my correcting her. There were signs that told me I would be learning a lot of things from her besides how to take care of a baby.

BABY DAY

I had been up all night with cramps. I was sure it was time for this baby to be delivered. I thought about whether it would be a boy or a girl. I prayed it would be a boy. For some reason I thought it would be easier to raise a boy than a girl and with Daryl's family having a history of boys, I thought it would take away the pressures a baby girl would bring. I called the doctor around 6 AM, and he told me to go to the hospital. I had no idea what delivering this baby would bring, but I would be glad to get rid of the belly I had.

We checked into the hospital and went through the normal process, I guess. I didn't know for sure. The nurses were very nice to me, but they kept calling me "little girl", which I found very annoying. I wasn't a little girl, but I must have looked it to them, seeing as they were all at least 50 years old or more. I had always looked younger than my age, but I didn't feel good about that here. I was the first pregnant mother in the labor room and it was nice to have the privacy. Soon two more women came in to share my space. As the morning progressed so did my contractions. By late morning, I was not enjoying myself. I thought this was the worst pain I had ever experienced. Daryl stayed by my side, but didn't know how to help me. The past eleven months had gotten us past the honeymoon stage in a hurry. Daryl had been quite focused on the things he wanted rather than the things "we" wanted. I was definitely a wife, subservient to the husband. We were still very much in love, but it was different. On this day I was not feeling that having a baby was as much fun as he had told me it would be.

Afternoon came. The other women had been moved to the delivery room and delivered baby boys. I was angry. I couldn't understand why they got to deliver before me; after all, I got here first. I should deliver first. In the progressing stages of labor I thought I would surely die. This was so painful and now the pains were closer together and longer. I was tired of doing this. I was tired of hurting. The nurse came in to check me and said it looked like I could go to the delivery room soon. At this point

I almost didn't care. I just wanted to get some sleep. They moved me into the delivery room and I wanted very, very badly to push this baby out of me. I wasn't in a mood to deal for anything else.

"You must stop pushing now until the doctor gets here." The nurse said to me.

"What? I've been here since early this morning trying to do this and now I have to wait?"

I was tired, in pain, angry and didn't understand. I came into this hospital to have this baby. (They left me for hours saying I wasn't ready to deliver and now they said I was ready but had to wait!) It was hard to hold off the pushing urges. I wanted it to be over—right now! The doctor arrived and told me I could push. The nurse asked me if I wanted to watch in the mirror positioned above me.

"No" I said, angrily. But when I looked up to see where the mirror was I could see the head of the baby coming out of me.

For some reason I could not take my eyes off of the mirror. I watched this baby come into the world and I could see very clearly that it was a boy. The delivery was a lot easier to go through than the labor and now it was over. The baby was crying and the doctor said he was fine. They laid him on my chest. I didn't know what to do with him. He was messy and crying. I touched him.

"Don't let him fall off." The doctor cautioned the nurses.

After a few minutes they took him and started cleaning him up.

The nurse nearest me began pushing her fists into my abdomen.

"Oh my God! What are you doing?" I cried out.

She started to explain the process of getting the afterbirth out of me. This was the procedure. I could feel my stomach muscles tighten in retaliation. It seemed like it took longer to deliver the afterbirth than it did to deliver the baby. I couldn't believe the afterbirth was removed that way—we never did that with the cows! It really hurt. They finally finished poking me at which time the doctor put in a few stitches. Then I was wheeled to my room.

The doctor went to tell Daryl the results. Daryl had been in the waiting room with his cousin, Rodney. It was ironic, but Rodney's wife, Annette, had delivered a baby boy just that morning. Now the two of them would have something in common. Our babies would share a birthday.

Daryl came into my room as soon as I got back and said he had seen the baby. We had talked about a name and decided on Dale Daryl; the first name that I wanted and a namesake that Daryl wanted.

I ached from my chin to my knees, not to mention—starving. The nurses got me a tray from the kitchen and Daryl soon left to tell the family of our new family member. I took a nap.

Around 6:30 PM the nurses came in with Dale all bundled up and not as little as I had expected. He weighed 7 pounds and 9 ounces and he really was a pretty baby. He had lots of blonde hair and blue-gray eyes. He laid there in my arms and I thought he looked like my side of the family. I held him and we started to get to know one another. I looked at him and thought this poor little baby; he has a mother that really isn't sure how to take care of him. I fed him his bottle of what looked like water and he didn't fuss or cry. The nurse came in to show me how, and when to burp him. I really didn't remember the details of the days of babysitting that I had done for years. Besides, this was different. This one was mine. He would be with me every minute for everything he needed and that was a scary thought.

Just before 7 PM the nurse came and took Dale back to the nursery. Visitors would be in any minute, and they couldn't have the babies exposed to all those outside germs. Daryl soon came to my room. He said he had been to the nursery to see Dale and he was looking beautiful. Daryl's parents had come to see him, too and I walked to the nursery to greet them. I really didn't want visitors, but people came anyway. I was feeling the excitement that everyone else was, and the maternity ward seemed like a family reunion. Rodney and Annette and both of their parents were there. Daryl, his parents and my sister Trixie all piled up at the viewing window. The visitation time passed and I was glad. I was tired and wanted to sleep. I still wasn't feeling very good. When the visitors left, the nurses brought the babies back. This time Dale got formula.

About a half an hour later the nurses came back and took Dale back to the nursery. They told me to get some rest. I didn't have to do the 2 AM feeding because I wasn't breast feeding. It was hard to go to sleep. I was very sore and every move I made hurt. There were lights on and people walking around the halls. I slept off and on. The next morning I was hoping to feel like new, but I didn't. The nurse came in and told me

I had to get up and walk; doctor's orders. So I tried to do that, but I still wasn't feeling well. I got up and walked the hall once in the morning, but it was a slow journey. That seemed to keep the nurse off my back for a while, but when I couldn't choke down lunch she commented about that as well. I just couldn't please her no matter what.

By afternoon I had to do another walk. Then I had bath training for the baby, then visitors again. I ate all my dinner, but it was a struggle. My time with Dale left me feeling more comfortable with him and my role as his mom. The other mothers unbundled their babies to see if all their parts were in place, which I had no desire to do. I saw Dale in the delivery room and he was all there. Now I just wanted him to be comfortable and warm, all wrapped up in my arms resting, drinking his bottle and burping. That was good enough for me.

That evening my mother came to visit us. She had gotten a job driving school bus and came after she got out of work, about 7 o'clock. She explained not coming yesterday because she thought all Daryl's family would be here and thought it would be tiring for me. Dad was in Montana on his hunting trip and Mom said she had talked to him and told him I had the baby. He seemed excited about having a grandson.

I felt uncomfortable with Mom there. After all, we spent years going through high school being reminded that having babies was a bad thing. Somehow that is just how it felt now. We were cordial to each other as we walked up to see the babies in the nursery. I couldn't help thinking how cute Dale was, even as a newborn. Mom didn't say much about him, only that he looked like me.

She asked when I was coming home. I told her I thought it would be Sunday. She said Dad would be home later that night, but wanted to wait for us to get home to see Dale. She offered to bring dinner for us on Sunday, so I wouldn't have to cook. I hadn't even thought that far ahead. My mind was still tired, but I gratefully accepted the offer, realizing that the apartment would be full of people when I got home. Dale was the first grandson on both sides of the family. Daryl's parents would definitely be there, and it sure would be good to eat some of Mom's cooking again.

Sunday

Soon it was time to pack up my things and take Dale home. He was doing very well and I was feeling better. Daryl told me that he had to call his parents when we arrived so they could come up and hold the baby. I told him that the books that I read strongly discouraged holding the newborn when they first come home from the hospital because of all the outside germs that could be transmitted. I knew that would be a difficult thing to tell his mother, but it was what the book said. I told Daryl it was up to him and he agreed that we should do what was best for the baby. He would tell her that she could hold him in a day or two.

We arrived home around noon. The landlord came up to see Dale first. Daryl called his parents and mine. Within an hour the apartment was full. Mom brought enough food for everyone. If there was one thing Mom could do well, it was cook for a crowd with all the fixings! Pork roast, mashed potatoes, gravy, vegetables, applesauce, pies and ice cream. What a wonderful welcome home present. Daryl's parents came to hold the baby, but were more than happy to eat Mom's country fixins'.

Everyone got to see Dale, but no one held him except Daryl and me. I knew Daryl's mother would be mad about that and it wasn't until later that night I found out how mad. By 4 PM Daryl Sr. and Jeanette gave their congratulations and good-byes so I could rest. Mom, Dad and Trixie left shortly after. We were finally alone with our new son. It felt good to just sit down and have some quiet time with the three of us.

Around 8 PM we got a call from Daryl's mother. I could tell it was her by the way Daryl spoke. He was trying to explain something to her and that he was talking about my parents too. I couldn't figure it out at first, but after Daryl hung up he told me his mother was terribly upset, crying and all, because she didn't get to hold Dale. She was sure my mother did after they left. That was unfair and on and on. Daryl told her that my parents had not held him either, and that they didn't get to do any more with the baby than she did. I don't know if she believed it or not, but it was true.

After a couple days of practice with our new baby, we allowed everyone to hold Dale. Jeanette was very quick to tell me all the things I needed to do to make sure he would be healthy. She even told me how many bowel movements he was to have every day or I should give him some home remedy of hers to correct it. By the end of the first week she was driving me nuts with all the suggestions. I was loosing my confidence to take care of Dale when I finally called my doctor.

When he came to the phone, I started reeling off questions so fast that it took him three attempts to interrupt me.

When I finally started to listen he said, "Who on earth have you been talking to?"

"My mother-in-law is telling me that..."

The doctor interrupted me sternly, "Stop right there and you listen to me! Do <u>you</u> have any concerns with what <u>you</u> are doing with the baby?"

"Well, my mother-in-law said..." I started again.

He cut me off again and said, "No, I said do <u>you</u> have any concerns with the baby? I don't care what your mother-in-law says. You don't need to listen to her. You just have to pay attention to what you feel and what <u>you</u> think, okay?"

I stumbled in conversation thinking that I really didn't have any concerns and finally responded with, "Well, yeah, I mean, he seems like he is doing okay. He's not sick or anything."

"You are doing just fine," He said, "if <u>you</u> need anything, please don't hesitate to call me, but it sounds to me like you are doing everything you should and you don't need to do things the way they were done thirty years ago, okay?"

"Okay. Thank you very much, doctor" I said, feeling quite stupid.

"You're welcome." He said. "I will see you in a few weeks, Okay?"

"Okay, thanks." I said, sheepishly.

I just got the shot of confidence I needed. I was suddenly eager to tell Daryl what the doctor said. I also reminded him that when he was a baby his father was in the service, overseas and his grandmother, Mattie (Jeanette's mother), took care of him until he was three years old. More than likely his mother was quoting practices from her mother which would be two generations back. I didn't think we needed to go back that far to get the techniques of caring for a baby. I had read all the current books on the subject and I had my gut feelings to fall back on. My doctor said to rely on <u>my</u> instincts. I also reminded Daryl that he could tell her to back off because this was our baby. In his own way he did, but it was much more subtle than I would have done it.

ANOTHER BABY DAY

The years passed as my life went on. The marriage was continuing like I thought it was supposed to and I had gotten pregnant for the second time. This pregnancy was not the walk in the park that Dale was. I was experiencing fainting spells and I got very large almost immediately with this baby. For the past month, the doctor had been telling me "any day" and my patience to accept that was getting old.

I finally said, "Lie if you must, but don't tell me 'any week' again!"

With a smile and encouragement he said, "If you haven't gone by Tuesday, I will induce labor, okay?"

"Okay," I said, with a discouraged voice. I didn't think he realized how difficult this pregnancy had become. I was so big that people stared at me in the grocery store. I had not seen my feet in two months. I couldn't even wear maternity pants because they would cut into my low hanging stomach! In one of my states of depression in January, I decided to measure myself. I had a waist line of 54" and it was only my eighth month! I didn't measure again.

By the end of my ninth month my stretch marks had become canals in my stomach. The cocoa butter lotion didn't help. I wasn't officially due until the 12ᵗʰ, but the doctor kept saying I would go early—he lied. Finally around midnight on Thursday the 10ᵗʰ I was starting to experience sporadic labor pains. Daryl had gone to work at midnight and around 3 AM I decided to call him. We only lived two blocks from the hospital and I didn't see a need to get there too early only to be sent home with false labor. Trixie came over to stay with Dale and take him to a babysitter before she went to work. I went to the hospital a little after 6 AM. The pregnancy, labor and delivery were just the opposite of what it was for Dale. The labor was easier, but when the doctor broke my water it shed new light as to why I was so big. It was as if someone opened the flood gates and the whole reservoir was emptying. This baby kicked all the way through the labor process and by 12:30 PM the doctor had arrived and I was ready to deliver. The delivery was tough and there were minor complications which I learned about later.

Finally at 12:45 PM a rather large baby boy emerged. I had hoped for another boy. I just didn't want to deal with the family going nuts and being partial to a girl. I didn't want Dale to be forgotten. This baby was 9 pounds and 1 ounce. He was born with the umbilical cord wrapped three times around his neck. The delivery was tricky and somewhat dangerous. But he was breathing and crying and everything appeared to be fine. The only thing we didn't have ready for him was his name. Daryl wanted Jason Frederick and I didn't. My doctor asked what his name was and I told him we hadn't finalized that yet. He suggested I select a name from my father.

I chuckled and said, "I just can't name a kid Marvin in the 70's. The poor kid won't live to graduate!"

Everyone laughed and the doctor quickly pointed out famous people named Marvin. In spite of their great suggestions he became Bret Alan. The cleanup process after the delivery went pretty well, even though I was in the delivery room a long time. Bret was doing just fine and he looked a lot like Dale. Lots of blonde hair, steel blue eyes, he was just two pounds larger!

I got back to my room around 1:30 PM and my lunch came immediately. I wasted no time devouring it. Daryl stayed with me until I finished lunch and then left to notify family members. I think he was a little disappointed that it was another boy, but I was not. I soon fell asleep thinking I would be able to tie my own shoes tomorrow.

It was late afternoon when the nurse brought Bret to me all bundled up and as she handed him to me, she said, "He didn't clean up," then walked out of the room. I thought that was an odd thing to say as I looked into my bundle of baby.

I couldn't even see his little face until I pulled the blanket away. It was at that moment I realized just how difficult the delivery had been for this poor baby. He had a hemorrhage in his left eye, his glowing pink skin could have illuminated the room, he had broken blood vessels in his face, which was large, swollen, and resembled a small muskmelon. I almost cried. This poor, helpless, not so little baby looked like he had been dropped and run over. The nurse brought his bottle and he began eating immediately. He responded to feeding and burping better than I remember Dale doing, but I knew from the start this baby would not be like Dale.

I went home first thing Sunday morning. I had been very conscious of my weight with this baby and had only gained 22 pounds. That was a benefit I realized when I got dressed to go home. I had carried a lot of fluid and a lot of baby, so when it came time to go home I was able to wear a pair of elastic waist pants and an oversized blouse. I did not want to wear maternity clothes home no matter what, and I didn't.

I was home by 10 AM and was feeling like a million bucks. Mom came over with dinner again to welcome Bret into this world. Daryl's parents were vacationing in Florida and called with their congratulations.

I felt bad for Bret that he looked as rough as he did, but he was a perfect baby in all other respects. He didn't cry very much and the family commotion didn't bother him either. Dale was at Daryl's aunt's house and was showing signs of a cold, so we were told, but they would bring him back on Monday. As the day quickly passed by, it was soon time for bed. Bret drank most of his bottle and I put him in his own bed for the first time. He must have been okay with that because he slept through the night, as did I.

The next day, Dale came home to see his new brother. He looked like he was comfortable with Bret; holding him and watching him. Dale was going on four years old and had been a very fast maturing child. Many times I would watch him holding Bret and wish that they would be close to each other all their lives. I wanted them to be best friends, like Trixie and I were, but I didn't want them to wait until they were older to develop that relationship. I wanted them to be close from the beginning.

Time passes so very fast when you are watching children grow up. I didn't realize just how fast until I had these babies. Dale was growing into a young adult at a very young age. He had started school at four years old against the wishes of Daryl's family, but I knew he was ready. And he was. Bret was the model baby even though he disliked formula and was on whole milk by 6 weeks. He had given up his bottle at 6 months and appeared to be modeling himself after Dale in a lot of ways, but he was doing it his own way. It was very evident that Bret had a very strong mind of his own.

We bought a house when Bret was about six months old. Dale would be able to start school from our new house and the boys would be able to settle into their own bedrooms before Dale started kindergarten.

As the boys grew, they looked more and more alike, just like Trixie and I had, with their blonde hair, blue eyes and slim structures. They certainly were a couple of handsome boys and though they looked exactly alike, they were two completely different boys in spirit. Dale was easy going and very quick to please. He didn't question authority, like teachers and family. Bret, on the other hand questioned just about everything. He was creative, stubborn, a quick study with a quick temper. He copied Dale every chance he got.

I had my ups and downs walking this path, but one of the highlights was my sister. She had gotten married to a guy that worked at the same place as Daryl and he played on Daryl's softball team. His name was Ronald and he was an attractive man with blonde hair and blue eyes and was welcomed with open arms into the family. Ronald had quite a bit more professional and personal polish than Daryl. It would occasionally remind me that once again Trixie had done better than me. She and Ronald lived in a very nice development just a couple of miles from us and there were lots of days spent together doing fun, silly and sometimes outrageous things. We had gotten to be very close and when Bret was just two years old, Trixie's daughter, Onicka came into the world.

We shared special times with our babies at her house and mine. Trixie and I were enjoying each other, our children and life. Daryl, however, was not enjoying the closeness she and I shared. At times he appeared to be jealous becoming annoyed with her and me. He didn't like Trixie and me having this much fun. At times he would create reasons, roadblocks, for us not to be together.

Trixie and I got together for coffee on a regular basis. We would have marathon coffee breaks and talk for hours. One day during one of these coffee marathons, she told me Ronald had been offered a new job and promotion. I was excited for her until she said they would be moving to Temple, Texas in about a month. I tried to be happy for them. But I was feeling the loss already. Trixie was ecstatic about the whole thing. There would be house shopping, and new furnishings, new surroundings, and friends.

She looked at me with her bubbling expression suggesting, "You guys will be able to come down on vacation to visit us!"

With all the enthusiasm I could muster I said, "Yeah, it'll be great. I've never been to Texas. You can show us around, we can go shopping, do lunch, the kids can play with the rattlesnakes in your back yard!"

We both laughed, but I wanted to cry. We continued speculating the future with our ridiculous jokes and Texas style humor through out the day. It was our last marathon coffee break.

Trixie's schedule got busy after that. There were flights to Texas, house hunting, movers and packing arrangements. That month was over almost before it began. I wanted to spend every day of that month with her, but it wasn't to be. There were a lot of good-byes from friends, co-workers, neighbors and family. The distance between Trixie and me was now real. We never talked about our feelings before she left. I think it was too awkward. We just made the standard comments "see ya soon" and "I'll call ya."

Daryl was almost too excited about Ronald's promotion and departure. The problem with visiting them on a vacation was that we never had any vacation money. We lived day to day, no matter how much we made. I didn't think I would ever see Trixie in Texas.

Life continued as I thought it should. I stayed home, cared for the boys, did some babysitting and at home jobs like sewing, baking, and even Tupperware for a while. Trixie had been in Texas for three years and it felt like a lifetime. We called occasionally and wrote even less. I kept pressing Daryl for a vacation in Texas when finally he consented. Trixie had another baby, a boy named Barry, and I wanted to see him, and Onicka and Trixie. We planned a three week stay with Trixie and Ronald during April, 1977.

The Turning Point

It was mid-April and we were within a few miles of Trixie and Ronald's Texas house. I was so excited I could hardly wait to see her, new baby Barry and Onicka, who must be twice the size she was when I last saw her. We were right on schedule, expecting to pull into their driveway around 8 PM on Monday. We had been driving for two days and now I just wanted to be there.

We pulled into their driveway at 7:45 PM. Trixie and Onicka came out to greet us. They looked great! Ronald was working swing shift and would be home after midnight. We unloaded kids and baggage and proceeded into the house to see Barry. He was about three months old now and he looked like he could have been Dale. We started jabbering like we used to do and there was nothing Daryl could do to stop us. The kids played together very well and everything seemed to be like it was before she and Ronald left New York.

The three weeks went by very fast. We went sightseeing, visited co-workers who used to live in New York shopped, went to lunch and we were having a great time. But as the weeks passed the tension from Daryl was getting to the breaking point. There was an outburst coming back from a restaurant where Daryl was screaming at Dale for something—no one knew what. But it was uncalled for and even Ronald stepped in and asked Daryl to calm down. We all knew it was past time for us to go back home. I just wanted to send Daryl back alone. I knew I couldn't do that. The next day we packed up for home. We said good-bye with hugs and tears.

A couple of days later we arrived home and immediately sank into the routine we left three weeks before. Daryl went to work and I took care of house and kids. I couldn't put Daryl's behavior at Trixie's out of my head. He was so rude. I was still feeling embarrassed. Even though Trixie comforted me at the time, I wish she could be here now.

Daryl was becoming more and more controlling of me each day. I was being turned into a servant. The love we once shared was just an emotion from the past. People are married for life—till death do us part! When you are in love, its not enough time. When you're not in love, its way too long! I did not know how to get out of this marriage. I knew about divorce, but in angry times when I threatened divorce, Daryl would guarantee me that I would never get the kids. He said he could prove I was an unfit mother. If I ever decided to leave him I would get nothing because everything was his, bought with his money, the house, cars, and furniture. To me that looked to be true. I didn't have anything with my name except the deed to the house. I just kept thinking I made a commitment for life, no matter what happened.

I really started feeling the void when Bret started school. I decided I needed to do something for **me**. I went to work for a bank and enjoyed that immensely. Daryl was very emphatic about my working. He told me that my bank job was my "hobby," meaning that if I expected him to help with the general upkeep of the house; he was not responsible because it was my choice to work. Therefore, I had to maintain "my hobby" and the household responsibilities.

I liked working and figured I could handle all the tasks at home and work. The money I made soon fell under Daryl's control too, Before I knew it I was working for his toys and not getting any more financially stable. I soon realized I needed a better job so I took a temporary position in the accounting department with the company where Daryl worked. The pay was better and I liked it very much, but it only allowed Daryl to increase <u>his</u> buying.

The boys were growing up and playing all the sports that kids play. Daryl became involved with coaching their teams. Our lives were becoming more and more distant, as were the communications with Trixie. After our Texas vacation, things just weren't the same. She and Ronald moved back from Texas the next year and bought a house in a town about 12 miles away. I was working full-time and our kids were in separate schools. We had definitely lost the connection we once had. I was sure Daryl's control was somehow involved. I learned to accept the fact that as long as he was in my life he would always have the control.

Over the next two years things went sour in the family. Dick told Dad he wanted his share of the farm so he could have one of his own—somewhere else! The cows were sold and Mom and Dad moved across the road to the first tenant house. The original homestead was sold. I had never been allowed to be a part of the farm after I left, and now the house I grew up in belonged to someone else.

Then there was the Trixie and Ronald split. I never knew exactly what happened, but one night the family (all members except Dad and me) converged on Trixie and Ronald's house while Ronald was gone. They took all Trixie's, Onicka's and Barry's belongings. There were several trucks to move Trixie into the "other tenant house" that Mom and Dad owned. It was on the next block over from the homestead, and Trixie and Ronald were officially getting a divorce. Trixie and I weren't even on speaking terms now and I had no idea why or how that happened.

During the next three years I found myself wanting to accomplish something else in my life. I found out what that was from one of the parents of Dale's little league team members. We always had a party for the Little League kids at the end of the season. We had an in-ground swimming pool and a huge back yard, so it made it an event the kids looked forward to each year. During the party I had a conversation with one of the fathers about career and education. I was embarrassed to admit that I had not gone to college. He started telling me about a program in the State of New York that was designed to accommodate the lifestyles of people like myself. It took into consideration people had a job, family and home to contend with before considering college. It was structured around our daily commitments. It was sub-titled "The College without a Classroom." He told me he would have the information sent to me so I could review it before I made a decision.

I thought about college a lot off and on over the years. I always had the gnawing question inside me that never got answered. *Am I really too stupid to go to college?* I thought it was about time I answered that question for myself, once and for all.

The information came in the mail about a week later. I read it from top to bottom. This looked like the type of college I was looking for. The program was fully credited by the State University of New York and all degrees were approved by the New York State Board of Regents. I thought about the program long and hard. I was sure it would take every ounce of energy that I could muster to complete, but I could use it to get a better job. It would have a positive influence on my future. I had to know if I **was** that stupid.

Before I could start this venture, I felt I had to do something to prove to myself that I had the commitment to succeed. I thought I needed to do something I'd never done before. What could I do that would push my commitment and drive to accomplish—something.

RUN; LIKE IN JOGGING; MILES! YOU HAVE NEVER DONE THAT!

In high school I had always been a very athletic person. I participated in track and liked to run, but short distances only. Jogging was very popular right now and was something I had never tried to do before. Maybe this **is** what I needed to do to prove I could run <u>long</u> distances, as in miles! I would have to be very determined and dedicated. This could be the perfect test to see if I could make it in college. The two subjects seemed unrelated, but in my mind it required the same level of dedication, commitment and yes, accomplishment that I would need for college.

I went shopping that weekend and bought myself a new pair of running sneakers

We lived just outside the back gate of a Veterans Hospital which had a road around the inside of the complex. I measured the road around the grounds and found it to be exactly one mile around. I spoke with the security people and they said there were lots of people that ran through the complex every day. It was open to the public all the time.

I started running Monday. I was surprised how far I could <u>not</u> run. But I was determined to keep trying. There was a lot about jogging that I did not know and learning how to breathe didn't enter my mind. I would run a little further each time. It took me almost two weeks, before I finally went the whole mile without stopping. Daryl suggested I try the radio he wore while he mowed the lawn, to see if I liked running to music.

The first time I tried the headset, I noticed immediately that I could not hear myself getting tired. I found I could run further with less effort listening to the radio. The headset was cumbersome and hard to keep on, so I decided to get myself a cassette player. I could hear music I liked without interruptions. It worked beautifully.

Soon I could run the mile effortlessly. I had reached my goal. But it didn't seem challenging anymore. I could run a mile without stopping, big deal. I did that in less than three weeks. It wasn't until I had a conversation with a guy at work who also ran that I realized I had not yet reached my goal.

"What's your time for a mile?" He asked.

I admitted that I never thought of timing the runs. He gave me some ideas of what times were good for starting out and how I should progress. From that point on I started timing myself and running against the clock not the distance. I found a new challenge. Now I was pushing myself harder and feeling like I had something to keep reaching for. The running got to be fun. I was going faster and farther almost every night. My schedule got to be more hectic with work, softball and home. I found that running at night was not only enjoyable, but schedulable. It was cooler and there was this calm inner peace that I felt when there was less visual distraction. Running in the dark, with only the street lights of the VA, became very therapeutic.

I felt the drive that I thought I needed to go to college. Thanks to the endorphins, (something new I learned about from running), my head was clear and running like a fine oiled machine. I filled out the application for college and sent it in.

COLLEGE

I had gotten my college acceptance letter in July. The school did not hold classes in the month of August, so I was scheduled to start in September. I was excited and scared. This would be the true test for my brain and my self esteem. Deep down inside I knew I could do it. I had mastered a lot of challenges in my life after high school. Running had gotten to be like bathing. Every day—no exceptions. Now, I was mentally prepared to do something that all the authorities in my high school had been telling me I could never do.

YOU'VE DONE IT BEFORE. REMEMBER THE TIME IN THE FACTORY?

I had to work in the factory to get a permanent job at Mobil. I had worked as a temp there for almost a year, but getting hired directly into the offices was next to impossible. The temp job I had was posted and given to a woman who worked in the factory. I told the personnel manager I would do anything, even factory work. I was offered a job as a packer working midnight to 8 AM in the Meat Tray Department. The company manufactured foam meat trays, dinnerware and specialty products like hamburger clam shells (the ones used in fast food restaurants) and cake plates for commercial bakers. The huge rolls of extruded foam sheet were fed into a thermoforming machine to mold and cut it into the required shapes. My job was to pack the rows of finished product into plastic outer bags, seal the bag, stack the cases onto a cart and hook the cart to the drag line that would take the goods to the warehouse for storage and shipment.

The rumors spread through the plant like grass fires. Daryl had been a supervisor in this department for years, but he had recently been transferred to another department. Policy stated that we could not work in the same department and that was a good thing. I knew a lot of the people who worked in the Meat Tray Department and I thought that would help. Much to my surprise and dismay, it didn't. Daryl liked to flaunt his authority and sometimes it could be construed as unethical.

He had a reputation with the factory workers and most of it was not as positive as I had thought. It didn't take long for me to realize that there was a huge difference between how I thought it would be and how it really was working in the factory.

I found out that most of the workers considered me to be "one of those prissy office workers" and they had bets that I wouldn't last a week. Most of them didn't know that I had pitched shit, milked cows, bailed hay, drove tractors, done street drag racing and been a real tomboy for most of my life. The other elements I had were my father's stubborn determination combined with a little hidden defiance and the drive to prove them wrong!

The first week was a real eye opener. I always wore makeup wherever I went. Going into this factory every night at midnight wasn't any different. The packers in the department were mostly women and they subtly let me know that I was invading their space. They were very distant and rarely talked to me. There was a really shy young man working on the machine next to me, and we got to be quite good friends. From time to time, he would tell me stuff the other packers were saying, and we would laugh about it. After a few weeks, I noticed some subtle changes. The women were wearing makeup to work every night. I always felt better if I knew I looked my best, even in a factory, at midnight. I hoped they thought that too.

The Lead Operator in charge of the machine I had been assigned was a woman. I had known her a few years through company picnics because she worked for Daryl. Her name was Penny. She was a warm, considerate, little tiny woman who helped me a lot. She made sure I did not fail. After a little while, I was working quickly and getting along pretty well with factory work. I was getting paid a lot more than I did when I worked in the offices and I really didn't mind the transition. At times it got rough. During the summer when the temperature by the machines could get to 105 degrees during the night, made it a real sweat box.

One night when I went into work I noticed the mold had been changed in my machine. It was starting up on our shift with the 1S or "three tomato" tray. I didn't think much about it until Penny told me that this tray was the worst tray to run and even worse to pack. It was so bad that the other lead operators in the department started another pool. They were taking bets as to when I would have to be moved to another machine because I would not be able to keep up. Penny told me about the bet and my father's stubborn defiance kicked in yet again. She comforted me by telling me that this tray usually ran only a few days at a time. I was sure I could make it through a few days.

There were problems with the machine as it didn't always punch the trays out consistently. For some reason the sheet would jam and leave cut pieces in between the trays. I would have to pick these pieces out before I could pack the good trays. The first night was a disaster. The machine went down several times, I got behind several times and there were trays and pieces flying everywhere. Penny was as frustrated as I was, but we kept doing all we could to deal with the circumstances.

The next night it was better and I was getting faster. Four nights we worked furiously hoping that the mold would be changed out over the weekend. I went home on Friday, the fourth day, and thought for sure by Sunday night it would be changed. Sleeping during the day was usually more difficult than at night, but not this week. I slept like a baby.

Sunday night came and I went into work to find the mold had not been changed. I asked Penny about it.

"According to the schedule, it's supposed to run for four weeks straight!" she said.

I thought I was doomed, but like the first week, I pushed myself to handle the demand of the machine. There were bad nights and some not so bad, but the boss never did give the order to put me on another machine.

I had gone to college orientation and was signed up for my first meeting with my professor. The structure of the college was one-on-one with a professor. I had to design my own degree program and everything was subject to approval by the Board of Regents. The first day I met with my professor, we talked about the type of degree I was looking for and the types of subjects I would be taking. My focus was business and I had been approved on a contingency acceptance, which meant I was still in a "maybe" student status. The professor suggested I start my studies with a six credit course for Macro and Micro Economics. I didn't even know what that was! I would soon find out when I got my first assignment, bought the books and started my college journey.

As I read about economics, I found that it was really pretty interesting and there were a lot of things to learn. I worked very hard at this subject and completed all my work on time. I wanted to make a good impression. When you are one-on-one with your teacher, you have to be prepared for any questions he or she might ask. There were tough spots, but together we would work through them. I was learning a lot and feeling good about it.

At the end of the economics class, I held my breath for a grade. My final grade was a B+. I thought I had done pretty well even though in my mind I was thinking I was supposed to get A's. In conversations with Adam, another student, I found out that he had taken the economics class in the structured classroom setting at the local community college. We compared grades. He told me he had gotten one of the highest grades in his class, which was a C. I felt really proud to tell him that I had gotten a B+. I especially enjoyed his "Oh, really?" response. Suddenly my B+ felt like an A!

I continued taking classes and the grades were averaging between B+ and A's. I was amazing myself as I found my other classes to be easier than the economics class. I was enjoying college very much. I wasn't stupid!

Over the next two years my classes continued and my schedule got even more hectic. I had finally landed a job in Customer Service after working in the factory about eight months. I was still running every day, playing softball twice a week, going to college once a week, worked some occasional overtime and there was still the house to maintain. I had become very disciplined. My routine was everything. If I missed a time slot, I would have to make it up somewhere else. That was usually near impossible.

As I got closer to completing my studies for my Associates Degree, I noticed Daryl becoming more distant with our already failing relationship. At first I attributed it to the sports schedule with the boys, but the closer I got to being a college graduate, the more annoyed Daryl seemed to get. I wanted to think he would be proud of me. It was difficult to ask him for help with anything because he would become so defensive. He critically reminded me that work and school were my choices and my problems.

THE BEGINNING OF THE END

The realities of my previous hesitations finally caught up with me, 18 years later. This was the month Daryl and I had met, and this is the month that I would finally leave him to seek a different life. I sat in my one bedroom apartment on Main Street of the town I had lived since I left the farm. I knew this was the right decision. I had always loved the country and yet here I sat in an apartment without a driveway, noises of others I didn't like, and constant sound of traffic.

DO YOU WANT TO GO BACK?

I always said, "No". But the hurt was much more than I expected.

The boys, were now 16 and 12, and had chosen to stay with Daryl. They were told by Daryl that he would buy them each a new motorcycle if they stayed. I couldn't offer them anything but me, and they didn't know what it meant to be without me. My apartment was only a few blocks from the school, and they came over for visits weekly. I really felt lonely with no kids, no dogs and no yelling. Inside, I still felt this was the right thing to do.

I had been to see a lawyer and started the paperwork. I was suing Daryl for divorce and he would be served with papers on Friday. He had become such an arrogant, threatening man that I feared his reaction. I tried convincing myself that he should be expecting the papers, but was surprised to learn that he wasn't.

***

I tried to finish my last class before summer, a computer language class. There was class time and lab time. I wasn't used to the classroom thing three days a week and it left me with very little spare time. The softball season had started and I was playing softball twice a week. The only way I kept my sanity was to keep running. My schedule was so full that it would be into the night when I ran, usually between 10 PM and 1 AM.

The VA Hospital had become a solemn refuge for me. I could feel at peace with everything. The security staff watched for me every night. They warned me about the skunks that would invade the parking area garbage cans. One night, when there was a partial power failure, the back sides of the grounds were dark. They volunteered to drive the patrol car through that section just in front of me so I would be safe. They were like family and I did feel safe.

By July my computer language class was done, and I decided to take a little vacation. I only had one more class to take before I would complete my studies for my Associate of Science Degree. August was a vacation month for the school. I just wanted a few days out of town to catch my breath. I needed to think things through. Daryl had been treating me like I was some kind of incompetent child that just got in his way for years. I was responsible for everything at home. He would remind me constantly that I couldn't even do that right because I couldn't keep the house clean—like **he** wanted. He was the breadwinner. He could decide that he didn't have to do anything except bring home the money. I wasn't allowed to have any money to spend because he dictated how my money was spent. This enabled him to have more of the things he wanted. Now all these things were racing through my head. Why do I have to do everything? Why does he get to decide everything? The answer at the end was the same. He will take the boys, the house, and my car and leave me with nothing.

As I started looking back at the past few years, I began to realize all of the things that had changed. I didn't feel I could go to my mom or dad about any of my problems because there would be that "I told ya so" thing. I knew they had gotten tired of his stories too. Daryl's parents certainly wouldn't want to hear anything negative about their son from me. After all, I was the one that made up that outrageous story about his father. I had to think this through and come to terms with it myself. I just needed someone to listen to see if I was talking delusional or realistic. The only one I had right now was Abby.

Abby was a woman I worked with. We had gotten to be good friends. She always listened while I vented my frustrations about Daryl. She didn't care for Daryl and he didn't care for her either. Any time we spent together, he got mad. Abby was single and in her mid-thirties. She came from a divorced family and lived at home with her mother and brother.

Abby and her Mom often took vacations all over the United States and told of wonderful sights they had seen. I wanted to do something like that, but didn't have the budget to spend on one of those trips. I asked her if she would go on a long weekend with me somewhere. We could get away from the "Daryl pressure" and do some shopping. We decided to make it a long weekend within driving distance to a place we'd never been.

One night I told Daryl, just as we went to bed, that I wanted to take a break from school, work, and home just for a weekend. I told him I wanted to go shopping in Cleveland, Ohio just to go somewhere. I explained I really wouldn't be alone because Abby wanted to go with me. I asked him if he minded if I went. He was very quiet and slow to respond. He told me he didn't think I needed to go that far away because I could go shopping in Rochester. I reiterated to him that I wanted to take a few days to unwind before I started my fall class. We didn't discuss it much after that. I knew he didn't want me to go. He knew I was determined to go. We left it that way.

On the 29th of July, Abby and I left for Cleveland, Ohio. One of my Cleveland customers recommended we go to the festival on the docks that weekend. He said it would be a great time and thought we would enjoy it. He suggested meeting us there for a drink so we could meet each other in person. I thought that to be fun and agreed to see him on Friday night.

Abby and I talked about Daryl most of the trip down. I expressed the need to sort out all the factors that I needed to weigh, in order to come to a decision about our marriage. I felt the need to do this while I was in Cleveland. This would give me an opportunity to think without the persuasion of guilt by Daryl.

I wanted closure to all the bad that was going on between us. The boys knew it was happening and they just avoided the whole family thing. They were always going to their friends houses and I was beginning to see why. Daryl and I were fighting whenever we were together. The guilt he instilled in me was overwhelming at times. He blamed me for failing as a wife and mother, and I, in turn, accepted that blame. I was supposed to make everyone happy. My fear was in control, encapsulating me, and I felt I had to somehow break out.

The weekend was great. We met Evan and had a couple of drinks. He and I danced while Abby sat by and watched. He acted like he was attracted to me, and I was feeling the giddiness of a teenager. At the end of the night he walked us to our room and Abby went inside. Evan and I talked in the hall for a while. We looked into each others eyes and saw something that we both wanted. We danced around the subject until finally Evan gave me a kiss goodnight (on the forehead) and left. I was feeling like I wanted to be close to someone like him. He was attractive, but very young. I didn't care. He made me feel good even though it was just a friendly acquaintance for one evening. He knew I was unhappy in my marriage and I found out later he had just broken up with his fiancé. I think we both knew how vulnerable we were and thought it best to walk away.

REBOUNDERS! THIS IS WRONG! THINK ABOUT IT, BUT DON'T DO IT!

I was in a fog. I didn't want to hear anymore commands.

On Saturday Abby and I went shopping and then onto the festival on the docks. It was a great time. There were vendors and all kinds of food concessions. The crowd was so thick you could barely walk through it. There was a spectacular fireworks show that sparkled over the water and bridges. It was an incredibly beautiful show and event.

Sunday morning we toured downtown Cleveland for a while and headed home about noon. I felt I had handled myself badly that weekend with Abby. I treated her like she was just along for my ride and my conversations. I spent so much time bitching about Daryl and that I didn't realize until much later that I could have at least asked her if there was something she wanted to do. My mind was almost out of control. My ability to think rationally had disappeared. The drive home was bad and the closer to home I got the more irresponsible I became. I was driving 80 MPH most of the trip home. I drove right up on the bumpers of the cars in front of me.

Abby was scared and would ask, "Do you have to drive so fast and so close to those cars?"

I felt invincible and shot back confidently with, "They will move over. It isn't like they are going to stop real quick or anything."

My behavior had damaged our friendship more than I could ever repair. She had helped me to deal with the Daryl situation. In our limited conversation on that trip home she helped me make a decision. She was a good friend. She was there when I needed someone. To this day I am sorry I jeopardized our friendship, but still very grateful to her for listening.

I had come to a conclusion by the time I got home. If Daryl showed me any evidence that he missed me, then I would stay. I would make a go of the marriage no matter what it took. If he showed the anger, I had seen in the past, I would tell him I wanted a divorce.

It was Sunday at about 5:30 PM when I pulled in our driveway. Daryl was not there. I went into the house and put my bags in the bedroom. Nobody was there, not even the boys. I was surprised. I decided to wash the car in the front yard.

I was almost done with the car when he came home. It was about 7 PM. He parked the truck, got out and started walking toward me.

"Where were you?" I asked.

With an argumentative, hostile tone of voice, **"I didn't know when you were coming home,"** He fired back. **"I had things to do. So what if I wasn't home when you got here. It's your fault for not telling me what time you expected to get back."**

He stormed off into the house. I finished rinsing the soap from my car. I thought it best if I took my time and let him cool off a little. But the decision about my future had just been made. I have to leave. I'll tell him I want a divorce.

About 15 minutes passed before he stormed out the front door.

"Why did you buy that colored underwear? Did you get it while you were in Cleveland? If that is where you went?"

"I just bought some new underwear. I bought the colored stuff because I just thought it was pretty. It was different from what I had." I replied.

I bought some pretty navy and soft pink satin bras and panties. I just couldn't pass them up. He had obviously gone through my luggage and found them. He was enraged and shot back with the statement that finalized the decision.

"You're a whore to wear that stuff. That's probably why you went to Cleveland anyway. I don't need to be associated with a slut like you."

He got into his truck and left, spinning the tires and racing to the end of the street. I finished rinsing and toweling the car, trying to understand. I was really confused with what to do now. I wanted to see the boys and I guessed they were at their friends' houses. I did know that I would have to start looking for somewhere else to live right away. Plain and simple, it was over.

The boys came home around 9 PM. We talked about the trip and I gave them some souvenirs. They asked where Dad was and I told them that we had another fight. He left very angry, but I didn't know where. Around 10 PM the boys and I went to bed.

Daryl came back about 11 PM. He came into the bedroom with his authority glowing.

"We need to talk and I want the boys to hear what I have to say!" He demanded.

He proceeded to wake them up, asking them to sit at the dining room table for a family announcement. As the boys and I congregated at the table, he went to the bedroom and took out his 38 pistol and a box of shells. He came back to the dining room to speak to us with the gun in full view of all of us.

Daryl started talking like he was in some kind of military pre-war prep meeting.

"Dale, Bret, your mother and I are splitting up. I can't live with her behaving like some kind of slut; running off doing who knows what. I don't expect you will see me again after tonight." He said as he turned and walked away.

He walked out of the house like he had just been called to duty. We could hear him get into his truck and speed away. The boys and I stared at each other in silence for a moment, but the expressions on their faces saying, *what was that all about?* The boys had seen enough episodes to take this, somewhat, with a grain of salt, and for that I was grateful. We didn't say much. I think the boys were still half asleep. I told them it would be okay, he was just mad and he would be back. The boys didn't say anything. We all went back to bed. It took a long time for my racing mind to turn off and go to sleep.

When I woke I realized it was time to get ready for work. There was no sign of Daryl. I showered and dressed thinking of where he might have gone. I didn't think he would actually shoot himself. He just didn't have it in him. I resented the grandstanding he did in front of the boys, but that was Daryl. He would go to enormous measures to reiterate he was in charge. He was the authority. I still couldn't help but wonder. I went to say goodbye to the boys. They were still both asleep. I woke them enough to tell them I was going to work. They both asked if their Dad came home and I had to tell them no. That stuck with me for most of the day. I never did know where he went. But the reality of the situation made me realize that I could not live with a man that would be so dramatic as to put on an act like that in front of his own children.

I went to work. Near the end of the day, a floral arrangement was delivered to the customer service department. The arrangement was for me and it was from Daryl.

The card read, "I'm very sorry, Love Daryl". This was typical of him. He figured I would have told everyone at work of the incident. Now, he needed to earn points with my coworkers by having the flowers delivered in front of an audience. I had not mentioned anything to anyone. When I got the flowers, coworkers were asking if it was our anniversary or something. I confirmed it was not and that it was probably my welcome back from my long weekend away.

When I left work to go home, Daryl was sitting in his truck, parked behind my car. He was waiting for me. I carried the flowers as I walked over to the truck. I opened the passenger door and placed the flowers on the seat.

"I see you got my flowers." He said.

"Yes," I said, "but you should have saved your money. You don't need to buy a slut, like me, flowers."

He started with the schmooze talk I heard so many times before.

I tried to remain calm, interrupting with, "It's over."

I shut the truck door and got in my car. He drove away and so did I.

The evening schedule held a softball game for me. Daryl was the coach. The evening went according to the schedule and the usual routine. Neither of us let on there was anything different than any other day, except I decided to walk home from the game. I didn't want to be near him, at all. I knew my feelings for him had changed. Actually, I knew that some time ago, but now I was dealing with the reality of it. I was committed to ending this charade he and I were playing. He was angry and his jealousy didn't allow him to trust me. He should have known by now that I did not, or could not, lie about anything. He believed Abby and I was out man-hunting. In Daryl's world, married women don't have single women friends.

When I got home he was already there. I quickly changed from my softball uniform to my running clothes, grabbed my radio and headed for the door while he tried to talk to me. I confirmed to him that the talking was over as I left.

I ran about 3 miles. I usually did 2. When I got back I showered and went to bed. Daryl was watching TV with the boys. When I went into the bedroom he followed. I suggested he sleep on the couch until I found a place to live. For some reason, he didn't say anything and left the room. He did sleep on the couch that night and the rest of the nights until I moved out.

The next night I talked to the boys. I told them it was over between their father and me. We talked about it for a while before I asked if they wanted to live with me. I told them I needed to know so I could get an apartment that would be big enough for all of us. I could tell by their expressions and lack of conversation that they didn't grasp what I was telling them. I knew they wanted to stay home. It was the only home they remembered and I understood that, but I could see in their eyes they were saying, "Mom, you aren't leaving—this is just talk. You are just mad—it will pass like it always does." I told them I would be close by and that I loved them and didn't want to leave them. They had to tell me now if they were coming with me. They were quiet for what seemed like a long time. They both said they would stay. It was their house too and I knew they just couldn't leave like I knew I had to.

I called on apartments that night and set up appointments to look at three on Saturday. The rest of the week went along as Monday did and the boys, Daryl and I knew things had changed. None of us knew how to fix it. None of us wanted to talk about the changes.

On Saturday I put a deposit on an apartment. That is when I found out that Daryl had taken all my credit cards out of my wallet. I cashed my Christmas club to make the security deposit. I could move in August 28, after the owners finished painting. It was a one bedroom upstairs apartment with a back enclosed porch. I liked the thought of taking my plants. It felt like it could be a comfortable place to live.

The boys were not home much anymore. The dogs knew that things were changing and that was even more painful because I couldn't take them with me. The boys said they would take care of them for me. I knew they would need them too. Shellee, a tri-colored seven year old

Sheltie, and was the mother of Missi, a five year old sable Sheltie. We also had Hio, Missi's father, who was a seven year old sable. Missi and I had been partners since her birth (actually the minute of her birth). It would be very hard to be without them.

Daryl tried to make amends, but I knew he wouldn't give up control. Not even a little of it. I knew, in my heart, this was what I had to do. I felt bad and guilty because of the boys. They were trying so hard to cope and yet I knew they didn't understand.

On Friday, the day before the move, I was packing bare necessities when Daryl decided to invite some friends over. I continued to pack during their visit and no one talked about what I was doing. It was so weird. I think it was his way to stop me from packing. He tried to continue the charade as we had done for years, but this time it didn't happen. I kept packing.

Mom came over the next morning with Dad's truck and we loaded my things. I wasn't taking very much because I wanted to leave as much for the boys as I could. I wanted their lives to continue as unchanged as possible. Bret was not handling this well at all. I told Bret that I would still be running through the VA Hospital. He could meet me there and we could talk every night if he wanted. He didn't respond. He was nasty and angry and very hurt. I wished I could have done this differently. He would not help me leave. He didn't help me load a single thing. I knew he felt that if he didn't help, maybe I would stay. But as the day went on, the harsh reality finally consumed him. He kept it all inside and shed not a tear. I wish I could have done as well. Saying goodbye to Missi and Shellee was the heart breaker. The look on their faces was something I would never forget.

The first night in the apartment was so quiet it was deafening. My mind was somehow peaceful yet unsettled. I didn't have much stuff to move, so settling was pretty easy. I only took the bare necessities. I could get the other stuff later. I was sure of that. I would get my phone installed on Monday. I could call the boys to help ease their pain and mine. Dale was at work or Gill's house through most of this and we never did talk about it.

By Friday things had changed again. I called the boys every day. They came up to the apartment after school a couple of times. Today they told me Dad had a girlfriend and a date for tonight. I tried to be positive about it. I told them maybe this was a way for him to be happier. He had never lived alone. He didn't know how to do it. He didn't cook. Cleaning, laundry, and paying of the bills, was woman's work. Fortunately, the boys had learned to do their own laundry. They cooked some, and I thought they could help take care of their father.

The new girlfriend left me unsettled. I knew Daryl needed someone to take care of him. But, I was disappointed that he didn't even wait a week before he replaced me. There was also the factor of the boys' feelings. He didn't appear to be concerned about that. Adjusting to life without me in the house everyday was tough enough for them, but getting used to a new face in my role was something I thought he should have waited a little longer to do. But, that was Daryl's way of showing me that he didn't need me. I'm sure he did it to make me angry. The part that bothered me was that the boys needed some transition time.

Through the weekend I continued arranging furniture, putting up new curtains and settling the kitchen and bathroom. Bret called me several times. He was giving me the scoop on the new girlfriend. It seems Daryl met her when she applied for a job and he had interviewed her. I guess the interview got "casual". It turns out that she was just newly divorced and had three children, two boys and a girl. Bret said they had been over to meet them on Saturday. Bret was mad about the situation and I tried to calm his anger.

"It will make him easier to live with," I told him, "It isn't that she's replacing me. She could never do that. I will always and forever be your mom, no matter what."

He seemed to feel better about that, and actually so did I.

The boys were showing signs of adjusting. We talked more now that we did before I moved. There were still a lot of things to deal with. I knew I had to get an attorney right away. This was another learning process for me. I never had the need to see a lawyer before, and now I had to find one and get him busy. I heard enough divorce horror stories to know it would be in my best interest to sue Daryl for divorce first. I checked the yellow pages for a local attorney. I found an ad for an attorney and an associate that specialized in divorce and family matters. The office was just a couple of blocks from my apartment. That would be convenient for consultations. I called and set an appointment.

It was Wednesday when I met with the attorney for the first time. He was the associate of this firm and appeared to be slightly younger than I. He was soft spoken with a distinctly deliberate manner. It was definitely a "let's cut to the chase" kind of meeting. I gave him the particulars and expressed my fears with the legal process. I had left the premises and the boys. He comforted me by telling me that didn't matter anymore in New York State. He recommended we sue first and fast. The bad news was that he needed a retainer of $800.00 to get started.

I told him I didn't have any money. He asked if I had relatives I might borrow from. I thought about Mom and Dad. I had never asked them for money, or anything else for that matter, before, but now was a desperate time. I told the attorney I would get the money by Friday, one way or another. He said he would get the paperwork ready for Daryl to be served with the summons suing him for divorce. I told the attorney Daryl would be hopping mad and that I worried about his reactions. He assured me it didn't matter. He would have him served on Friday and the Sheriff's Office would handle the serving of the summons. We set another appointment to gather more details for the next step. In the meantime I had to get some money. I would have to go see Mom and Dad.

***

The drive to Mom and Dad's was about 20 minutes. My mind was filled with all the ways I would ask for money.

As I walked into the mud room, I could see into the kitchen. Mom was sitting at the kitchen table. I figured Dad was probably in the barn. It was about 7 o'clock and I was nervous, almost terrified, to go inside. I pushed myself through the door.

As I walked in, Mom looked up and said, "Hi! How are you doing?"

"I'm doing okay..."

"How are things?" She asked.

"Good, actually," I said, "I saw an attorney today and he plans to summon Daryl on Friday. I'm suing him first. I think we both know how that will go."

She said in a knowledgeable tone, "Yes, we do."

I felt a little better after that. We had talked about the divorce during the move, but there was so much going on that day, it was hard to really talk about the emotional side of. We were feeling too much of Bret's emotional upheaval.

I told her what the attorney reassured me that moving out won't hurt my case and that suing Daryl first was quite important. It would give us the upper hand in dealing with the situation.

She agreed that it sounded like the attorney knew his way around handling divorces.

"He told me I would have to get a retainer to him as soon as possible," I said, "and I wondered if I could borrow some money to get this started."

"How much do you need?" She responded eagerly.

"$800.00." I said and paused for some kind of reaction.

"I'll give you the money," she said, "it is about time you got out from under this bad situation anyway. I don't know how you put up with it this long!"

I was stunned by her response, but relieved. We had more candid conversation about things between Daryl and me. She wrote the check while we talked and we continued our conversation even after Dad came in from the barn. It appeared he knew as much as Mom did about everything and he supported my actions. We had pie and ice cream before I went home.

It was Friday night when I got a very angry call from Daryl. It seems the sheriff tried to deliver Daryl's summons to him at work. The security staff prevented it from happening, but it did crank up the rumor mill. The sheriff's deputy then served the summons to him at home.

When Daryl read the summons he exploded in anger. He was screaming at me over the phone, asking me what I thought I was doing. I left him and I had no right to sue him for divorce. I guess he expected me to sit in my apartment and wait for him.

I was surprised at how stupid he thought I was to think that I would be waiting for him to act out the threats he had been giving me for years. I wasn't much of a procrastinator and after living in fear of this event for so many years, I guess I just wanted it to be over as soon as possible. He wasn't happy about any of it (it was one of his friends on the sheriff's department that served him)! He got so mad he couldn't talk any more and hung up on me. It wasn't much of a conversation—I don't remember saying anything back to him!

Daryl always thought he was invincible. He had met this woman, dated her for a week and then proceeded to move her and her children into the house before consulting with an attorney. He had always thought of himself as being the exception to most of the rules. If he ever got caught, he thought he would just consult with one of his powerful friends to fix it for him.

Bret met up with me in the VA during my run that night and told me the gory details of the summons. Bret said the sheriff came to the house looking for Daryl around 5 PM and the girlfriend went to the door and told the sheriff he was not at home (when actually he was hiding in the bedroom). The sheriff's deputy said he would come back later. After he left, Bret said Daryl waited about 20 minutes, then called the sheriff's office to find out about the summons. They told him they would send the officer right out with the summons, which they did. He accepted the summons politely, Bret said, but as soon as the sheriff left he exploded and proceeded to call me.

IT ISN'T LIKE HE DIDN'T KNOW IT WAS COMING BY THEN!

Well, I wondered how he would deal with it. I guess I found out. It went about how I expected.

The painful process of divorce started on a downward spiral after the summons. Daryl started being as brutally uncooperative as he could and tried talking up his new girlfriend every chance he got.

THE DIVORCE

By October 3, my attorney sent our grounds for divorce to Daryl's attorney, requesting his counter reply. After the summons, things between Daryl and me started to get really dirty. The phone calls diminished considerably and most of our communications were done through lawyers. I would come home from work and find boxes of my belongings on the porch at my apartment. It seems that the girlfriend decided she needed more closet space and started cleaning things out.

The next few weeks were spent waiting for the several counter suit replies from Daryl and his attorney. He hired an attorney from a large, prestigious firm in Rochester. It seems the attorney that took the case was the father to one of Daryl's little league kids. The firm had an impressive reputation which made me nervous, but my attorney comforted me and told me not to worry. In the meantime things got even worse between Daryl and me.

As much as I wanted to shut the door on Daryl and his existence, I could not because of Dale and Bret. Dale was a senior now and there were things to take care of that we had been waiting for 16 years to do. First there were his senior pictures. After the proofs came back I realized I would have to show them to Daryl so he could pick the ones he wanted for himself and his family. I decided I would just show up at the house with the proofs, unannounced, just to watch Daryl squirm.

Daryl came to the door. He closed it immediately behind himself. I told him that I would need to spread the pictures out on the table or counter so he could get a good look at them. He was still resistant, but Bret heard me at the door he opened the door from the inside. We all merged together like water through a funnel. Just inside the door were the girlfriend and her four-year-old daughter. It looked like she may have been trying to listen to our conversation. With me inside, she didn't have to strain to listen. I walked past her and into the kitchen where I spread the pictures out on the counter. Daryl was quick to follow, stumbling over his words as he tried to introduce the girlfriend. Neither of us wanted to know the other, but Daryl was trying to do the polite thing. Bret was trying to ask me a question about how to get a stain out of his favorite shirt while Daryl was viewing pictures.

Before I could finish responding to Bret, the girlfriend cut me off.

"I'll get that stain out for you, Bret." She chirped. "I will take care of it tomorrow."

Poor Bret looked confused. He looked at me and I assured him it was okay. Neither of us said anything more.

Daryl made his selection of Dale's pictures and told me he would call the photographer to order the ones he wanted. I gathered up the pictures and left as quickly as I could. I was very uncomfortable. I felt the girlfriend getting a defensive attitude with me. I didn't want to get into a nasty verbal exchange with her in front of Bret. I cried all the way home.

SOMETIMES SWEET REVENGE IS NOT SWEET!

December brought the counter to the counter sue and that is when I got all the list of demands from Daryl and his attorney. My attorney said there were 25 line items of reasons listed and that most were typical, but we had to discuss line item number 25.

"I didn't tell you before," he said, "because I knew it would upset you. Daryl is claiming you were having an affair with another woman."

My mouth fell open. I was shocked to the point of being speechless.

"Daryl's attorney wants you to mutually agree on the terms." My attorney continued, "That way none of the reasons will need to be discussed any further."

My mind raced. I tried to refocus my thoughts.

THINK, THINK, COME ON YOU NEED TO RESPOND, HERE.

I was thinking of my class from college, Business Law. I suddenly remembered a term from my class that might apply here. The term was slander.

"NO, NO," I demanded, "I will not agree to mutual terms. If he wants to slander me, he will have to prove it in court and I know he can't." I looked straight at my attorney and waited for his response.

He took a deep breath. His eyes welded to mine, said, "I thought you might react that way. I am going to do something that ethically could get me into trouble as an attorney. I will ask for a trial date to be placed on the Supreme Court calendar for the divorce. This will force them to scramble preparing their case. Divorce attorneys don't do this—it is considered a risky move, but I can see this divorce getting very ugly. It could go on for years, and I know you can't afford it. This way it evens the playing field for all participants. If we can't come to an agreement by the date then a Supreme Court Judge will decide."

I felt immediately better. My attorney said I should have a good Christmas and he would call me as soon as he heard from the court clerk and Daryl's attorney. He assured me I would get through this and this action would help to shorten the suffering. I thanked him and wished him Merry Christmas.

I went home to my apartment and thought about the conversation with the attorney. I was glad to know there was a pinhole light of hope. I knew, however, there were still more hard times to come until the divorce was officially over.

Christmas was always a storybook holiday for me. It had to be traditional—food, presents, family gatherings, cookie day, the works. This year would be different. Daryl had filed paperwork to have the boys for Christmas morning. He knew how important it was to me to do all the things that go with Christmas morning. I would get up very early to make cinnamon rolls, put together a huge fruit basket, and I always had to get the turkey stuffed before the boys got up for presents. We all would gather around the Christmas tree and start opening up presents, taking a break on occasion to bite a warm cinnamon roll and have some juice or hot chocolate. After the presents, came the arrival of all the grandparents and other relatives for dinner. The house was full of laughter and celebration. It was always a happy time, even as the boys grew up and the myth of Santa Claus faded.

This year Christmas would be very different. Somehow I got the strength to commit myself to enjoy Christmas Eve with the boys the best way I could. I bought a 5' Douglas Fir tree and decorated it with all the ornaments I had painted when the boys were very little. I put electric candles in all my apartment windows, all 6 of them, and decorated wherever I could in the apartment.

Through some unusual turn of events, I wound up having all the kids at my house for a while on Christmas Eve. There was Dale and Bret, my niece, Onicka, and nephews, Barry and Bruce (Dick's son). We could all barely fit in my makeshift living room, but everyone piled in and opened a present or two. The kids seemed to be have a great time and we celebrated with Christmas cookies and milk. The time flew and soon it was time for me to deliver everyone to their destinations.

I returned home to a silent apartment, but it was still glowing with Christmas lights and the echoes of children laughing. I would have all the silly snap shots the kids took when we were all together. I couldn't wait to see them. I felt very lucky. I settled into bed leaving all my window candles lit. The three rooms of the apartment had a warm yellow-orange glow that was very comforting.

On Christmas morning I awoke and looked out the window. My candles were still on, but the orange glow was gone. It was overcast outside and looked cold. There was still a covering of snow on the ground and the trees, which gave the appearance of a typical New England winter. I went to the kitchen, made some coffee and went to my living room to see my Christmas tree. I had been sent a gift from one of my salesmen from work. I saved it to open on Christmas morning.

I bent down and picked up the small gift. I tore away the paper to find a porcelain Christmas bell. I smiled and thought—this will be my only gift this Christmas season and the only person thoughtful enough to give it to me was a co-worker.

There was a peaceful quiet in the apartment as well as in the streets. Everyone was celebrating Christmas. I thought of Dale and Bret and what they must be doing. I wanted to call, but didn't. Whoever was fixing Christmas dinner at our house certainly wouldn't be feasting the way we did. Oh well, their loss I guess, but I was the one feeling the loss, too.

MENDING FENCES

It was just past the New Year. I was so hoping it would be a better year than last, but I knew there would be some rough roads still ahead. I hadn't heard from my lawyer, but I knew the holidays would slow things down. I did have an odd conversation with Mom though. She called to tell me about something my niece, Onicka, had asked her about during the holidays. Onicka was now 11 and Barry 9. Onicka asked if Mom knew why her mom and Aunt Laura didn't talk anymore. She said she really liked me and wished we would get back together. Mom told her she didn't know why we weren't speaking. Mom suggested, if I wanted to, I could call Trixie and bury the past. Daryl was the influencing character here—maybe it was time to end the silence. She gave me her phone number.

BUT YOU DON'T EVEN KNOW WHY SHE STOPPED TALKING TO YOU!!

I thought about my sister and how our relationship had literally died. Daryl had always hated us being together. Maybe it was time to clear the air. Maybe **I** needed to call her first. I had my hand on the phone for the longest time before finally I just dialed her number. All kinds of things went through my mind while I waited for the telephone to ring. It rang once and I thought about hanging up; no one answered the second ring. I'm thought more seriously about hanging up and then no answer again. I almost hung up but I thought that she might answer. It rang a third time.

Now I was ready to hang up, but before my brain could tell my hand to hang up I heard the "Hello?" My brain went blank. I couldn't speak and panic hit; I stumbled with a greeting.

"Hi, Trixie?"

There was a pause. "Yes?" she questioned.

I was incredibly nervous as I said, "Hi, this is your sister."

I was preparing myself for the click of a hang-up, but it didn't come.

She said with friendly enthusiasm, "Hi!"

I wasn't sure how to tell her why I was calling, but I decided I would just have to start talking and not thinking about what to say.

I started, "I was talking to Mom and she told me something that Onicka had asked her over the holidays. Onicka wanted to know why her Aunt Laura and her mom didn't talk anymore. I think it might have something to do with Daryl, but I'm not sure. I thought maybe we could get together and talk. Seeing as I am divorcing Daryl, maybe we could bury the hatchet, like over lunch somewhere."

She replied, "Yes, I think we could do that."

I explained, "I was thinking about taking a couple of days of vacation and maybe I could come down and you could show me where you live and I could get reacquainted with my niece and nephew and Kyle, whom I really don't know."

Trixie answered in excited voice, "Yes, I can show you how the southern part of the state lives. We could go to the Mall for lunch."

I cut her off and said, "Where is the Mall?"

Trixie said, "Buffalo."

In a startled voice, I said, "Buffalo! I thought you lived south of here?"

She confirmed, "Yes, but when you are out in the sticks as far as we are the nearest place to get a really nice lunch is Buffalo."

I replied in stunned voice, "You are serious!?"

"Yup!" She replied in her quirkily humorous voice.

I told her of my thoughts about coming down on Thursday and staying for the weekend. She thought that would be great. She gave me directions to her house, which filled the page of my notepad. She told me the trip would probably take two and a half hours. I was a little nervous about making the trip alone, in January, but I had to do this. We talked about things with our families for a short while and then ended our phone call with a "see ya later."

On Wednesday evening after work, I talked with Dale. He said Dad was ripping mad that I was going out of town. He said he wasn't babysitting for my dogs any longer. He said Dad was planning to take the dogs to a local dog shelter on the weekend—after I left to go to Trixie's house. Dale knew I would be upset. I told him I would see if Mom could take the dogs for me until my lease ran out and I could get a place to have the dogs. I asked him if anyone else was there. He said he was alone. I told him I would be over to pick up Missi and Shellee and when I arrived I wanted him to just let them out the front door of the house. I knew they would get in my car without hesitation and this might keep Dale from getting into trouble with his father, or so I thought. I told Dale I would get Hio after I got a sheriff to help me. We hung up and I drove to the house. Missi and Shellee did get into my car without hesitation and Dale came along to help.

I drove to my apartment and got the dogs settled inside, and then I called my attorney. I explained what had transpired and asked him what I should do about picking up Hio. He suggested I have someone else pick up the dog with a sheriff escort. I told him I could have my mother get Hio and he thought that would be good. I hung up and made respective phone calls to Mom and the sheriff's office. Dale and I waited at the apartment with Missi and Shellee. Hio was strictly a kennel stud dog and was very uncomfortable inside the house. Mom came to my apartment while we waited for the sheriff to call with his arrival time at our house (even though I thought of it as Daryl's house now).

The sheriff called, and Mom was on her way to get Hio. She planned to come back to my apartment to let me know everything went okay.

Dale, Missi, Shellee, and I waited. We talked about how furious Daryl would be and how he might react. After about 20 minutes Mom appeared at my door with Hio. She was excited about all that was happening, but said that Daryl was as friendly and cooperative as he could be. She no more than emptied her mouth of that sentence when my phone rang. Dale picked it up. I'm not sure he even said "Hello," when he pulled the receiver away from his ear and we all heard the shouting. Daryl was VERY mad! After shouting for a couple of minutes, he hung up on Dale. We all laughed and proceeded to load dogs into vehicles to take them to their new temporary home on my mom and dad's farm.

Dad had a Bassett hound named Sophie and was well practiced in spoiling animals. Now he would be able to spoil 3 more dogs for a while. It would be great to spend some more time with the dogs and the boys together.

Thursday morning came and I still went to my sister's as planned. Mom was more than happy to take the dogs for a while and told me not to worry about them.

I arrived at Trixie's about 10 AM. She and Kyle were still in the barn. Shortly after Trixie divorced Ronald, she started seeing Kyle. She knew him previously from being involved with the cows when we were kids. Trixie had always stayed involved with the cows and the state cow associations after she left 4-H and the farm.

As I drove into their driveway I could see the brown A-frame house placed neatly on a sloped lot overlooking the barn across the road. I parked my car and got out to get a breath of fresh country air. The sun was shining and the winter air was crisp and very clean. I was enjoying the moment when a voice called to me.

"Hi, I see you made it okay," yelled Trixie. "I'll be right up, please make yourself at home."

I waved back and shouted, "Okay"

I gathered my things and went into the house. The house had small rooms, but the living room, dining room and kitchen were all one quite large room. I settled my bags and was looking at the pictures on the walls of the kids and cows when I heard Trixie come in the downstairs door. She was asking if I had found the coffee yet and I answered that I had not. When she arrived in the kitchen, she started to make coffee as we made conversation about my drive down and the road conditions. It felt good to be with her again.

After coffee and a shower, we got into her car and headed to Buffalo for lunch.

The drive was a little less than an hour by the time we arrived at the mall. She parked at Sibley's so we could go to the restaurant upstairs. We had lunch and talked—mostly about Daryl. She told me she found out Daryl was saying some pretty nasty stuff about her that wasn't true. She was mad and she hated him for saying those things. She wouldn't go into the details and I didn't feel I needed to know them at this point. She seemed glad we were reconnecting and I was glad too.

After lunch we went shopping. Shopping with Trixie was always an experience because she was always clowning around. We were laughing and giggling to the point of almost being asked to leave in a couple of stores. It was fun being silly like a kid again. By late afternoon it was time to head back home and we decided to pick up fast food for supper.

Kyle was still in the barn when we got home, but we ate with Onicka and Barry and told them some of our childhood stories. The kids were quite entertained while we had fun reliving those times. Kyle came up from the barn, ate and then watched TV.

Trixie and I talked about our divorces and the horror stories that went along with them until midnight. It had been a long day, but a good one. I slept on the couch and was happy to be in a different place.

The next morning I was awakened by the sunlight pouring in the windows of the living room. I found the coffee and coffee pot and made coffee. I looked out the window of the front door to see an absolutely breathtaking sunrise. The sun was a beautiful burnt orange that crept through long threads of clouds, accenting the sky with streaks of gray and steel blue. In front of the dark shadows created by the woods were sparkling stars of reflection from untouched snow. Sunshine illuminating the silos and barn roof made the picture complete and perfect enough it could have been a postcard or Christmas card. I stood enjoying the sight and the warmth of the sun coming through the window until I could hear people stirring upstairs.

Within a few minutes my sister came downstairs for coffee after she woke Barry and Onicka to get ready for school. She asked if I slept okay and I confirmed I had and commented on the beautiful sunrise. She said that was pretty typical every day and that fall is especially beautiful.

The kids went off to school and Trixie had to feed calves. I hadn't done that for years, but she suggested I participate. The process had changed and I was about to be instructed on the new process. I borrowed some "barn clothes" and Trixie and I went to the barn.

The calves were housed outside because of disease and vulnerability to illnesses. Each calf had a hutch (a dome shaped plastic doghouse-like object) with a little fenced outside area. Each calf was given milk. Older calves got larger portions of milk in a pail, while the new baby calves got milk in a 1 or 2 quart bottle, depending on the calf's size, with a nipple. The hutches were constructed with bottle and bucket holders so you could place the bottle or bucket and go on to feed the next. We had to feed over 20 calves and then give them some grain and hay.

Trixie and Kyle had some hired help, but did a lot of work themselves. The farm was pretty large, milking over 200 cows and probably another 300 in smaller stock. All the cows were registered. They always competed in cattle shows wherever and whenever they could. I remember the farm and fair routines, but I didn't feel a part of it anymore. It was fun to revisit it, but I was glad I wasn't living it.

After chores we all went to the house for breakfast. It was closer to lunch than breakfast, but we ate the typical farmer breakfast. It consisted of bacon, eggs, toast, fried potatoes and juice. We didn't need lunch now! Trixie, Kyle and I talked about old times more during breakfast and Kyle asked if we had plans for the afternoon. We really did not, so he suggested showing me the Cattaraugus sights. I had no idea what that could possible entail, but I would soon find out. We showered and by 1 PM we all loaded into their pickup truck and headed for town.

I quickly found out that going to town pretty much meant going to see the local bar owners and patrons. The first place we stopped was called The Waverly Inn. The post office was across the street and was bordered by vacant buildings except for one. That building used to be an old hotel, called The Otto Hotel, and was also a bar. The clientele was made up of mostly local farmers, farm hands, construction workers and carpenters. January was a light time of the year for work so it was pretty easy to take some time off during the day. I met many of the locals and of course they were all very friendly with great humor. Most of that humor was directed at men, but I got the impression that the women folk were to understand that and went along in jest. I did.

At the Otto Hotel I got the "test" to make sure I was mentally fit to drink in their establishment. The test was made up of three questions: 1. How do you spell Otto? 2. How do you spell Otto backwards? (And finally) 3. How do you spell Otto inside out? (Toot☺) Well I am proud to say I passed the test and the drinking began. Everyone at the bar was shocked at how much Trixie and I looked alike. We had that "identical twins" question asked many times. Usually people thought Trixie to be the older one. When we were teenagers, that bothered me a lot, but as I got older it felt a lot better. I always looked younger than my actual age, but now it was becoming an asset.

We made the rounds that day. After the Waverly Inn and the Otto Hotel, we went to the next village. It was larger with probably 2500 residents and the usual mix of businesses with a couple of diner type restaurants mixed in. The next stop was to The Village Inn. This was a small building just outside of town, but the mix of people was about identical to the Waverly and Otto Hotel. Everyone was very friendly and seemed to be very glad to meet Trixie's sister. The last bar we stopped at was Chuck's Lounge. This was in downtown and this establishment was also a restaurant—serving real food. But by the time we got there and had been drinking all afternoon, food was the last thing on our minds. It was getting late, close to 6 PM, and we still had to do chores.

We left Chuck's and went home to feed the calves. I was drunk enough that I had to concentrate on walking to keep up with Kyle and Trixie. They seemed to be loosened up by the drinking, but not as drunk as I was. One of the hired men had started the process for us so it didn't take so long. I was glad of that. I believe we ordered a pizza for dinner, which pleased Barry and Onicka and me too actually. We all turned in quite a bit earlier than the night before.

The next morning had a similar routine even though it was Saturday. Get up, make coffee, get barn clothes on and go to the barn for chores. After chores, breakfast and then we had time to spend with Barry and Onicka. More fun stories and hearing about what was going on in their lives.

In the evening Trixie and Kyle and I went out to dinner at the Waverly Inn. They served prime rib dinners on weekends and it was very good. We had a few drinks after with the locals at the bar and Trixie and I went home earlier than Kyle. Someone would bring him home later and did, but after we were asleep.

Sunday came and soon it was time for me to pack up and head for home. Trixie wanted me to stay for as long as possible and I did, but I finally headed back toward home around 6 PM. She went to feed calves and I started my two and a half hour journey back home to my apartment.

I didn't actually arrive at home until near 9 PM. I gathered all my things and went upstairs to my apartment and I heard the phone ringing. I dropped everything and ran to pick it up. It was my Dad. His voice was upset and sounded like he was crying. He was trying to explain something about the dogs. For a moment I couldn't think what he was talking about, but then it hit me. Missi and Shellee! He told me he had let the dogs out to the backyard so they could go to the bathroom and they both ran away. They headed for the back woods through an open field. He was trying to apologize and was crying at the same time. He said they had been gone since about 6 PM. He asked if I could come over and maybe they would come to me if they heard my voice. I told him I was on my way and not to worry, we would find them.

I got into my car and started driving as fast as I dared to get to the farm. My mind was racing. Poor Dad! He sounded so upset and consumed with guilt for letting them out without their leashes. Poor Missi and Shellee; they had never spent a night outside in their lives, not to mention in January.

It would take me twenty minutes to get to the farm. I couldn't stop thinking about Dad and the dogs, but suddenly there was a car in front of me that was driving erratically. It pulled to the side of the road but was still moving slowly. I was impatient so I pulled around him and continued on my way. About half a mile down the road I suddenly noticed red flashing lights reflecting in my mirror. I realized it was a police official of some sort. I pulled over and put the car in park. I started fumbling for my license and registration. After a minute, I wound down my window to see where the police officer was because I didn't see him. When I wound down the window and looked back toward the police car I saw a female county sheriff with her gun pulled and pointing at me. I had my paperwork in my hand and held it up so she could see.

She yelled in her very authoritative voice, **"Why didn't you pull over when I put my lights and siren on? I have been chasing you for over a mile!"**

I was surprised by her question and scared looking at the gun. I immediately started to cry. In my blubbering crying voice, I tried to tell her about Missi and Shellee and that I had been out of town and they were pedigree dogs and they were lost and my Dad wanted me to come help find them and…

She cut me off, put her gun away, and said, "Look, I understand but you can't get your dogs back if you get into an accident and kill yourself."

I was still crying, but nodded in agreement.

She continued, "Just slow down and get there obeying the speed laws, okay?"

I started to recompose myself and promised I would slow down. She went back to her patrol car and waited for me to leave first. I took a minute to put my license back and gather my thoughts about what had just happened and tried to get my rationality back. I drove away and got to the farm a little after 9:30 PM.

Dad started crying again as soon as he saw me and I did too. We walked out to the back yard and I started calling the dogs. Shellee was hard of hearing and couldn't see well anymore, but I hoped Missi would help guide her to my voice. There wasn't any response. I walked into the open field towards the woods. No sign of the dogs. It was dark and very difficult to find tracks. I was about three quarters of the depth of the field calling Missi and Shellee as loud as I could. I had a flashlight hoping I would get a glimpse of their eyes reflecting light back to me. After about twenty minutes of looking, I thought I saw a shadow of something in the field just outside the edge of the woods. I flashed my light back again: eyes! I could see a pair of eyes reflecting in my flashlight. I called again. The object started running. I called again. It stopped and was now coming toward to me. It was Missi. I called to her again. She came bounding to me. After hugs and a complete wash of my face, we walked back toward the woods looking for Shellee but could not find her. Missi, Dad and I went back to the house.

By now it was 11 PM. Mom had been away on a bus out trip and had returned while we were out in the field. We talked about what to do next. Mom said she would call all the neighbors in the morning. Shellee wouldn't be in good enough shape to go very far and she was probably nearby. I cuddled with Missi for a bit and thanked Dad for his help and Mom for her ideas for finding Shellee. I told them to call me at work if they heard anything tomorrow. I would go home (slowly and safely) and worry all night about Shellee.

The next morning I called Mom before I left for work. She hadn't called any of the neighbors yet and Shellee had not come back either. She said she would call me when she heard something. I left for work thinking about what I should have done different to prevent this from happening. I didn't come up with anything except enormous guilt.

Work was busy and that was good; it helped keep my mind off Shellee. Around 9:30 AM I got a call from Mom. She said they found Shellee. She was at the neighbor's house just on the other side of the woods. She was barking at the door of their house this morning. The neighbor called Mom and asked if she knew anyone that had lost a cute little black and white dog. I was delighted to hear the good news and so were Mom and Dad. Now I could feel better that all three dogs were safe.

By the end of the month I had gotten information from my attorney that he had asked for a trial day to be placed on the judicial calendar. The date was April 17. He told me that Daryl's attorney wasn't happy about that move and it was a risky one for an associate attorney, but it did create the kind of reaction my attorney wanted. Now we had to prepare my arguments just in case we couldn't settle out of court before the trial date, April 17, 1986

***

Trial Day

The day had come. This should be the end of the Daryl reign of terror for me and maybe the boys too. I was scared and anxious. We were to go in front of the Judge by 9:30 in the morning. I was there and met my attorney by 9:15. He had prepared me for what was to come in our meeting the night before. He and Daryl's attorney would be discussing possible settlement agreements up to the moment we go into the courtroom. He asked me in that meeting if I would settle for mutual terms and I again said "No." He said Daryl's attorney pretty much told him that they would not pursue aggressively for conditions because he also knew Daryl was just telling a story about me having an affair with another woman. When I wanted to sue for slander for the statement, Daryl's attorney backed down and asked what I wanted to settle. I wanted to be rid of Daryl and our debt and I wanted him to pay for my attorney's fees for the divorce.

Just before we walked into the courtroom, my attorney came to me with their last offer. He said that if we could keep this from being an actual trial it would save a lot of money, money which neither one of us had. The final offer was that Daryl pays all the joint debt from the sale of the house, we settle on grounds of cruel and inhuman treatment and loss of loving environment, but I would have to pay for my own attorney's fees. I would get half of the house settlement after the bills were paid and some of his retirement equity. My attorney said it was a good deal and that I could pay him after we sold the house. I agreed. He also asked whether or not I wanted Daryl to be in the courtroom during courtroom proceedings for my testimony and the judge's declaration. I told him I did not want Daryl present. He also asked about my name change. Would I keep my married name or go back to my maiden name?

We walked into the courtroom and everyone sat in their respective places, my attorney and I on the right side of the room and Daryl's attorney on the left side. I was asked by the judge to take the stand which I did. I remember shaking, so scared I could hardly speak. He asked me what Daryl did to justify the cruel and inhuman treatment. I remember sharing the abusive verbal conflict with Daryl and his girlfriend. The judge said his decision was a declaration of divorce effective immediately on this day, April 17, 1986. He told me I had the right to take my maiden name back if I wanted or keep my married name. I explained that either name could be a problem for me because my brother's ex-wife kept her married name (being my maiden name) and that Daryl was dating another Laura and if they were to marry that would be two of both names and we all worked for the same company. I asked if I could pick a name under the circumstances. He agreed and that he would forward paperwork to make the legal change as soon as I chose a new name. Court was adjourned. I was divorced.

My attorney and I walked out together and he said he would be in touch with me for any paperwork finalization, but for the time being, I was divorced and I should be happy with the results. I definitely was pleased with the results when all the details started to sink in. I didn't have any old bills to pay and all of our debt would be taken care of when the house sold. I would get half of the house equity, which wouldn't be very much actually because of Daryl's spending habits, but it would be more than Daryl would get when all was signed and sealed.

I went back to my apartment to digest my feelings. I saw Daryl at the courthouse, but I didn't speak to him. I remembered how mad he would get and this would be one time I didn't have to watch it, hear it, or deal with it. I was very happy that his stories about me were recognized as lies. It may only be the attorneys that find out, but that was enough for me. Eighteen and a half years of this unhappy, unfair, one-sided lifestyle and now I could find a life where I could truly be happy.

I called my friend Abby and asked her if she could meet me for dinner on Friday to celebrate my divorce and help me pick out a new name. She agreed and I proceeded to call the rest of my family to let them know it was over. I was divorced—officially and it was done in six months. I knew of others whose divorces went on for years. Children would be used to transmit pain to the opposing parent and I just couldn't watch that happen to Dale and Bret. The boys could decide when they wanted to be with or see each of us and that worked out very well. Dale had been staying with me since January and Bret and I got to see each other whenever we wanted. There would be no child support because of our joint custody and the boys chose the visitation days and time (so far, so good).

On Friday Abby and I met at the diner for a light dinner. I gave her all the gory details and we started thinking about my new name. We took a lot of things into consideration like keeping my initials the same, having it sound sophisticated, not having too many syllables, and being a name people would easily pickup during the change. We had a lot of fun in the process. Laughing was just the medicine I needed at this time.

I settled on Dennis. I would soon be Laura Dennis.

I had time to think and digest the events of the past few years. That thought process usually took me into deeper memories of my past.

WRITE! ARE YOU LISTENING NOW? WRITE ABOUT WHAT YOU HAVE JUST GONE THROUGH AND MAYBE OTHER WOMEN WILL GET THE COURAGE TO CHANGE THEIR LIVES, TOO! JUST DO IT!

NEW LIFE

This would be the first spring season I would not be planting flowers in my yard. My life had changed dramatically in the past six months and when you are blinded by divorce, you don't see all the changes that it causes. Many times I had thought of the days when I couldn't wait to be without Daryl. I don't regret that, but I had not prepared myself for the silence that followed.

My friends were "our" friends because those were the people Daryl allowed me to have as friends. Abby was the exception, yet, after the divorce and my name choosing, we didn't see each other. I am not sure why. I may never know, but this spring was becoming difficult to face. I kept running every night, but started running farther and farther. I would run past the softball fields where I used to play. I would see some of the girls I used to play with and thought of those fun times.

SOMETIMES, YOU CAN NEVER GO BACK. IT IS LIKE GOING BACK HOME. YOU CAN NEVER GO BACK. FIND SOMETHING ELSE TO DO.

There's one thing about divorce that was refreshing. The weight loss! Everyone I had ever known who went through a divorce lost weight— noticeably! I did too. I began this emotional journey weighing in at 136 pounds. Now I was 109. I was in clothing sizes I had never dreamed I could wear. It was fun. I knew I would probably gain some back after the emotional drain leveled off, but right now it was feeling good. I was feeling better. People were beginning to notice the physical and social changes in me and I was finding out how to make new friends.

The month of June brought the reality of Dale's graduation. Daryl had always made big promises about getting Dale a car for graduation and now Daryl was crying poverty. Dale was not allowed to drive any of Daryl's cars so he would borrow mine on a few occasions. Dale needed a car so I told him I would get him a loan for the car as his graduation gift, but he would have to make the payments. I had a friend that was selling her car and it would be a very good one for Dale to have. He agreed and we started the process of getting the loan and the car.

Dale's graduation day came on the third Sunday of June. The day was perfect, but I knew I would have to contend with seeing Daryl and his parents all together for the first time since the divorce. After the ceremony, I put on my cordial face and smiled while exchanging the typical hellos the best I could. I think I passed. I'll never really know. I decided to get the pictures I had taken of the ceremonial walk to the 1 hour photo shop so I could spread them out on the table at Dale's party.

I promised him a graduation party and I planned to have it at the apartment in the backyard. The people downstairs had moved and it worked out beautifully. All of my family was there except for my brother Dick and his family and I didn't expect them to come. Trixie came with Onicka and Barry, and Kyle's kids, Heidi, Hanna and Clark, from his previous marriage. I had not met them before. They were in the same age range as Onicka and Barry and seemed like a fun group of kids. It was wonderful to see how many people showed up to the party. My brother Lyle came, and that alone was a sheer act of God. Lyle was still driving tractor-trailers and usually wasn't in the same place longer than three days. He had a very young companion with him, like 20 years old, which sparked some ribbing from the family, but he took it all in stride like he always did.

Trixie and Kyle threw me a curve when I tried to introduce them to one of my co-workers. I found it very awkward trying to explain Kyle as my sister's boyfriend or live-in partner. I was stumbling to get some kind of explanation out of my mouth when my sister interrupted me and said, "Husband".

I turned and looked at her and said, "Husband? When did that happen?"

She replied "June 1."

In shock I responded, "Why didn't you tell me sooner?"

As it turned out, no one in the family knew. They just got married in front of a justice of the peace in a nearby town where their friends from the cow association lived and they made all the arrangements, promising to keep it a secret. I think she wanted to make the announcement at Dale's party, when most of the family would be there. It certainly added to the festivities.

The day after the party I got a call from Daryl telling me that his family was upset because I had not invited them to Dale's party. I suggested to him maybe he should have had a party for Dale himself. I didn't get a response from him on that comment and he just hung up. I thought at the time that Daryl wasn't acting like he understood that being divorced meant we don't do things together like we did when we were married. I know he felt rejected and for that I had no regret.

After Dale's party, life went back to normal for me, but only for a short time. I had been running one night when I literally ran into the group of women I used to play softball with. I was running past some of the vehicles they were getting into after their game and they recognized me and stopped me to see how I was doing. They invited me along for a couple of beers and I decided to go.

It was a lot of fun socializing with the team players again and they were curious to know what had happened between Daryl and me. They also had their versions of what they saw between us, especially at the end of the season last year. They asked me if I could play on the team with them next week. They needed a catcher in order to have enough players. I was game and they already knew I couldn't throw, but I could catch ANYTHING! I agreed to play and the evening ended with stories from last year and a plan for next week.

The night came for me to play and I was psyched. I got to the field in plenty of time so I could warm up—a lot! The game was against a good team and the pressure was high. I assumed my position and was able to handle the spot pretty well. During the 6th inning, there was a play that would change my routine (again) for a while.

The batter was up for the other team. I was in my catching stance and trying very hard to intimidate the batter (catchers are supposed to do that). The pitch came in and the batter hit the ball about mid-center field. Everyone scrambled; the runner on second base ran toward third base, the batter rounded first and headed for second. I watched the ball—where it went, who had it, were they watching the runner rounding third base? I noticed the second baseman. She had the ball and tagged the runner and was looking at me to throw. This woman had an arm like a gun and I saw her wind up and throw the ball—hard and fast. I positioned my glove, set my posture for a tag, and looked out of the corner of my eye to check the runner, and......BAM!!!

When I turned to look for the runner; which I never should have done, I lifted my glove ever so slightly. When I looked back for the ball, it had already hit my front leg bone just above my ankle. Then the runner plowed into me like a locomotive. The ball ricocheted off my leg to the first baseman. We had one out and one run. I got up, dusted myself off and assured the team members I was fine to finish the game, which I did.

The game ended with our team losing by 2 runs. That felt a little better than losing by the one run that I let score. We all went to the bar again to wash the dust off and laugh about the game, the day and life. While at the bar I could feel pressure on my leg. I ran my hand down my leg and found a huge lump. It was large enough to fill the palm of my hand. Well, just about softball size, actually. It was starting to burn and when I looked at it, it had already turned black. I thought at the time that was one nasty bruise.

The night grew late and we all went home. I could still feel the burning on my leg, but went to bed and slept soundly with the help of the alcohol I had consumed.

I always had an automatic alarm clock. I would always wake up when I needed to. I don't know how I acquired this talent, but I was always grateful for it. This morning I woke up at my usual "get ready for work time" and it wasn't until I set my feet on the floor that I remembered the softball bump on my leg from the game. Suddenly I had this intense burning sensation on my leg that was nearly unbearable. I thought, I had to go to work—I had to. Maybe I could just walk it off. I tried that and I don't know if I got used to that level of pain or I just convinced myself it wasn't that bad, but I did get ready and drove to work. It was my right leg—of course. The one I use on the accelerator in my car so the whole drive in was with extreme pressure in this gigantic lump on my leg.

The only way I got through the day, was to prop my leg up on a box, but then I had to walk back to my car and drive twenty minutes to get home. I just didn't realize how difficult it would be because I was forgetting I was alone. Alone, without any help from anyone! Dale was working now at Mobil Chemical (with the help of his father) on a midnight to 8 AM shift. He usually spent evenings with his friends. I was quickly reminded about the painful trips to the bathroom, to the kitchen, to turn on the TV, to answer the phone, and of course, all these trips would be necessary just as I sat down somewhere. One of the phone calls was from my friend Dottie.

Dottie was a great friend. She was married to Daryl's cousin and was going through a nasty divorce too. She would have liked hers to be over as quickly as mine, but we helped each other deal with the day-to-day traumas. I told Dottie about my leg and she told me I should go to the hospital. I was nervous about that, but she did convince me I could probably get some help with the pain. She volunteered to go with me, so I agreed and told her I'd be over to pick her up right away.

At the hospital, they took an x-ray of my leg and when the doctor read it, he told me it looked like I might have a hairline crack in my leg bone.

I asked the doctor if I was going to get a cast and he said, "No. I want you to go home and stay in bed with your leg above your heart until the black goes away."

KEEP YOUR LEG ABOVE YOUR HEART? HOW ON EARTH CAN YOU DO THAT? DO YOU REALIZE WHAT KIND OF POSITION THAT REQUIRES?

As he told me this, my brain tried to process the instruction. I was just learning how to live alone. It was just me! No one else would be there to help me! I was replaying his words in my head envisioning lying in my bed with my leg above my heart! How on earth can I do that?

I jerked myself back to reality. I looked at the doctor and asked how long he thought that might take and he said he didn't know, probably a week or two at best.

I asked if he could give me some crutches, and he promptly said, emphatically, "NO, because you will not rest if I do that. Stay home, get some rest—heal! " I hobbled out of the examining room to the waiting room where Dottie was waiting. I told her the outcome and together we went to my car to go home. I was in pain and in shock, but I did have my instructions.

The next morning I called my boss and told her my terrible news. She tried to comfort me and told me to rest and not to worry about work, which she would handle. Then I called my friend Lori and told her about the doctor's orders and asked her if she could pick up some groceries for me. She said she would be happy to and she would be over after 6 PM tomorrow. I thanked her and went to bed.

The next evening I told Dale when he was getting ready for work. When he left, he let me know that he didn't have much spare time in order to help so I just went back to sleep.

Mid morning I heard a knock at the door and I went to the top of the stairs and yelled for them to come in. It was a delivery person with flowers and a stuffed cow from my boss and coworkers wishing me a fast healing. I wished it would be fast, but it didn't look like that was going to be the case. I went back to my position—leg above my heart. I had no idea how many things I couldn't do in that position. Watching TV was about all I could handle besides talking on the phone. Going to the bathroom took a few minutes and eating involved grabbing something from the refrigerator and praying it was still good enough to eat.

I borrowed a TV from Mom when I moved into my apartment. I didn't have one and couldn't afford to buy one at that point. I had no idea where she got it, but I knew it was old and today I would find out how old. I was watching the usual afternoon soaps when suddenly the TV stopped talking. I had picture but no sound. I was desperate to get the one thing that connected me to anything in the outside world fixed. My leg was now black all the way to my knee and if I put it down for a second it burned like a blow torch. I called the local TV repair place and asked if they could come and look at it. The person said they could send someone out by the end of the day. I told them I would be waiting.

By late afternoon I heard someone yelling from the downstairs door of my apartment. It was the repair man. I told him to come up but to please not laugh at my situation. He had to come into my bedroom because I could not get out of bed to greet him. When he peeked in my bedroom door I could see a little hesitation and a curious look on his face. I told him about my "almost" broken leg and how the doctor wouldn't give me crutches so I was stuck and now without a television. I begged him to fix it because I could not afford a new TV. He smiled and said he would try his best to fix my television.

Within thirty minutes I was hearing my TV talking to me again which made me very happy. I wrote the repair man a check and thanked him for the repair, pleasant conversation and understanding.

After two weeks I went back to the doctor and he told me I would have to give it more time. I was still showing black in my leg, but the lump was mostly gone. He told me another two weeks, probably. I was heartbroken, but I was still feeling pain so I didn't argue much. I was able to go to my mailbox now and get my mail once a day, but that was about it. I worried about my running. I wanted to do that again as soon as I could.

One day when I got my mail, I received the new lease agreement for my apartment. It didn't seem like it could have been a year already. I had mixed feelings about the lease. I liked my apartment now, yet I wanted to get a place where I could have Missi and Shellee. I missed them very much. They had been my best friends through all this mess and they deserved to be with me. I did not know what to do. I lay in my bed thinking of places I could start looking for an apartment. I wondered about how I would see my friends if I moved out of town. But since I hurt my leg, I hadn't heard from any of the softball team members I thought were old friends. Dottie, well she and I would always be friends.

During this thought process, my phone rang and it was Mom. She said she had to call because the tenant in grandma's old house just gave her notice that she had bought a house and would be moved out by the 1st of August. She asked me if I would be interested in renting it. I couldn't believe what I was hearing. It was only minutes after thinking about getting a different apartment and now I could have a whole house in the country with my dogs and near my job and family. The rent was realistically possible and I hoped I could survive the fuel bill in the winter. I told her immediately that I would take it which kicked my level of excitement up just when I needed it.

It was like a prayer had been answered—right then! I had not been very close to my grandmother and yet I remember her as a very kind person with a soft voice and a continuous smile on her face. We always spent Thanksgiving and Christmas with them. Grandma prepared dinner with all the traditional fixings until she couldn't, due to failing health. I remembered her characteristic things; Cashmere Bouquet soap in the bathroom, a beautiful blue bottle of Evening in Paris perfume on the window sill and her ever famous cinnamon rolls and apple pie. I could smell the pie and cinnamon rolls from the driveway as we arrived for dinner.

My father's brother and sister and their families would also be there. All together there would be sixteen people. The house was small and most of us kids had to sit in the kitchen at the kitchen table (or the little table as they called it). In different combinations depending on our ages, the offspring would take turns at the little table. I remember mostly Trixie, me, Mel and Fawn. We were the closest in age and able to feed ourselves, but Fawn and Mel always had to wear bibs, even though I thought they were too big to be doing that anymore. Their mom (Dad's brother, Harley's, wife) was so afraid the children would soil their good church clothes. I swear they were almost teenagers before they lost those bibs.

My father was the oldest child. His brother, Harley was 5 years younger than he and his sister, Irene, was 5 years younger than Harley. I always marveled at the exactness of the spacing of these children. Most families had children closer together. It seemed pretty unusual that they were precisely five years apart.

My grandmother passed away on December 3, 1971. I remember it well because I was seven months pregnant with Bret and my doctor had advised me not to go to the funeral. I stayed at the house and helped some with the luncheon for the family members. I thought how Bret would never even meet his great-grandmother. Bret was able to know his great-grandfather a little, but he passed away in April of 1980.

Now I would be living in the house that left me such good memories. I knew my mother didn't have those good memories in this house, and I didn't think she understood my feelings about the house or why the memories I had were very special. She had lived through some pretty tense times with her in-laws, but I didn't have those memories—they were hers. This was a wonderful turn of events for me and I was very excited about it.

The next day in my mail I got an invitation to my twenty-year high school class reunion. I had mixed feelings about this and I was not sure if I even wanted to go. I had gone to the ten-year reunion and had a degrading comment made about me that upset me terribly. I didn't go to the fifteen-year reunion because of the fear of more degrading comments. I thought about it a lot for the next few days. I weighed the pros and cons. I was a new person now and I was alone and could use this event to do something different.

YOU WOULD GO TO A SOCIAL EVENT ALONE?

I could do that. I looked good. I was thinner now than I'd ever been in high school. Besides I was now a college graduate with a good job, two great kids and one ex-husband. I decided to send back the RSVP that I would be attending.

The next obstacle I would have to conquer would be walking and doing it in high heel shoes. I found a dress in a catalog which offered matching shoes, which I thought was perfect. I wouldn't have to shop at the mall for a dress which I couldn't do for another two weeks.

Five days before the reunion I saw my doctor and I told him about my reunion and the need to return to work. He said I looked like I could do both, but I should be careful for the first week. I could return to running slowly after another week.

I was healed and ready for this reunion, a huge step in my next phase of life. I was 38-years-old and learning how to go into restaurant alone for the first time. I was scared and excited at the same time.

***

Reunion Night

I started to get ready hours before I needed to, but the excitement was almost overwhelming. The dress I ordered came and fit me perfectly (a double plus). The only thing about the outfit that was a little concerning was the very low cut front and even lower cut back of the dress. This would have been totally unacceptable for Daryl, yet I felt like a prom queen in the dress. I fixed my hair and makeup and kept checking the front and back of the dress, making sure my underwear didn't show. It looked great—each time I checked. Finally I decided to leave the apartment (slowly) and drive to the restaurant.

As I parked the car I looked around to see anyone else going into the restaurant that I might know. I had prepared myself to forget the past and things said and enjoy myself. I would not have Daryl there to talk for me and I would have to do this alone in front of people I knew 20 years ago.

I got out of the car after one more check in the mirror. I still looked good. I walked across the parking lot and up the sidewalk, holding my head high. I felt good about myself. My leg was holding up very well and I felt the confidence of that movie star I had always dreamed about being. Tonight in my own way I was just that person. I pulled the door of the restaurant open and walked into the entrance near the banquet room. I walked a few steps and stopped to look for people I knew. As I started scanning, I thought for a moment I might be at the wrong banquet area because I didn't see anyone I knew. I was beginning to panic. I took a couple more steps and looked into the banquet room where our dinner was to be served. People were around in both areas talking to other people and there still weren't any that looked familiar.

Now the panic was beginning to crawl up my spine and I started looking around at the tables set up with pictures and name tags. Whew, names I recognized. Thank God, I am in the right place. Just then Jessica came up to me and asked if she could help. She introduced herself and I knew her from her voice which had not changed one iota. I smiled and said I recognized her voice and told her who I was and she came back with a reaction I wasn't expecting.

She exclaimed, "Oh, Laura, you look great! We saw you come in, but none of us knew who you were and we were trying to figure it out. I'm so glad you came!"

I said, "I was very nervous that I might have gotten the wrong party until I saw the name tags. Thank you for coming to my rescue."

She said, "You're welcome. Didn't you see Patty and Wayne? They are over there (pointing to some people near the bar) and James is over there talking to Seth and Fred."

I was feeling like I belonged now and my panic was gone. Jessica walked me over to Wayne and Patty (class president and valedictorian, respectively). They both reacted to me with much surprise and friendly interest in what I had been doing with my life. I began to tell them. Patty was an aid at school where their children attended and Wayne had recently gotten a professorship at a college near their home. They were both surprised I had gone back to college. I was proud of that. Patty said she had not gone back to college after her first year and wished she had. I was shocked. I actually had a higher level of education than our class valedictorian!

WOW! CAN YOU BELIEVE THAT?

It was almost time for dinner and I mentioned to Wayne I wanted to get a drink before dinner. Wayne said, "Well you remember the guy at the bar don't you?" I looked up and saw a tall thin man with very bushy blonde hair and a full beard, that I didn't remember at all.

That is until he opened his mouth and said, "Hi, Laura."

It was my dreaded, condescending, arrogant classmate, Paul. He was smiling now and obviously impressed with how I looked (it was smeared all over his face). He said I looked wonderful and asked if I had been modeling.

CONSIDER THE SOURCE OF THAT QUESTION!

I laughed, and said, "No. Oh, no. I got healthy and divorced and that alone works wonders for the human body."

He laughed and agreed with me. Someone called to us to come in and sit down for dinner. He asked if he could sit with me, and I told him I would like that very much.

During dinner we had a lot of conversation about life. Paul was always good at that; he was always telling us about the things he had done, things that, as young people, we weren't supposed to do. Yet he never got in trouble, or we never <u>knew</u> if he got in trouble. But then our worlds were a universe apart, in commonality and personality. This was the first conversation <u>I</u> had with a man without looking over my shoulder to see if Daryl was watching me, and I smiled at that, and it felt fantastic!

The time came when everyone had to stand up and tell what we were doing currently and previously. I was surprised at the answers some classmates gave. Alex was the salutatorian for the class and he was now living in California and was a computer programmer. He said after 10 years he finally went to college and got his masters degree and was a successful computer programmer. He credited his wife of seventeen years and their four children for his success. Alex never even dated in high school! Fred, who was the class clown, was the owner of a very reputable restaurant in Rochester! He never took anything seriously in school!

When it came to my turn, I stood and proudly stated I had worked for Mobil Chemical for six years and had gone back to college to earn my AS Degree in Business Management. I also told everyone I was in the process of writing a book. I got applause when I sat down and was a little embarrassed, but I felt proud for the first time in a long time. This was the first time I had said out loud that I was writing a book. What was I thinking? I only had a few pages of notes from the divorce.

GOOD! NOW YOU WILL HAVE TO START WRITING MORE THAN JUST JOURNAL NOTES, AND IT'S ABOUT TIME!

Paul was my date for the evening with interruptions from others who were glad to see me after all these years. People that wouldn't speak to me in high school were now very friendly and glad to listen to my stories.

The evening passed very quickly and soon it was near midnight. Sue invited everyone to breakfast at her house and Paul asked me if I wanted to go. I told him I'd like to and he encouraged me to come join the fun. So I did. I sort of remembered where Sue lived and Paul told me to follow him so I wouldn't get lost. We left the restaurant for Sue's house. Sue and her husband were married around the same time as Daryl and I. She even had similar wedding colors and bridesmaids' dresses. But the biggest difference was that she was still happily married and I was starting over. Some days this was exciting and some days it was frightening. Today it was a little of both.

We got to Sue's house a little after the rest of the crowd and some of the women were cooking already. I sat with Paul among classmates and we just told stories endlessly. It was lots of fun. After breakfast, people started to leave. I thought it was also time to go, so I gave my thanks for a wonderful time and a great breakfast and Paul walked me to my car.

I opened the driver's door and stood inside the door and turned to tell Paul goodnight. He was standing just the other side of the door only a few inches from me. I told him I was glad I came to the reunion and breakfast and I was glad we had a chance to spend an enjoyable evening together. He smiled with an ever-so-inviting, warm smile that left me feeling we had connected in some way. We talked about highlights from the party and after a while the small talk began to wane. I told him I was moving in about 3 weeks to my grandmother's house. He knew exactly the house because his grandmother lived two country blocks east of that house. Again the conversations softened and we found ourselves staring into each others eyes speaking few words.

I tried to make a decision whether I should be so bold as to kiss him or wait to see if he intended to kiss me. It seemed like a long time and the spoken words didn't seem to be making sense anymore. I finally said I should go home. Paul suggested the people inside might be wondering how long we would be standing in their driveway at this point. We both laughed and I moved out from my car door to give Paul a hug, for which he was very receptive. The hug was comforting and tender and we held each other for nearly a minute. I told him I was moving on the last day of the month and invited him to stop by if he happened to be near his grandmother's place. He acknowledged the invitation and I got into my car and drove home.

The next week was a busy one at work and my friends, Jackie and Val, had a ton of questions about the reunion. We chatted whenever we could about the night and if I thought Paul would be back around. We giggled like school girls talking about our first encounters with a boyfriend, speculating outrageous outcomes of the imaginary relationship.

By the weekend I had moved on to my usual routine and only thought about Paul in mini flashbacks of that night. I was thinking I might see him when I moved over to my grandmother's house in two weeks. In the meantime I needed to pack and try to get Dale to pack his stuff too.

About noon on Saturday, my phone rang and when I answered, I was surprised to hear a man's voice. It took me a few seconds to recognize the voice, but it was Paul. He was inviting me to go on a motorcycle run with him on Sunday. The motorcycles were congregating in North Rose for the trip and then back for a party at the local tavern there. I couldn't remember the last time a man called me on the phone asking me for a date, so I was still trying to digest the invitation. I was totally unfamiliar with "Motorcycle Runs!" I tried to contain my excitement and ask what I would have to wear and do. Paul was laughing slightly at me and he assured me that jeans and t-shirt would be fine and maybe a leather jacket if I had one which I did. He said he would be over to pick me up around 11:30 on Sunday if that was okay. I assured him it was and gave him directions to my apartment. He said he would see me then and hung up.

I used to ride motorcycles and owned one when the boys were small. Daryl and I would ride with the boys on short trips. Now I was trying to remember how I dressed for that. I had never ridden with another person very much. I was suddenly so excited about this date I was almost bouncing around the apartment. I was thinking of all the possible scenarios that might be involved with this "run." I would be sitting with my arms around him for most of the afternoon. God, how fun!

I was desperately trying to think of someone I could call and tell about this date. I called Dottie and told her what had just happened. We were giggling like kids about my date with that schoolgirl excitement again. Gosh, two times in a week!

Sunday came, and just like Paul told me, he arrived at 11:30. I let him come to the door and knock just so I wouldn't look really goofy running out of my back door—so anxious to be with him that he would barely have time to stop the bike before I got on it.

We exchanged our hellos and Paul asked if I was ready (little did he know I had been ready for a while). I said I was ready and we went out to get on his Harley Davidson motorcycle. He gave me a helmet to wear and he climbed on, started the bike and then I got on. I knew I would need to relax because I remembered how difficult it was to drive a motorcycle with a rider that didn't ride with the motion of the bike. I remembered learning how to lean into the curves as Paul started the bike and we were on our way.

It was a perfect day for a motorcycle ride. The sun was shining and the temperature was in the high 70's. There were soft billowy clouds scattered randomly in the sky resembling a pale blue ocean. I had time to start digesting this new experience as we rode. I thought about Jackie and Val and how they would never believe what I had done this weekend. I thought about Paul and my meeting and how this day had come about. This was the day I realized my new life was headed for unknown paths— and I was having the time of my life.

While Paul was registering us, I looked around. I wanted to fit in with this crowd, but I was new at it and it showed. Paul went on to talk to some of the bikers he knew while I waited at the bike. I felt a little nervous until Paul came back. When he did I asked him if I was a comfortable rider. He said I was and asked why I asked. I told him I had not had much experience as a passenger and I know how wiggly riders can interfere with the comfort and maneuvering of the bike. He assured me I was fine and looked at me with that smile that I saw in the shadows after the class reunion. I felt better.

After a short wait for the rest of the bikers to arrive and the local police to direct us through town, we were on our way. I was shocked at how many bikes there were in this pack. As we drove out of town, the line trailed for as far as I could see. There had to have been over two hundred bikes lined up in pairs. The sound of that many bikes together gave an ominous roar to the area as we rode. People would gather at the edge of the road to watch the group go by. Kids were waving and older people were just standing and watching with almost fearful expressions. It looked like some people thought they might be under siege with Hells Angels or something. It was funny in a way, but the general consensus appeared to be awe at this incredible sight.

In each town we passed through, we had police escort which helped us get through traffic lights so the group could stay together as much as possible. It was an incredible ride and I was a part of it. I couldn't wait to tell Jackie, Val, Dottie and the boys. The boys really wouldn't believe it!

It was mid afternoon when we arrived back at our starting point. We parked the bike and went into the tavern that was set to receive us for beverages and a little mingling. Paul found us a table and ordered us a couple of beers. We sat and talked by ourselves mostly with interruptions from a few of Paul's biker friends. Paul was quick to replenish the beer supply when our bottles were empty. I usually could hold a few beers without much effect, but this time I was finding that was just not the case. At one point I excused myself to go to the ladies room. It was then that I realized I was more impaired than I thought.

When I came back from the bathroom, I asked Paul if we could get a little air. He smiled that smile and said, "Sure." I could tell by the look on his face that he knew I was drunk and trying to cover it up, but he didn't make reference to it until I stumbled into him during our walk around the block where we had parked the bike. He laughed politely when it happened but suggested we go somewhere else to get something to eat. I thought that was a great idea.

We went to a small restaurant just outside Canandaigua. Paul recommended the linguini and white clam sauce and asked if I liked that. I confessed that I had never had it, but I did like clams and would love to try it.

The food made me feel much better and we continued getting to know each other; actually we talked more about me than about Paul, but I wasn't used to talking to someone who was interested in hearing about me or what was going on in my life. It was very nice, refreshing actually. Paul had a way of looking at me that made me feel different somehow. His crystal blue eyes had a calming effect and just looking into them made any fear or apprehension disappear.

After our dinner he took me home. I asked him if he wanted to come up for coffee and he accepted the offer. As we walked up the steps of my apartment, I could feel the excitement about our day continuing for a little while longer.

YOU DON'T HAVE A LIVING ROOM, REMEMBER?

I tried to think as fast as I could of what options I might have to entertain him in my bedroom. It didn't matter—we were at the top of the stairs before I could come up with an answer. I walked into my kitchen, and offered him a chair. I started explaining the living situation in the apartment and that the TV was in my bedroom.

BOY—WHAT A WAY TO MAKE THIS GUY'S DAY!

I wanted to believe that Paul would understand and continue to be the gentleman he had been all day. It worked—he was. I made the coffee and we took our coffees and retreated to my TV bedroom. I had this magnificent bookcase bed which was one huge unit with mirrors in the headboard, recessed lighting in the top, and dresser storage on each side. There were drop down shelves which I used for end tables. I turned on the TV and we settled onto the bed and continued talking. The conversation this time was about my apartment and moving and all the circumstances involved. I told him I was excited about the move and was expounding on the details when I heard the door at the bottom of the stairs open and footsteps coming up. It was Dale.

When he got to the top of the stairs he turned and looked into my room and saw Paul and me sitting on the bed propped against the pillows with coffee cups in hand. He stopped dead in his tracks. He tried to say something but his voice froze. His mouth was open but nothing was coming out.

I broke the ice for him and said, "Hi, Dale this is Paul."

Paul said, "Hi, Dale."

Dale, closed his mouth and spoke, "Hi, ah….Paul."

We all just stopped for a moment like we had been "freeze-framed" on TV. Dale was stuck and Paul and I knew he did not know what to say or do, but he finally came out with, "Did you see the motorcycles go through town today? There were hundreds of them."

Paul and I laughed as I said, "Yes, as a matter of fact, we were on one of them."

Dale, looking embarrassed for a moment, said, "That must be your bike out front, huh?"

Paul smiled and said in a comical way, "Yep."

Dale told me he was going to work after he changed his clothes and told Paul it was nice to meet him. Paul and I laughed about Dale's uncomfortable look and I explained that I had not seen Dale to tell him what I was doing this weekend. In further conversation, I told him that Dale and I had pretty separate lives, because he worked nights. After a few minutes Dale said his goodnights and goodbyes and left for work

Paul and I continued our conversations, but they started to wane. Soon we were lying more comfortably on the bed and I found myself looking into those blue eyes of his and not saying a word. I remember doing that for a very long time. It was like I didn't have to talk to communicate with him. He held me and we were just close and quiet. It felt good to have arms wrapped around me again. I would like this date to lead somewhere. I wanted to see him again. But during this quiet time, I realized I didn't know much about Paul. He had been such a good listener and comforting companion for the day. I really didn't know much about who he was or what he was like.

We stayed wrapped in each others arms for a while and I could feel myself dozing off. I knew Paul could feel it too but I didn't feel comfortable enough to ask him to stay. I had thought about it and decided it wasn't a good idea.

GOOD CHOICE!

Paul finally said he should go and we got up from the bed and walked to the stairway. He turned and looked at me with that ever so comforting smile and his hypnotizing blue eyes and reached for me to hug him again. I sank into his arms one more time and thanked him for the invitation for the day and dinner. I told him I had a wonderful time.

We released our arms from each other and he softly said, "You're welcome".

He looked into my eyes as he told me he would call me and I told him I would like that very much. I reminded him of my move and to stop over for some food if he wanted. He just smiled and walked down the stairs. At the bottom of the stairs he said "Bye" and walked out the door. I couldn't see the street from my apartment windows, but I could hear him start his bike and drive away. I thought about the day as I prepared to go to bed. This was one of the most incredible days I had ever lived.

I fell asleep chuckling to myself, "I can't wait to go to work tomorrow!"

THE END, A BEGINNING

The next two weeks were filled with arrangements. I had to finish packing, figure out how to get stuff moved, clean the apartment, and force Dale to get packed. In the meantime, our old house had sold and we would be getting all the paperwork in order for the divorce settlement to be finalized. I was excited about that. I would get money to buy new household furnishings. I definitely needed a new couch. I had to get a washer, dryer and TV. My attorney contacted me a week before the move and handed me a check for just over $7,000.00. I felt rich (again) for a moment.

I went shopping at a local appliance store for my washer and dryer and found sales on TVs, microwaves and a tiny freezer. I listed all the appliances I thought I would need and asked the manager if I could get a volume discount. I knew the trend for women getting divorces was to get new cars, but I was very happy with my car. It was one of a kind. It was a Monte Carlo, which wasn't unique, but it had a diesel engine and that was rare. It was a great car and I had won its ownership in the settlement. Daryl was still paying for it, and that gave me some kind of personal pleasure. The only thing I was missing was a stereo system. I went to several electronics stores to price stereo systems. The CD rage was just beginning, and I wanted to get one.

I found a store that would sell me a system, deliver and set it up. They also offered to have someone show me how to use it while they were setting it up. I also got a volume discount for the number of pieces I bought. I got all the components necessary to have a great sound system, plus a VCR. I made arrangements for them to deliver it to my grandmother's house, now owned by my mom and dad. My mom was the landlord of several houses they had bought from family members as they went out of the farming business. Mom always managed the rentals and did all the remodeling of them as well. This one would be mine—I hoped forever.

The house had been vacant now for about two months and Mom had been remodeling and cleaning. We would use Dad's one ton stake rack truck to load all my belongings with the only help I had, which was Dale and Mom. The worst piece of furniture would be my bookcase bed. There were four cabinet pieces with a light bar, two mirror sections and a queen mattress and box spring. It was oak and really heavy, but one piece at a time would be okay.

Moving day was the Friday of a long Labor Day weekend. I left work at exactly 5 PM to hurry home so I could dismantle as much stuff as possible. When I arrived at the apartment and parked in my usual spot behind the garage, Dale was standing there with one of his friends. I hoped he was going to be there to help with moving, but as I got out of my car and quickly asked, I found out something quite shocking.

Dale told me there was some guy in my apartment moving the big stuff onto the screen porch. I was dumfounded for a few moments and asked him who he was talking about.

"You know," He said, "that guy you went motorcycling with that weekend."

I was stunned. In all the scurrying around, I had forgotten about Paul. I quickly went upstairs to my apartment.

I found Paul at the top of the stairs with a chunk of my bed in his hands.

"Hi!" I said

He returned with an almost formal, "Hello".

Grinning, I continued, "I see you caught Dale by surprise."

"Yes, I did," he said laughing.

I told him I had to unload Dad's truck at the house before I could load anything more. Paul suggested we load his truck with the rest of my stuff and then go unload both trucks. I thought that was a great idea. He placed the last piece of my bed on the porch and went to the street to get his truck and park it at my porch door.

I changed my clothes and called Mom. She thought the plan was a good one because she was still doing things with curtains and cleaning. I told her I would see her when we got there. We had a great plan.

Paul was already loading his truck by the time I got off the phone with Mom, and we continued discovering that just about everything fit into his truck. There were a few small things I put in my car. Dale was downstairs talking to another one of his friends when I asked him when, where and how he was loading his bed and belongings. He said he would move his stuff on Saturday because he was off work on Sunday. I accepted his answer and left.

We arrived at grandma's house, and I went inside to find Mom. She was upstairs putting up curtains in what would be my bedroom.

"Hi," I said, "you have obviously been very busy. The house looks great. Those curtains look very nice in here."

"Yeah, they were ones I had from the other house." She replied. "I hope you like it here."

"Why wouldn't I?"

"I don't know. It just makes me uncomfortable in here. It seems kinda spooky."

I didn't respond to that comment. I just told her Paul and I would start unloading the trucks. I headed downstairs.

Dad's truck was parked in the driveway with furniture and Paul backed his truck up to the front porch. We would be able to walk off the tailgate of his truck directly into the house. Paul's truck had "the bed." We soon found out that my queen size box spring was NOT going to go up the stairs. The door at the bottom of the stairs was just too small. This house had been built near 1900 and didn't have a lot of structural considerations for modern furniture. Paul measured and found he could take out the upstairs window and we could get it in that way.

The box spring task was like watching some kind of circus act on TV in a room with the lights turned off. We had to figure a way to get the box spring up to the window from the outside of the house. Of course we didn't have any ladders or anything like that, so we had to improvise somehow. Between Paul and me, we decided to use Dad's truck. The idea was to have one of us stand on the top of the rack and support bar while balancing the box spring until it could be stuffed into the window. It was dark by now, but I was confident we could make this happen.

I moved Dad's truck, backing it up under the window to the bedroom. Paul helped me place the box spring on the top of the truck rack support bar. I told Paul I was sure I weighed less than he did and would probably stress the racks less. I didn't mind doing the monkey act to make this work. We both laughed and he agreed and went in the house and upstairs to receive the box spring.

I used the house walls to support my balance as I started maneuvering the box spring. Paul was hanging out of the window to help as much as he could. I was walking across the steel support rod when I lifted the box spring up, hoping it would be high enough to meet Paul's outstretched hand. With a little weaving and missed catches I gave one huge heave-ho and Paul caught the board that framed the box spring. He pulled it up out of my hands and I was then able to lift the back enough so it would just slide through the window with ease. It actually only took a few minutes, and I gave a big sigh of relief. We both gave a cheer and chuckle marking our success. I climbed down and Paul started putting the window back in its casing while I went onto the next task.

Mom and I continued unloading Paul's truck and then Dad's truck. Paul finished putting in the window and then started to assemble the bed. In the unloading process, Mom, Paul and I scurried about putting things in their places. I didn't see Paul unload the mirrors to the bed, but in the process of assembling the bed, I noticed there was only one mirror in place. Paul could see I noticed the missing mirror.

He responded immediately with a sheepish smile almost laughing, "I owe you a mirror, and that is all I am going to say about it". It seems he had some kind of altercation with it, but he wouldn't tell me what.

We were getting things put into place and Mom said she thought she would go home. She had put my food items in the fridge and it was near midnight. She said she and Dad would be back first thing in the morning with the dogs. They would try to make a run for the dogs. That would prevent them from getting into the road. That was something I had forgotten all about until she said that, and I was happy to think I would finally have Missi and Shellee back home with me. A few months ago a friend at work with four children desperately wanted a dog. I told him about Hio and my desire to get him a good home. It was getting hard for Mom and Dad to maintain all the dogs. In May, Hio left the farm to live in town with the family.

Mom left and I went upstairs to find Paul putting the box spring and mattress on the bed frame.

It wasn't until he said, "Well, let's make the bed, shall we?", that it dawned on me…is he planning to stay here tonight, with me? I was trying to avoid the obvious by thinking about only making the bed. All sorts of things started going through my mind.

WHAT DO <u>YOU</u> WANT TO DO?"

Paul and I finished making the bed and we went downstairs. Paul went over to my refrigerator, opened the door and pulled out a bottle of wine. He said he won it as one of the door prizes at our high school reunion and thought we might drink it in celebration of the move and my new life. I was in favor of that and tried to find some glasses of some kind. Paul and I sat on chairs in the living room and talked. Our conversation was very comforting and the wine helped me unwind. I was able to talk to him with a confidence I had not known before. I didn't have the feeling he was looking for any "special favors" from me. He acted as though he was truly glad to help me.

The night was getting long and our wine was nearly gone. In a silent moment as we stared into each others eyes, I softly asked, "Where are you sleeping tonight?"

Paul smiled back, "Wherever you are."

I smiled. It was comforting, in a way, to have someone in the house with me. Especially after the comment my mother made about the house being "uncomfortable" to her whenever she was there. At the time, I just thought she was bringing back memories of the past that upset her reliving the family traumas. Now it was just Paul and me with all the boxes from the move. We put our glasses in the sink and went upstairs to bed.

I located a nightshirt in the bed drawers and Paul just undressed. I slipped under the blankets while he turned off the light. As he climbed into bed, he asked me if I was ashamed of my body.

I thought that was an odd question, but maybe a valid one. I told him that I was always self-conscious about my shape. It was not as perfect as it used to be, especially after two kids. Running kept it respectable although I still didn't feel it was good enough to show off. He told me I shouldn't think of myself that way and that I looked just fine. He leaned over and kissed me.

This kiss was one of the most loving gestures of affection I had ever experienced. It seemed like we kissed this first kiss for a long time and neither of us made any motion to stop. We wrapped our arms around each other in a truly loving embrace and drifted into a state of sexual ecstasy, taking me to arousal levels I had never known.

I remember drifting off to sleep still wrapped in Paul's arms thinking it had to be near dawn. I was glowing and safely protected by Paul.

It was about 7 AM when Paul and I awoke. We went downstairs and both of us started looking in boxes for the coffee pot. I noticed Paul would help with anything. He found my frying pans and suggested breakfast. He didn't ask if I was cooking it, but rather what I would like to eat. He asked if scrambled eggs were okay with me.

In shock, I said "Yes."

He proceeded to find food Mom and I had put in the refrigerator and began making a scrambled egg combination of potatoes, onions, eggs, salt, pepper and oregano. After he put this all together he topped it all with grated cheddar cheese. I found plates and silverware and coffee cups and set the table. This was great! This guy cooks! What a find!

We had barely finished our breakfast when Mom and Dad arrived with Missi and Shellee. They danced around me with excitement for a long time. Paul made his introductions to Dad and they began talking about putting together a fenced area for the dogs. This road was traveled by cars going about 55 mph or more at times. The house had an old woodshed attached to the back which made a perfect indoor pen. Dad and Paul put up some fence and dug a small hole in the stone foundation so they could go outside.

Mom and I started putting away my kitchen stuff. She didn't ask me if Paul stayed overnight, and I hoped she wouldn't. All was going very well and I didn't want to end the momentum of settling the house. Dale and a couple of his friends came by early afternoon with his bed and clothing. By evening I was feeling like I had things pretty well settled and tried to scrounge up some dinner. I had some Italian sausage and sweet corn from Dad's garden. It was during this meal that I found out that Paul was a vegetarian. He told me after I cooked the sausage. I felt like I should find more food to fix, but he assured me he was fine and I was not to worry.

Paul stayed at the house all weekend and left on Labor Day. He had given me a wonderful weekend and had been a great help and companion. He also made the transition of sex after the divorce a very memorable and enjoyable experience. He was a very mysterious man. Even though we had spent the weekend together I found I still didn't know him, but I was enjoying his company and really hoped to see him again. He didn't tell me if I would for sure, but he did give me a kiss goodbye and said he would see me soon—very open-ended.

After the holiday, I returned to work and told Val and Jackie about my incredible weekend. I told them they must come over to my house in the country. Now that we lived much closer to each other, we would be able to see each other more often and that would be great fun. Val lived at the end of my mother's road about 4 miles away and Jackie lived in town about seven miles away. I had friends now and maybe a boyfriend.

Paul would wander in and out of my house and my life whenever he felt like it. I was always glad to see him no matter what. The element of surprise seemed exciting in a way. He would leave me presents or things for the house that he found at a yard sale or flea market whenever he did not find me at home. He knew where I had hidden the extra key and I would only know he had been there when I found something new hung on the wall, placed on my bed or sitting on the table.

September brought my graduation from college with my Associate of Science Degree in Business Management. It was an accomplishment I had worked hard for and now it felt good to have the time spent studying behind me. There was a small graduation ceremony that I thought I would skip, but Paul asked me to reconsider and maybe ask my mother if she would like to attend. I thought that was a little unusual, but I did ask. Much to my surprise, Mom said she would attend the ceremony with me. She suggested I invite my good friend, Dottie. She also asked Dale to go with us, which I thought was odd too. But I was used to discounting my thoughts and feelings when I was told to do something by the other people in my life, so I did again here. I didn't know life any other way really, and didn't question it now. After all, it was my mother, and I would be expected to obey her suggestion.

The ceremony was at 1 PM and all the graduates were asked to sit up front. There were no gowns or any of that because we went to the "college without a classroom" which was very untraditional at the time. The president of the college asked each graduate to say a few words to the audience about our accomplishments. I had learned to speak to groups of people without feeling tense, but I had to think of something to say!

The exact words came to me in a flash and when it was my turn to speak, I walked proudly to the podium and said, "As a single parent I was always reminding my son about his homework responsibilities and would often ask him, 'Do you have your homework done?' Going to college at this stage of life gave me a greater respect for college and its accomplishments and rewards. It also gave my son the opportunity to ask, "Mom, do you have your homework done?" That was a reality check that we both enjoyed. Thank you to Empire State College for the support and opportunities."

After the ceremony we all walked out to the lobby for refreshments. In the process, it got very crowded and we were standing in a very close line when my mother reached up and put her arm around me and attempted to give me a kiss while saying she was proud of me. The action caught me off guard and rightfully so. This was the first time I ever remember my mother giving me a hug or a kiss since I was a very small child being tucked into bed at night. It was also the first time I ever heard the word proud come from her mouth directed at me. The moment, awkward as it was, meant more to me than she will ever know. Dottie, Mom, Dale and I got into my car and drove to Dottie's home, which took about 45 minutes. She invited us up for something to drink, and as I walked into her apartment I noticed congratulation decorations all around. The table was already set with plates, cups, a punch bowl and a cake. I should have known there were too many oddities to ignore. Dottie and Mom laughed as Dale asked where the food was, in jest. I laughed and Dottie went to the kitchen to get sandwich fixings: rolls, meats, cheeses and all the relish fixings one could ask for. Dottie always did attend to details of a perfect table. We were gathering food for our plates when there was a knock at the door. Dottie asked me to get it for her, which I did. Much to my surprise it was Paul. The look on my face had to show my surprise and delight. I now saw the reasons for the earlier oddities and suggestions. Come to find out, Paul went to my mother after I said I probably wouldn't go to my graduation and asked her what she thought. It was all planned from there.

October 1986—The Cabin and Annabelle C.

I talked about holiday times with Paul, and I told him I absolutely hated Valentine's Day and Mother's Day. Both of those days were ones that Daryl never felt he needed to observe. Valentine's Day was to be celebrated by unmarried people so they could get married and Mother's Day was to be celebrated by kids with their mothers. Because I was not his mother, he didn't have to buy me a gift. That was the responsibility of the boys and they were too young to have any money, so I didn't get anything. Well, one year for Mother's Day I did get a brand new screen door for the front of the house. That was memorable and functional. However, during the conversation I also expressed my special affection for Christmas. It had to be my all-time favorite holiday, even when I spent it alone.

Paul would suggest things we could do together that were always new for me. We would go for walks in the woods behind the house, which I loved. I used to go into the woods to hunt when I was younger and I remember trails I used to walk where the deer ran. It was a place I could go for a connection with nature. I could think more clearly about things in my life.

It was October when Paul asked if I would like to go to his camp for a weekend. This was the first time I had heard about a camp, and it sounded like a great idea. He told me there was a cabin in the Adirondack Mountains near Speculator, NY. It was about a 3-hour drive and very remote. There was no electricity, running water, or bathroom, but there was an outhouse a short distance from the cabin, which was comforting. I was excited about the trip and told him I would put together the food and we could go as soon as I got out of work on Friday. This was something I had never done with Daryl and it seemed to fit exactly into the type of lifestyle I thought I would enjoy forever.

Friday came and so did Paul. He was at the house when I arrived home from work. It only took a little time and effort to load the food and clothes into Paul's truck and we were on our way. The trip to the cabin was filled with conversation. I was getting a little more information about Paul and what his world was all about. He was not currently working; he was on disability because of stress from his job. He had been a residential caregiver for an ARC (Association for Retarded Citizens) ever since he left high school. That really surprised me because I had an opinion about him that did not fit with him being a caregiver, but then I didn't really know him in high school and I didn't really know him now. I just listened whenever he talked about his world. I just liked the things we did together and enjoyed hearing the stories he told.

During this trip he also told me about his grandmother. She lived in a small trailer in the woods just two country blocks from my house. Of course I knew the location—I had grown up there and had relatives on that road. He said he also had a trailer in that area that he stayed at most of the time when he wasn't with friends. He was portraying himself as a handyman turned vagrant, but I found him incredibly exciting, back to basics and earthy like my father. Paul was a crafty person and made things from wood and sold them to people and at craft shows sometimes. I thought it took a special kind of person to be that independent and self-maintaining, which made me feel a lot better about living in the house alone. If Paul could live on almost nothing and make it work, so could I.

We arrived at the cabin and drove into a makeshift driveway that led to a small clearing in the woods. It looked as if loggers had been there and there were large ruts filled with water almost everywhere. Paul drove through a couple that looked like we might get stuck, but we didn't and he parked on a high spot beyond the water holes. I looked around and saw nothing but trees. It was almost dark and the shadows of the trees camouflaged the area making it difficult to see anything.

Paul and I piled out of the truck and I grabbed my duffle bag and purse. Paul grabbed a couple of bags of things I assumed to be clothes and I followed him into the woods. We walked along a small slightly worn path down a bank. The bank was steep and slippery. Paul cautioned me about the unpredictability of the path. Just ahead of us was a wooden structure that looked a lot like a large outhouse. It had a front porch and steps leading to the front door, but there didn't appear to be any windows. I didn't say anything and I just followed as Paul set his bags on the porch and then walked to the front of the cabin, turned around and came back. He had gotten a key for the padlock on the front door. He explained to me that this cabin belonged to members of his family and they all used it from time to time. It was locked up like that because of the bears. They tended to break in when they smell anything resembling food.

BEARS!

Bears! I didn't even think about the possibility of bears. I just realized I was in a different world from the one I was used to at home and just the thought that it might be <u>that</u> different had never occurred to me until this moment.

I asked, "What do you do with the bears when you are here?"

He smiled back with a grin that said he was enjoying my innocence and naïve thinking and then answered my question in great detail. We would not be able to dump ANYTHING in the woods, not even dishwater because it generated a smell of food that would attract the bears. Usually the bears would stay away from the cabins with people in them because of the smell of the wood stoves and the noises humans make. As he talked, he was opening the door and we entered the cabin. It was much roomier inside than it looked from the outside. To the left of the front door were a set of double size bunk beds, which had been stick-built into the cabin, and another set across on the other side of the cabin. Between them were some large, round corrugated containers with steel band lids. There were things on the walls hanging in various places: a set of snowshoes, kitchen utensils, and a picture of a cowboy in a provocative stance, which I thought resembled Paul, in a way. Just to the right of the door were the wood stove, the table and some counter boards with a small gas 2-burner cook top. This was really quite nice and I liked rustic living.

Paul offered to get the rest of the food and things from the truck, saying he would be right back. That gave me a chance to look around a little. This was a very cool cabin. As I heard Paul coming down the bank, I opened the door for him and he came in with the cooler. He then offered to show me the outhouse. The outhouse path was around the front of the cabin and up a slight incline. It was a little further away from the cabin than I realized.

MY GOD, YOU'RE IN THE WOODS!

I decided to use the outhouse while Paul started a fire. The temperature was dropping and I had a feeling we would need the fire quite soon.

When I returned, Paul had a fire going and we decided to grab a sandwich for dinner. I started making the sandwiches and Paul started opening the lids on the large round containers. They protected the bedding such as sleeping bags, comforters and pillows. He said that mice can make a mess of stuff like bedding during the winter. I never thought about mice, either.

THERE ARE PROBABLY A FEW THINGS YOU HAVEN'T THOUGHT ABOUT IN THIS WILDERNESS—AND THIS IS THE WILDERNESS!

After we ate our sandwiches Paul got out some leatherwork. He had been working on as a Christmas present for one of his friends. It was a handmade leather belt jack knife holder. I watched his precision craftsmanship as we talked. We talked about family and he was talking to me more comfortably. We talked about our marriages, his mother who was deceased and his brother and sister who I remembered from school. He told me about his father's remarriage and how difficult it was having a stepmother. I got the distinct impression he had been very close to his mother who passed with cancer at a rather young age. I felt he was finally getting comfortable with me, or at least enough so to share a little piece of his world.

After Paul finished the knife sheath, we went to bed. Paul had already made up our bed and going to bed with Paul was always the same. Wonderful! We always went to bed at the same time and curled up into each other's embrace. We always kissed each other goodnight with incredible sensual enthusiasm. Our sexual encounters were like none I had ever experienced, and each encounter was more special than the last. I wanted Paul to be in my life. I thought his recurring visits were growing into something for the future. I hoped that was the case.

The next morning we got up and had one of those great breakfast concoctions. Paul and I made meals together, which was great. After breakfast he showed me how to clean up without attracting bears. Then Paul suggested we hike one of the trails. He told me how to spot a marked trail. There were spray paint marks on the trees (orange in this case) that you had to follow to maneuver through the woods without getting lost. The scenery was incredible, and at one point I saw a tree with pieces of bark curled downward almost like strands of hair. We stopped and looked around and Paul asked me if I knew what that was. I told him I guessed it was marks from a bear clawing into the tree. He confirmed that was exactly right and I took a couple of pictures.

There was a point where we took a break by a creek and just relaxed for a little bit. Paul asked if I was tired and I told him I was not. I suddenly got the impression he thought I was a bit more pristine than I actually was, and I suddenly felt a little too pampered. We didn't talk during our break. We just enjoyed the sounds of the forest and babbling water coming from the creek. Soon we moved on, and for a little while I thought we might be lost. I couldn't find any orange circles and Paul was taking the lead. We found our orange markers again and spent the rest of the day in the woods enjoying nature and each other's company.

There were no clocks or timepieces to check the time—we were living the weekend without a schedule. We got back to the cabin near dusk and I volunteered to prepare the special dinner I had planned. Paul rekindled the wood stove. I soon found out I would need to do the cooking process a little differently from how I was used to, but I managed to prepare a delicious dinner of Dijon chicken, potatoes and squash and it all worked out in the end.

THIS GUY EATS _ALL_ VEGETABLES—THAT'S A TREAT!

I also found out that I took too much food. I was thinking about feeding a hungry man and thought it required a lot of food when actually it did not.

After dinner and clean up we each did some crafting tasks. I was into painting small wooden Christmas ornaments and Paul was making more leather pieces for Christmas presents. We talked about Christmases of the past for each of us and what was special and memorable. Paul told me about Christmas with his brother's and sister's families where nobody was allowed to buy commercial presents. Everyone had to make the gifts for each person. He said it was very special and everyone usually had a genuine attachment to the gift and the giver because of it. I thought that was a really terrific idea (but I knew it would never fly with my family).

This conversation brought back memories from my childhood. We always kept Christmas a constant. The Sunday before Christmas was spent with Dad's family while Christmas Eve was always spent with my cousins from my mother's brother's family. There were two boys, Wade and Warren, and a girl, Wendy, in that order. Wade, the oldest boy, was just 18 months younger than me. Warren was close to my sister's age and Wendy was just a baby. We had great fun together and enjoyed all the special Christmas foods that represented the holiday. My favorite was my Aunt Wilma's fruit salad. It was made with grapes and mandarin oranges—my favorite and always a family tradition. Christmas day was spent opening presents after all the chores were done and we had gotten dressed up a bit for the occasion. Mom liked to try to take pictures, but didn't get that accomplished very often.

Our evening at the cabin ended in a sensual fantasyland and a wonderful night's sleep. Sleeping in the woods was the most relaxing experience I ever had. Even though there were times you could hear the animals walking in the night, it was not alarming because you knew it was a sound of nature. Drifting back to sleep was almost instantaneous.

The next morning started with the great breakfast and Paul suggested a walk down the road to see another cabin. This cabin was owned by his grandmother. I would get a chance to meet her because she was at the cabin until the end of October.

We walked about a quarter of a mile before I noticed a car parked off the side of the road. It looked like it was abandoned, because there was chicken wire fence wrapped around the whole car. The fence was about 4' tall and was staked to the ground. I asked Paul if the car belonged to his grandmother, because we seemed to be walking toward it. He confirmed that it was as we proceeded down another steep path.

While making our way down this very crooked path for what seemed a long way, I saw a cabin. It was similar to Paul's, but smaller. There were more buildings; one that held wood, keeping it dry and an outhouse overlooking a small courtyard with a campfire ring in the center. As we approached, Paul called to his grandmother. After a moment, the front door of the cabin slowly opened and a tiny old lady emerged. She was dressed in black knit pants, with sweatshirt and jacket. She had white hair of medium length and large curls over her head. She wore gold rim glasses and had a smile that made her whole face glow.

This was Annabelle. She had obviously passed her friendly warm smile onto her grandson, because that smile was the same as Paul's. Paul introduced us and he further explained where I had just moved. She was familiar with the area and knew my father's brother's family that lived just down the road from her.

We talked about our stay and I got to explain my new experiences with camping and the bears. That triggered her stories about shooting bears. I gathered she had been a hunter most of her life. She appeared to have an active role with her late husband hunting in the Adirondack Mountains and working the farm they owned as a younger married couple. Annabelle was Paul's father's mother; and what a woman she was. She told me about her life and Paul would smile like he had heard the stories at lease a dozen times, but for me it was the first time and I was interested in her stories and her life.

Annabelle offered us some lunch and beverages, which we declined because it was about time to start packing up to go home. Annabelle thanked us for stopping by and said she was glad to meet me. As she did that, she looked me squarely in the eyes and I felt at that moment like we had been friends for years. I found myself unable to stop staring into her blue and almost hypnotizing eyes. This would be a friendship I would remember forever.

We said our goodbyes and made our way up the path to the car with the chicken wire fence around it. On our way back, Paul told me that the raccoons would crawl up into the undercarriage of the car and chew off the brake lines and electrical wires, leaving Annabelle stranded. I told him Annabelle sounded like an amazing woman. He agreed that she actually was the most incredible woman he had ever known as he continued telling me stories of her life.

Back at the cabin Paul and I started packing up. There were things to put away to make sure there was nothing available for critters to chew. Paul had not made a fire in the woodstove that morning so that when we left he could cover the stovepipe so animals would not enter the cabin from the roof. All the bedding was put back in the barrels and the cooler was packed and now loaded in the truck. We began our journey back home..

I reflected on the weekend during the drive back. I thought about learning to stop looking for a clock to find out what time it was and feeling the frustration of not knowing. But why would I have to know what time it was? In the mountains, it was either daylight or dark. Daylight was time to do things like hike, sightsee, and take some really breathtaking photos of nature at its best. There were things in the woods that I never really paid attention to until this trip. I thought of the moss covered tree stump near Paul's cabin. How vivid the green colors shown as the sunlight highlighted its presence. For some reason, the green of the foliage was more vibrant than I ever remembered. Even as a younger person, my family would have picnics in the woods every fall, but I didn't remember this kind of beauty.

I always thought of myself as a country person. The picnics in the woods with Mom and Dad and all of us kids were something we all enjoyed. Even after moving into my grandmother's house, I walked through the woods almost every weekend. I didn't know of too many people that enjoyed doing that on weekends. Now I see Paul did and it looked like he had been doing that longer than I ever did. It made me feel a little insecure about myself, but I looked at it as a new experience. I needed to experience more of life. I was just beginning to realize just how much life I had missed. Somehow I needed to make up for those things I'd lost.

The three-hour drive back home went very quickly and I was finding myself wanting to ask Paul if he was staying the night at my house with me. I didn't feel he ever wanted to commit to any type of schedule, so I didn't ask and he didn't tell. We unpacked the food and my stuff at my house and he gave me wonderful hugs and kisses and told me he would see me soon. I looked into those hypnotizing eyes and believed every word he said. I wasn't thinking about how "soon" might be measured. I knew in my gut that Paul wanted it that way. We said goodbyes again and he was gone into the darkness.

There were a lot of things I loved about Paul, but there was one thing I was having a hard time with. His total lack of commitment for anything, I found hard to deal with. He would just show up, and if I was home, we would do something. If I wasn't home, he would leave me a small gift announcing his visit. In some ways, it was comforting and in other ways it was disheartening, yet I knew he lived to be mysterious.

I waited. Some days the waiting and watching for Paul was obsessive for me. I would find myself racing home to see if he was there. If he wasn't then I would scour the house for little things that he might have left. After the searching, the reality and letdown from the "no-show" would become painfully apparent and it would usually trigger a bit of depression. I would occupy my time with phone calls to friends or go visit with Mom and Dad. I never let on that I was feeling down in the dumps. During one of these times I decided to go visit Annabelle. What a wonderful visit it was.

***

Annabelle C.

Annabelle was a worldly woman even though she had lived her whole life in the local area. She told me about her life and her husband. She was married to a man that she loved with every depth of her being. She was a farm wife in a sense because she would tend the work at home both outside and inside. She would grow a garden large enough to feed their family during the winter. This also meant she would have to can and bake and feed chickens and all other small animals which also took residence on their property. Her husband was a hunter, as was she, and they both enjoyed the outdoor living. That is how she came by the cabin in the Adirondack Mountains.

Stories of hunting in the Adirondack Mountains told me more about Annabelle than I thought any human being could possibly do, but the sincerity in her voice and the look in her eyes as she told me stories made me believe she was probably the most genuine person I would ever meet. She told me that her husband died when she was 69 years old. She knew she had to take care of herself, but she didn't have a driver's license. So she practiced driving with the family car in the fields next to the house until she could build her confidence to take a driver's test. It didn't take long and she passed her test on the first try.

She was now able to drive anywhere she needed to go and returned to the cabin often. Her three children were grown with families of their own. She told me most of the time she would stay at the cabin from May until the end of October or the beginning of November. There were times the bears would invade her space and for the most part she could scare them off, but she told me that twice she had to take action against two of them.

The most recent bear invasion happened when the bear decided he wanted some of her food in the cabin. Annabelle told of the bear coming onto the porch of her cabin and starting to come through the only door the cabin had. She owned a custom rifle that her husband had made just for her so she would be able to handle herself in situations such as this. She always had the gun handy she said, and she grabbed it, aimed and fired. The bear fell back onto her porch. It was dead. She was relieved that the danger was over, but now she had to find the ranger to help her remove the carcass. Annabelle said she walked up the hill from her cabin and got her car out of the critter fence and drove to the ranger station in town. The ranger had known Annabelle a number of years, and I am sure had great respect for her, as I did. He would have to file a report about the incident because it was not bear season. He would need to measure the bear for the report. The ranger and a few guys came to help drag the bear out. It measured six feet tall. Annabelle was 82 years old at the time.

The conversation lasted several hours. I found myself wanting to stay and yet I knew I had to go. It took a few minutes for our goodbyes. I felt Annabelle wanted me to stay too, but I had to get back home and feed the dogs and get dinner. She waved from her front door as I drove away. I waved back and smiled. I was thinking I had never met such an amazing woman.

Mom and I didn't talk about Paul's visits, but I always knew she had her opinions and she wouldn't have liked the way he appeared to be using me. In some ways, I was being taken advantage of, a lot like Daryl used me. Paul just did it in a different ways. Daryl used my work ethic to get me to do as much work as I could so he didn't have to do it. He also used the guilt technique of saying it was "woman's work" so he didn't qualify. Paul, on the other hand just enticed me sexually and that seemed a lot less painful, but the reality of that was becoming more visible to my blinded sight.

THE HOUSE

It was the third week of October when I had the first encounter in the house. I remember it was Sunday morning around 4 AM when I woke up coughing. I remember thinking my mouth was terribly dry. I was almost panicky about getting a drink of water. I went to the kitchen to get a bottle of water. After a few more swallows, I went back to bed.

I woke up with the sun shining in my bedroom door from the east hall window. I again felt like my mouth and throat had been coated with baby powder. I was so dry I could hardly swallow. I grabbed the bottle of water and drank the rest. During that process, my mind was trying to find a reason for my incredible thirst. That is when I realized there was a fragrance in the room. All I could think of was the powder that used to be in the bathroom when my grandparents lived here. It smelled like Cashmere Bouquet soap. My grandmother always used Cashmere Bouquet.

I tried to rationalize the situation, but just talked myself out of that kind of thinking. I went downstairs to make some coffee, fix my usual Sunday breakfast and feed the dogs. The dogs usually slept in my bedroom, and they looked like they were anxious for breakfast today and ran down the stairs ahead of me.

This Sunday was a beautiful one and would be a great day to do all kinds of things, which I did. The dogs and I went for a long walk in the woods enjoying the colors of the leaves and the even more beautiful color carpet on the floor of the woods created by the fallen leaves. I saw a couple of deer standing frozen and erect listening and smelling for danger. I walked the dogs away from them so we didn't disturb or scare them. I thought of Dad. He would watch deer at the edge of the woods every spring when he would till the fields. One year he told about stopping to watch a mother deer and her three fawns. They didn't run away from him, and he would sit on the tractor and talk to them and watch them graze on the plush green spring blades. He would many times revisit this sight and talk to them and they always let him. Dad had a very soft side to him that wasn't always apparent, nor did he reveal it often, but I wasn't surprised he could communicate with wild animals.

Monday morning I rose to the smell of fresh baked apple pie. The smell was so strong that I went downstairs to actually see if I had left something in the oven or somehow forgotten to turn it off the night before. I was searching my memory for answers when I realized I hadn't used the oven on Sunday. Needless to say, there wasn't any apple pie. I just thought again my brain was playing tricks on me and went to get ready for work.

Tuesday I woke to the powder coating my throat again. I was beginning to think maybe these were not just coincidences, because first of all I didn't believe in coincidence and secondly each incident was something that made me think of my grandmother. I would shake it off and go to work.

Wednesday and Thursday mornings were the same as Tuesday and by this time I was really trying to make sense of it all. After work, I decided to go visit Mom.

It was about 5:30 PM when I arrived at Mom and Dad's house after picking up Missi and Shellee. Mom was starting to fix dinner. She asked me if I wanted to stay and I told her I would.

Then she asked, "How are things going at the house?"

I suddenly had a chill hit my spine that made the hair stand up on the back of my neck.

I said, "Why would you ask me that?"

"I don't know" She replied, "I just thought that house always made me feel a little uncomfortable and I wondered if you felt that too."

I had to take a minute to get my thoughts together.

I looked her in the eyes and said, "I have had a couple of strange things happen that I thought were just my imagination, but I'm not sure that is really the case. I don't want people to think I am nuts so I haven't mentioned it to anyone."

She asked, "What kind of stuff?"

We sat at the table while I told her what had happened. I found her to be listening to my every word (which was unusual).

When I finished she asked, "Did you know it was Grandma's birthday today?"

For a moment, I was frozen with the thought that my Grandmother might be trying to communicate with me in some way. That thought triggered a bunch of other possible explanations. It appeared to me that my Grandmother could be haunting the house. We talked a while about the events that happened and when they occurred. Mom was able to give me information that seemed to make sense to the events.

My grandmother had a very Dutch routine. A Dutch wife would always have certain days for specific tasks. Monday was always my Grandmother's baking day. People would often come to help in the fields with planting and harvesting and it would be the responsibility of the farmer's wife to feed everyone. This being October, harvest time, thrashers (men who would bring thrashing equipment to harvest crops like corn or beans) would come and she would have to feed them; thus the apple pie smell on Monday. Mom thought all the events made perfect sense and that Grandma might be hanging around the house.

Soon Dad came in from the barn for dinner. The dogs were dancing around Dad appearing delighted to see him and glad it was dinnertime. We all talked and ate, but I didn't dare tell Dad that his mother might still be in the old house. I just didn't think he would understand. I went home after dinner and riffled through my desk to find a birthday card. I made the card out to Grandma and wrote on the inside that if she was here I just wanted her to know that I had good memories of her. I was happy to be living in her house. I signed it, I Love You, Grandma, signed your granddaughter, Laura.

The next morning I woke without any powder sensation in my mouth and throat. This was almost as powerful as the experiences themselves. It was at this point that my life changed spiritually. I don't mean to say that I became a spiritual advisor or psychic, but I just realized I was not alone in the house. I found that to be comforting. I talked to Jackie and Val about these events and that opened up a whole new communication between us. Jackie and Val both had many stories of spiritual encounters and it was very comforting to know my mind had not failed me. Things like this happen to other people too.

This newfound revelation spiked my curiosity for communication with my grandmother. I had heard stories and watched television programs about this kind of thing. In some ways I did believe and in some ways I did not. But after these events I decided to test my level of spiritual awareness.

Jackie and Val had told me things to try to do to communicate, but they always said it was a very individual thing. Some people see things, some hear things, some sense things, and some people just know by intuition or gut feeling. Sometimes these things were difficult to explain, but the one thing that was constant was that each person had their own way to communicate with someone spiritually.

My grandmother's spirit intrigued me. I wanted to see if I could learn more about communicating with her. I had all the time in the world to test this while I waited for Paul to show up. Somehow it filled in the void very nicely. I wasn't the kind of person that could date other people while seeing someone, even though I knew Paul would never make a commitment of a solid relationship with me. It just wasn't like him to do that, so I waited and occupied my time with my grandmother.

I started becoming more aware of things in the house. During the next month I noticed a lot of things going on in the house that I found reason to attribute to my grandmother's spirit. One night in particular, I noticed the dogs' behaviors. They usually would sit or lie near me wherever I sat while watching TV or talking on the phone. If I sat on the couch, they would be either on the couch with me or on the floor in front of the couch. This night they were lying on the floor in the living room in front of the chair next to the television. They were in a begging stance with their heads looking up to an empty chair. It was the same position they used while begging my dad or me when we ate. Dad had ice cream every night and he would share it with the dogs. I watched the dogs and they acted like someone was sitting in the chair eating something and they were hoping to get some.

They held that position for over 20 minutes. Then they both got up and moved out of the way as if someone was walking between them. Then Shellee walked toward the kitchen. Missi stood in the living room and watched Shellee. She stood with her ears perked like she was listening for something. I had been watching a program on television, but the behavior of the dogs had captured my total attention. After a minute or two, Shellee walked back from the dining room and stood at the bottom of the stairs. She stopped and her head moved like she was watching someone walk upstairs. When she appeared to have followed the person all the way to the top of the stairs and perhaps out of sight, she turned and looked at me. Missi had moved near Shellee and watched too. Now they were both looking at me as if I could solve the mystery of why they didn't get any ice cream from that person.

The days went by and I got used to the behaviors of the dogs. It got to be almost comical. I could sit on the couch and feel drifts of cold air in short little waves go past me. People would come to visit me and also notice that I had a very drafty house. My grandfather had it fully insulated a while ago and I knew that it was not from outside drafts. Jackie and Val knew what it was and we would all laugh about it and say "Hi Grandma" as she made her presence known. It was very comforting to have someone there. I didn't feel alone. I could call to her and she would come, or rather her fragrance would, and I was grateful for the calming sensation it brought to me. Getting to know my grandmother in this way was a new experience and most unexpected. But it was one of the most memorable times in my life.

DECEMBER 1986—THE DREAM

By December I had gotten into a routine and Paul was making more frequent visits. I was really enjoyed the time I spent with him. I asked him if we could go to the cabin for Christmas. He said we could and we set our plans for the weekend after next. I was excited about going back to the mountains again, and being close to Christmas, there should be snow. I told Jackie and Val about our plans and they were happy for me.

I had started running again and one night when I was running a strange thing happened that I couldn't tell anyone. I enjoyed running in the dark and in the country it was REALLY dark. The road I lived on was away from the traffic, which made it very private, but very dark in December. I would run through what I called (and everyone else) "The Pines." This was a stretch of land made up of a couple hundred acres of pine trees. The trees were full grown and the property had been purchased by a developer and filled with new houses on 5 acre lots. The houses were buried into the trees and hardly visible from the road. The mailboxes had all kinds of reflectors on them which created the only light and visible only when cars drove by. Very few cars passed by this time of night.

This night I ran one mile and was heading back to the house when I looked up and suddenly saw what looked like a huge red light smack in front of me. Still running, I jumped to the left instinctively to avoid what I thought could have been taillights of a truck or something even bigger. Suddenly I realized a few paces later there was nothing there. I kept jogging at a slightly slower pace, telling myself I was imagining things. I was desperately searching my mind for a reason for this obvious error in brain or sight function. Maybe my endorphins were out of control. I discounted the vision as nothing I needed to pay attention to and kept running. I was almost home when the red flash came into my vision again. I jumped again and this time stopped.

WHAT THE HELL WAS THAT?

I started walking. Again it was there and then it was gone. I didn't know how to explain it a second time. I felt unsure of myself. I could not figure out what was going on. I wasn't in fear, just confused. What was I supposed to do with this situation? I started walking to cool down and gather my thoughts back. I walked past my driveway, thinking, analyzing, and trying to come to terms with the visions. Suddenly there was another flash, but this time it was white with an object in the center of the light. The object in the light was the rear view mirror in Paul's truck. I could see the bead necklaces hanging from it. It was as if I was sitting in his truck.

Another flash, the windshield! I am in the truck and everything is moving so fast—I am going through the windshield! I can see my face hitting the windshield and now I am flying through the windshield! I stopped, blinked and then rubbed my eyes. I could feel my heart pounding in my chest. My mind was racing. I just saw myself in an accident in Paul's truck.

Trying to rationalize, I started talking out loud. "I am standing on the side of the road away from my house. It is dark. I can see the neighbor's mercury light through the trees. How could I see something like that and it appear so real?"

I looked back toward my house. The lights were on, but there wasn't a sound anywhere. I slowly walked back to the house. The flashes visibly shook me. I always said there was no such thing as coincidence in life.

DO YOU THINK YOU DIDN'T SEE THESE VISIONS? THIS IS A WARNING! PAY ATTENTION! IF YOU GO TO THE MOUNTAINS WITH PAUL YOU COULD DIE IN AN ACCIDENT. THAT IS WHAT THE VISION IS TELLING YOU! PAY ATTENTION!

How else could I explain what just happened? I had never experienced anything like this before and yet the message seemed crystal clear. The vision was of an accident in Paul's truck. Do I pay attention to this? Do I tell Paul I can't go to the cabin with him? I didn't know what to do.

When I walked into the house, Missi and Shellee were waiting for me in the kitchen. They looked at me like they knew something was wrong. I tried to ease to their visible concerns. I petted them both and gave them snacks and that seemed to help. I couldn't help thinking about the visions, but I went into the living room and watched some television. Soon it was bedtime and the dogs and I went upstairs to bed.

I remember climbing into bed and comfortably curling into the blankets, and that was all I remember until the dream. It was dark and I thought I was sitting up somewhere, somehow. I was looking around to see if I could see anything in the dark. Suddenly there were strange flashes of stripes, but they were moving. It looked like I was going past a Zebra very fast, a movie of flying zebra stripes. Then there was darkness again. My vision became larger and I realized I was sitting in Paul's truck and I was talking to him while he drove. I don't remember the conversation, but we came to a "T" intersection in the road and Paul stopped and then turned left. We were driving on a secondary road that was winding around a very rural countryside. The sides of the road were lined with trees backed up with forest and an occasional sprinkling of buildings like barns or garages. The road became steeply inclined and winding. In front of us were the headlights of a large truck. It was a logging truck, loaded with logs. It looked like it was going too fast and coming straight at us. Paul quickly swirled to get out of the way of the truck and veered off the road.

The truck lunged and bounced off the road, down an embankment and suddenly there was a ditch. The truck hit the bank of the ditch and the vision of the rearview mirror and the necklaces came into my dream. My face hit the windshield and I broke the glass and kept flying out of the truck. I landed in a snow bank and things stopped moving. Suddenly it was quiet. There was no sound. No truck sounds. No motors, no voices, no wind. I was trying to grasp where I was and what was happening. I opened my eyes and saw Paul kneeling next to me. He had a cut on his forehead and the expression on his face was confusing. He looked like he was scared, and Paul was never scared of anything. If he were, he would never show his fear, yet fear was on his face at this moment. I wanted to ask him why he looked scared. He looked like he was trying to talk to me, but couldn't get the words out of his mouth.

Suddenly there was another flash.

I was flying up, very fast. I looked around to see if I could figure out where I was. It was dark all around me again, but I looked down and saw lights from an accident. A logging truck was tipped over on the side of the road and resting against some trees. Some of the trees are broken and some tipped from the weight of the truck and its load. There was another truck, a pickup truck—yellow with its nose plunged into a ditch bank.

There were people walking around and there was Paul. He was kneeling in the snow holding someone.

YOU ARE DYING IN PAUL'S ARMS IN THE SNOW!

There was another flash. I bolted to a sitting position feeling panic and looking around trying, again, to figure out where I was. I was in my bed, at my house, and Missi and Shellee are sitting next to my bed looking up at me. My breathing was fast and I had chills running down my spine. My mind was thinking of only one thing.

IF THERE ARE NO COINCIDENCES IN LIFE, THEN WHAT THE HELL WAS THAT?

I couldn't answer.

Sleep didn't come back to me that night. I couldn't ignore the apparent message in the visions while I was running and this horrible dream of an accident. I wanted to put this whole thing behind me, but I didn't know how. I wondered if I should tell Paul about the dream, but that seemed unrealistic. The dream gnawed at me the rest of the night and even while I was getting ready for work. I just needed to think about this for a while. The trip wasn't planned for another week.

It was Tuesday and my bowling night. This would be good. The women on the team were fun loving jokesters and would definitely take my mind away from the day before.

The rest of the bowling team was there when I arrived and bowling started as usual. The team we were bowling against wasn't fooling around as much as we normally do so the mood was a little more somber. During our bowling rotations one of the bowlers on my team told me she wanted to tell me something, but she didn't know just how to tell me. That was really strange coming from her because we were friends, but not terribly close. She began telling me she had a dream about me a couple of times during the weekend. She said she was afraid for me and proceeded to tell me that her dream was about me getting into an accident. She was having a difficult time telling me any details, but did say that the ending was upsetting for her.

THIS IS NOT A COINCIDENCE!

I pondered the thought to tell her I had the same dream just last night and I knew the ending. The concerned look on her face gave me the confidence to share the events of the past two days of my life with her. It did, however, put her further into shock with details of the events because they were identical to her dream. She strongly urged me not to go on this trip to the mountains with Paul. I told her I was thinking seriously about not going, but wasn't sure how to tell Paul. I wondered how I would explain without sounding like I needed that reservation to Willard that was offered earlier in my life!

Bowling ended that night without being as much fun. By the time I got home, I was ready for some sleep. I went to bed and slept soundly all night.

When morning came, I felt refreshed and didn't think much about the conversation at bowling. I got to work and took care of my customers as usual. At 11 AM the mail came and I checked my mailbox (like always) and there was an inner office envelope for me that caught my attention because it felt empty. I took it back to my desk and opened it to find a small card inside.

I opened the card and the message on the front said, "I was thinking of you..." and on the inside it said, "I just wanted you to know." It was from my friend Colleen. She and I became friends after she was hired to take my job in the accounting department. There were some major politics going on at that time and the situation was so bizarre that she and I became friends because of it. There was a handwritten message from Colleen saying that for some reason she felt afraid for my safety and just wanted to tell me for reasons she couldn't explain. I dropped the card like it was on fire. The hair stood up on the back of my neck. I sat at my desk frozen.

The phone rang, and it startled me so much I jumped. It was a call from a customer placing an order, which jolted me back to reality.

The day dragged on while I struggled to stay focused on my work. Each time I tried to think of work tasks, my mind would always come back to these "coincidences." By 5 PM I was leaving work to go home, hopefully relax and try to make sense of what was happening.

YOU CAN'T GO ON THIS TRIP!

The haunting phrase kept going through my head over and over and in reality I knew I could not go, but how could I back out of this trip? Paul would think I am crazy. Maybe I am crazy! I just wasn't sure anymore.

When I got home Missi and Shellee were waiting for me and showing me their happy faces and wagging tails. I gave them their treats and then dinner before I changed my clothes. I sat on the edge of the bed to take a deep breath and try not to move or think for a few minutes. That downtime lasted maybe five minutes before the telephone rang. Jackie was on the phone. She asked if I was going to be home this evening because she and Val wanted to come out for a visit. My energy level was low, but not low enough that I could tell her no. Jackie said they would be out about 7 PM. Now I had a little time to relax and get myself some dinner. I didn't feel like running tonight.

Jackie and Val drove in my driveway right on time. Before I could get out of the kitchen they were coming through the front door. Jackie was yelling for me as she came in and laughing in her usual contagious way. They both gave me hugs and we went into the front room to sit and chat.

Val started the conversation with, "We've been thinking about you lately and we just needed to tell you about it. Jackie and I are afraid for you."

My heart sank. I held my breath for a moment. I didn't dare respond to her statement. Jackie continued with the information that I knew (somehow) she was going to tell me. It followed the same train of thought as the other people in the past few days in that she and Val both had dreams that I would be in a fatal accident. Each gave sketchy details, but those details were basically the same as the ones I heard at bowling, the note from Colleen, and my own visions. This is too much! I can't believe this is a coincidence!

The next step, of course, was for me to tell them everything. I felt they needed to hear about all the people with this dream and what they had been telling me for the past several days. They were both shocked and even more concerned for my safety. They made me promise not to go with Paul to the mountains next weekend. They further explained the feelings they had were very bad and they just wouldn't allow me to discount all the events that indicated a message of real danger for me.

We talked until 10:30 PM and upon their leaving they made me promise not to go. I had expressed my concern about how to tell Paul. I was afraid about what he would think of me. I thought about lying about it, but I always feel too guilty to be a successful liar. They were relentless about the promise, which I made, but I knew they sensed I was still undecided. They gave me hugs and reminded me about my promise before they left.

Now I had the still of the night to try again to sleep. Maybe it would be okay, but I still thought about all the people that had come to me with messages. With those thoughts I went to bed (Missi and Shellee too) for a good nights sleep.

Morning came without incident and like the new day, there was a new lease on my life. I was starting the day with a positive attitude for an uneventful day. The day progressed just that way and the stress of all the events from earlier in the week appeared to be in the background of my mind. My routine continued as it usually did (until this week that is) and I felt good. I was sitting in front of the television with a bowl of ice cream when the phone rang. I answered the phone and it was my cousin Zack. Zack was my Aunt Irene's son. He would call me from time to time just to see what I was doing and we would talk. He was going through a divorce and sometimes needed an ear to bend.

After an initial greeting Zack said he had to call me, but he wasn't sure how to tell me something that happened to him this week because it was pretty scary. I assured him I could handle scary, especially this week. I meant that as a joke, but he didn't laugh. There was a pause, and I suddenly thought he was going to tell me a tale of my forthcoming fatality.

Zack started his scary story with him having a dream about me. At that point I sat down and started shaking. I couldn't interrupt his story, but I knew exactly what he was going to say. When Zack asked me if I was upset, I told him yes and no. I gave him the abbreviated version of the events of the week and he was silent. I continued talking calmly and asked what he was thinking.

"What are you going to do?" He inquired.

"I'm not going on the trip. After all this, how could I?"

This was the sixth person with the same dream and warning. How could I possibly ignore the situation? Zack assured me that was the best thing to do and that he would call me in a few days. I said goodbye and hung up the phone.

I sat motionless by the phone. I knew what I had to do, but I didn't know where Paul was to tell him or even how to get in touch with him. I had to wait until he appeared. This was unsettling for me. It was bad enough to have to deal with all the warnings that I would be killed in an accident, but to have to wait maybe a week to tell Paul was a lot to think about. There was nothing I could do, but wait and suffer.

It was Friday. I had been waiting for over a week for Paul. Today was the day I was to leave with Paul. When I got home, there were only the dogs waiting for me. I fed them as usual and changed my clothes when I heard a knock at the door. It was Jackie and Val. They said they thought I could use some moral support and didn't think I should be alone. I knew deep in my heart they came to prevent me from changing my mind.

It was only minutes after Jackie and Val arrived when Paul came. He came in smiling and asked if I was ready to go. I told him we had to talk.

Then Jackie yelled from the living room, "We aren't going to let her go."

Paul looked puzzled and I asked him to come into the kitchen for a minute. He followed me to the kitchen.

"Do you want something to drink?" I asked to soften the moment.

"No thanks." he replied.

I took a deep breath, let it out and quietly said, "I had a dream about a week ago that scared me. In the dream we got into an accident and I was thrown through the windshield of your truck. I died in my dream. But that isn't the whole story. In the past 10 days five other, unrelated people told me they also had a dream about me and the outcomes were the same that I would die in an accident. I felt I just couldn't deny the turn of events from so many different people."

I took another deep breath and looked into Paul's eyes. He was smiling as he looked at me and then wrapped his arms around me, holding me close to him.

He spoke softly in my ear, "Sometimes I have gut feelings that, at times, I can't ignore either. Perhaps we could go another weekend before Christmas."

He stood looking in my eyes with those incredible blue eyes that radiated a level of understanding I'd hoped for.

I pulled back from the embrace and said, "Thank you for understanding. I was afraid you would think of me as some kind of fruitcake and I'd watch you running for your life down my driveway." He smiled and said, "I like fruitcake," as he hugged me again.

We held each other for what seemed to be a long time.

Paul said, "As long as we aren't going, I have some things I could get done. I will be in touch, okay?"

"Okay."

He turned and walked to the front door, saying goodbyes to Jackie and Val as he left. I went into the living room to sit with Jackie and Val. It was over, and everything was fine. I felt relieved and glad I was not alone. I decided we should break out a bottle of wine to take the edge off. Everyone agreed. The three of us finished the bottle before Jackie and Val left just before midnight.

Now the house was quiet and I was alone except for Missi and Shellee, and they were looking at me as if to say, "It's bedtime!" I had to smile as I told them that it truly was bedtime and I turned out the lights and we all went to bed. As I climbed into bed, I wondered if I would sleep peacefully. I didn't have to wonder long because I fell asleep without remembering to look at my clock as I usually do. I slept soundly and didn't remember any events of my dreams.

Paul and I made plans to go to the cabin in two weeks. Just like the original plan he would pick me up after work and we would drive the three hours to the cabin. I just knew it was going to be okay.

During the trip to the cabin there was a freaky little thing that happened at the "T" intersection. We had been driving for about two hours and it was very dark. Paul stopped the truck at the stop sign of the "T" intersection and then attempted to drive on but the truck stalled. Sometimes that happens in manual shift vehicles, especially in winter, and I didn't think much of it at the time.

Then Paul tried to start the truck and it wouldn't start. The starter was trying to turn over the motor, but it just wasn't working. After three tries Paul got out and pushed the truck off to the side of the road. Now it started to feel a little freaky. He got back into the truck and didn't say anything, nor did I for a few minutes. Then he tried to start the truck again. It started right up without a hesitation and we drove away.

"Does your truck do that often?" I quietly asked.

"No." He replied, "Actually, that was the first time."

We didn't mention it again—too freaky!

We arrived at the cabin without incident and had a wonderful time. We tied ribbons on branches of one of the pine trees outside the cabin window in celebration of the holiday. Paul and I spent time doing crafts and chatting. We went for a walk to see the freshly fallen snow on the trees and woods. We curled up together and talked about our favorite stories of life from the past, as children and adults. Paul told me about his daughter and that he cherished the time he spent with her, especially at Christmas.

Sunday, after lunch, we packed up and started for home. The sun was shining brightly and the reflections off the snow made it look like a sparkling white wonderland. As we drove through Adirondack Park we drove through a section of road that had pine trees growing on both sides of the road. They were spaced perfectly and as we drove into the tree section it gave the illusion of a narrowing tunnel. Then the zebra stripes appeared. The sunshine was creating stripes of shade and sunlight and as we drove it was just like in my dream. The zebra stripes were flashes of sun and shade coming through the windows of the truck. My vision of the zebra stripes had been exact to this very real light show. As we drove out of the trees we came to the "T" intersection and I wondered if the zebra stripes were somehow connected to the intersection, like in my dream. I didn't say anything to Paul, but I felt better. I was comforted knowing I had done the right thing by changing the date of the trip and that I hadn't lost my mind either.

Paul would come and go and I was getting used to doing my own thing, realizing I wasn't to count on him. This was teaching me a valuable lesson I needed to learn, but it was very painful at times. I enjoyed being with him and doing things with him, but as time went on, the things we did only evolved around my house. We would watch TV or talk over a pizza or maybe a bottle of wine and he would spend the night. This would refresh my belief in "our relationship," which never was. I just wouldn't admit it or do anything to interrupt the routine. The on again, off again relationship continued for about a year and a half. The visits became less and less frequent, farther and farther apart.

In February Dad was diagnosed with cancer. The whole family was in shock and sheer terror at the thought of cancer. Dad was almost excited about it and that bothered me. I tried to talk to him about fears he had and he just wouldn't talk about it.

I remember him saying, "Yup, its cancer!"

He wore an expression I would see on him at happy times. It bothered me that his attitude was that of being a "lucky guy." The cancer was colon cancer and the doctors said it was quite treatable. We all felt optimistic about that, but there would be an operation to remove the tumor and additional tests to check for cancer cells.

The day of his surgery we all took the day off work, except Lyle. He was on the road and couldn't get back. The surgery lasted about three hours. The doctors were optimistic they had gotten it all. We felt relieved. But a few days later the test results from the colon biopsy came back. The doctor said there were cancer cells at the cut end of Dad's intestine and that was not good news. They warned of a strong possibility the cancer would spread to other parts of his body. Within a couple of months he was diagnosed with cancer in his lymph nodes. He began chemo and radiation treatments. They seemed to work, but it made him very sick. Two weeks after the treatment the cancer came back and grew even faster.

It wasn't long before Dad had lost his excitement about having cancer. He was tired and always cold. He talked about suicide and Mom kept a very close eye on him and didn't leave him alone. In the spring he tried to drive his tractor and bush-hog over the now weed-covered fields. I think he felt he had to do something with the fields because that is what he had always done in the spring, except this time he wasn't planting and growing, he was just cutting down the overgrowth of weeds on wasted crop land. He would go to the barn and care for the few goats he had and a couple of pigs, just to keep farming. Soon he was resting more than working and we watched a valuable man turn into a helpless body. He was 66 years old and we all felt he would be leaving us way too soon.

WHAT GOES UP...?

I had been laid off from my job of over seven years and wasn't seeing work friends very often. Jackie was busy with her daughter and her fiancé and Val had gotten a divorce and was in a new relationship that had swept her off her feet. I was on severance pay and learning to live on a tighter budget in preparation for the decrease in income. I was finding the jobs being advertised in the paper were far below what I was making and I would have to settle for less all the way around. The job I had was comfortable and the routine was a little boring, but the fear of finding something brand new scared me. I didn't have much faith in the old saying, "When one door closes another one opens." I had sent my resume to a few places, but I wasn't terribly serious about the job hunt. I was enjoying the time off with pay. I had three months of severance pay that started in July. I would be entitled to get unemployment—which terrified me. There was something about going to a state organization to prove I was not trying to get money fraudulently without working. It just felt wrong to me, but for now I was comfortable in taking every cent of my severance pay to the bank and enjoying the time off.

By mid-August I had been offered a job as a Marketing Assistant. This job wasn't paying much, but it was a job that linked to my Associates Degree. My job responsibilities included soliciting local businesses for work that would teach physically and mentally challenged adults a skill.

The first company I solicited was the one from which I was laid off. I already knew the marketing people and had an idea to help assemble sample kits of products for the sales people to distribute to their customers. There were a few months of brainstorming, trials and experiments to perfect the packaging, but it came together and my idea was a success. I was having fun with this job. It took me into places of business and allowed me to help them with new concepts and share ideas. I was now a marketing person, like the ones I used to work for, but now I was working with them and loving it.

By spring I was getting contracts with silk screening requirements. I would get orders for softball teams for shirts and hats with team names and/or sponsor's names. I was allowed to solicit contracts from anywhere and I had been asked about quoting an order for shirts and hats for my sister's husband, Kyle's softball team. I had been to their house many times and had gotten to know a lot of their friends. In April I had an order to deliver to Kyle's team for hats and T-shirts. Because of the distance and the urgency of the team to get the shirts, I offered to deliver them personally, rather than sending them. This would give me an excuse to visit my sister.

It was mid-April when I delivered the order to the bar in my sister's hometown. There was a party atmosphere when I took the shirts and hats to the bar. Trixie and Kyle were there with me and we all enjoyed the fun trying on shirts and hats. As the evening ticked on, other people from town arrived and partied with the team. There was one man that seemed to be a well-known person, yet he was dressed like he had just come from a desk job. It was about 10:30 PM when he came in, and the guys greeted him as "the professor." My sister introduced him to me as Jim.

Jim was a man of medium height, just less than six feet with almost black hair and eyes that didn't reflect any specific color. His glasses highlighted his full beard which was very neatly trimmed. He was slim in build, very attractive, and after a few beers, became more involved in the party. He and I started to have conversation about motorcycles with the person sitting next to us at the bar. Both gentlemen were quite surprised to learn I had a motorcycle. When I explained the make and model of my bike, that seemed to really open up the conversation. Jim's friend was obviously a Harley Davidson owner and was busting on me pretty heavy about my rice burner. I defended it the best I could, but I was not about to win this battle. Jim also favored the Harleys even though he did not own one. Jim and I conversed comfortably the rest of the evening. It was near closing time when I left and Jim stayed for last call.

Jim was one of those people who just looked out of his element. One of the local patrons nicknamed him the professsor. I thought it was because he had gone to college. But Jim had been through some rough times with his marriage, an after-marriage relationship, and some job woes with company layoffs. I felt a connection to him. He spoke confidently of the business world and I guess that gave us something in common.

In the weeks that followed, my girlfriend Val announced her wedding date. Rickie, the lucky guy, was the one who had swept her off her feet not long ago and I knew him because we had all worked together. Val's brother was always asking me out for a date. He was married and made it apparent he wanted to have an affair while staying with his wife. Now I was a little concerned that if I went to the wedding, as I should, he would be all over me like bees on honey. I decided I needed to take a date to this wedding to be safe. Now I just had to find someone that would go with me. I had not seen Paul in several months. I figured he had moved on to greener pastures. I was feeling rejected and angry with him. I thought he could have at least ended the visits with some kind of goodbye for closure. At least then I wouldn't be looking for him. But that didn't happen. There was a time I hoped Paul and I would grow into a serious relationship which might have lead to marriage, but Paul told me, on several occasions, that we could never be a couple. I just wouldn't believe it. I could only believe now that I was on my own—I finally had to face the reality of this non relationship.

The first weekend of May, my sister asked me to come down to watch the guys play their first softball game. I thought that was a good idea. In the back of my mind, I thought about asking Jim to go to the wedding. Then I dismissed the thought. I just didn't think he would drive that far to go to a wedding when he didn't know anyone except me.

I arrived at Trixie's house and we left immediately for the softball field. Kyle had already gone for warm-ups. We talked about the game and how the team was excited to start playing again, but really it was just an excuse to drink beer. Celebratory drinking would follow the game by both teams. The game was important, but the drinking was more important. All the guys were born and raised as farm workers, carpenters, county workers, or were self-employed garage owners. This made for a very good softball competition because of the physical strength of the players. Of course, they all acted as if they just left high school regardless of how long ago they graduated. It was fun to watch and cheer.

Kyle's team did win the game and the celebrations took place in various places. We wound up at the local tavern, the one closest to their house. I was glad of that because of small town police.

We got wings and beer and talked about the game throughout the evening. It was about 10:30 PM when Jim arrived. We exchanged the usual greetings as he stepped up to the bar to order a beer. Conversations, jokes and incessant teasing continued through out the evening. Trixie and I talked about all the guys and she was filling me in on their special talents.

Jim, excusing himself, walked between us to go to the men's room. Suddenly Trixie got an expression on her face as if a light bulb just gone off in her head. (She did that every so often.)

She turned to me and said, "Hey, why don't you ask Jim to be your date for that wedding?"

I looked at her and said, "I thought about that, but I didn't think I should ask him and obligate him to drive that far."

Trixie said, "He doesn't do anything except work part time for the pipeline company. Maybe he would be glad to get out of town for a free meal."

"I don't know," I said, "I guess I could ask him."

As we were talking about this arrangement and invitation, Jim returned and again excused himself as he walked between us. Trixie was always quick with comments flying out of her mouth, usually when I wished she would keep her mouth shut, but in this case, the timing was perfect.

She grabbed Jim by the arm and said, "Hey Jim. My sister needs an escort for a wedding. Would you be her escort?"

I was flabbergasted by the bluntness of the question. I felt embarrassed for Jim, but he turned around and looked at Trixie and then looked at me and said, "No, I don't think so."

Trixie was relentless and continued, "Jim, she just needs an escort, you don't have to marry her."

Jim now appeared nervous about the statement and everyone close enough to hear the comment joined in to tease. He stepped closer to me and said, "I really couldn't be your escort."

Embarrassed, I said, "I understand. Sometimes my sister gets a little brassy about things, especially after a couple of beers."

We were both silent for a long minute. I felt I had to say something. My sister had engaged in conversation with others at the bar.

I looked at Jim. He was looking at the floor. I said, "The wedding is in two weeks and I can't go to it without someone as an escort. The bride is my best friend and her brother has been hitting on me for about a year even though he's married. I just don't want to deal with that situation at her wedding."

Jim looked up at me with kind expression. "I couldn't...I'm just not in your class of people." At that he turned and resumed his position at the bar.

I felt he was being hard on himself and obviously his self-esteem had been destroyed by someone or something. The topic didn't come up again. Shortly after that Trixie and I went back to her house.

In the car she asked, "So, tell me, is Jim taking you to the wedding?"

"No. He said he couldn't because he was not in my class of people."

She didn't add anything and we dropped the subject.

Monday was a typical day at work and spring was in full swing. I had lots of work to do at home.

YOU NEED TO RAKE THE LEAVES OUT OF THE FLOWER BEDS!

I was changing my clothes when the phone rang.

As I answered, Trixie's voice spewed, "I only have a minute. Jim is going to call you right now. See ya."

"Wait! Wait! What are you talking about?" I called back into the phone.

"Jim just called. He wanted your phone number. Said he had been thinking about my offer and decided he didn't really have anything to do that weekend. His friends had told him he had nothing to lose and he should go. So, he was going to call you any second."

"Okay." I said, "Thanks for the tip."

WELL, HOW ABOUT THAT!

I smiled and stood by the telephone...waiting.

It didn't ring for five minutes, then ten minutes.

YOU KNOW IF YOU GO TO THE KITCHEN AND GET A DRINK, IT WILL RING.

I walked to the kitchen and pulled open the door of the refrigerator. The phone rang. I ran to pick it up, but paused to take a breath. I picked up the phone and tried to sound calm and uninformed.

"Hello."

The voice spoke with soft kind tone, with a hint of fear, "Hi, Laura this is Jim".

In surprised happy voice, I said, "Hi, Jim".

He continued, "I called your sister to get your phone number."

I felt the need to tell him the truth about this whole situation and interrupted him and said, "Yeah, she just called me."

He came back with, "I thought she might. Anyway, I was thinking about your need for an escort and I really don't have a reason not to come up and go to the wedding with you."

He paused like he was waiting for me to respond, which I did. "Jim, I would really appreciate it. I have been in a panic about this wedding for over a month and I just can't go alone."

Jim asked, "Is it a fancy wedding? What should I wear?"

"No, not fancy," I continued, "but the groom is Puerto Rican and I expect to see some cultural differences from a traditional wedding. I admit I'm not sure what to expect. All I know is, it's a 6 o'clock wedding."

"I have a corduroy sport coat I could wear with a shirt and tie. Would that be sufficient?" he asked.

"I'm sure that will be just fine."

"What time do you want me at your house?"

"If you're here by 5:15 that should give us plenty of time to find the church and get a decent place to sit."

After giving him directions to the house, we talked for a few minutes repeating the details. Jim gave me his phone number in case something came up. I thanked him for calling as we laughed about my sister's invitation. We hung up with the plans set for Saturday. I stood by the phone with a smile. I felt a lot better about my wedding commitment. I actually had a date! I called Trixie to tell her, and thank her.

The week passed very quickly and Saturday left me trying to get all my outside work done and the house cleaned before Jim arrived. I thought he would stay overnight because, after drinking at a Puerto Rican wedding, he wouldn't be driving two and a half hours to get home. I didn't know if I felt like sharing my bed with him, but I would cross that bridge when I got closer to the proverbial river.

By 5 PM I was dressed and ready for the wedding. I was nervous about Jim arriving. I paced back and forth from the kitchen to the dining room to the living room and back. I didn't make too many trips before I could see the silver Grand Am coming down the road and then slowing to turn into my driveway. I watched as he got out of the car and I thought he looked very, very handsome. I turned and went into the kitchen like I was busy and not waiting for him so I could actually walk to the door when he knocked.

He knocked and I exited the kitchen to the front door.

"Hi, Jim, come in," I called opening the screen door.

"Can I get you a beer before we go?"

"Sure." Jim said.

"Did you have any trouble finding my house?" I asked.

"No. Your directions were great." Jim said.

"Good."

We paused to sip the beer. I continued, "I'm not sure what to expect at this wedding, but I'm glad you're here."

He responded, "I'll admit I've have never been to a Puerto Rican wedding, so I guess it will be new for both of us."

We continued casual conversation as we finished the beer. We soon left the house to go to the wedding. Jim was clearly a gentleman as he opened the car door for me, getting in and out. I liked that.

The wedding was beautiful and the reception was not huge, but the majority of people attending were from the groom's side of the family. We had a little to eat and drink, but Jim and I felt a little out of place. We didn't know how to dance the Puerto Rican dances. Other people that I knew were caught up in the dancing and music while Jim and I sat quietly at a table watching the celebrations for a while.

Soon I turned to him and said, "How about we split?"

Jim looked at me with an immediate look of approval and nodded. We gave our best wishes and goodbyes to the bride and groom and went back to my house. It was still early in the evening, according to Jim's standards, so we decided to change our clothes and go out to a local bar where we could talk and feel more relaxed.

We went to a country western bar, which was a little odd because neither of us were lovers of country music. There were a couple of songs played by the band that were slow and "waltz-type." Jim asked me to dance. I always felt self-conscious about dancing. I had not done much of it. I accepted the offer and we walked onto the dance floor.

Jim took my hand and I put my arm around his neck. I could feel his arm go around my waist and pull me close to him. We danced in slow, sensual moves as the music swept us into a place that felt like we were dancing in a ballroom built just for us. As we danced, I felt a special closeness with Jim. We danced as if we had been doing it for years. I felt comfortable and confident about dancing. As the music ended, we slowed our steps and slowly pulled apart and looked into each others eyes. At that moment I felt a special sensation between us. It was powerful, hypnotizing and as I am frozen in the moment, Jim leaned toward me and kissed me with the tenderness of a prince in a fairy tale. The kiss kept the music playing in my head. I had always been self conscious about displays of affection in public, but on this day I felt like the princess. If the world was watching I didn't care. Jim was the prince and I was standing in a dream. As we parted the kiss I noticed we were the only ones on the dance floor. I was still floating as we walked back to our table. We sat and started talking with a casual comfort that two people acquire after they have known each other for years. This was turning out to be a magical evening.

There were more dances with nearly identical pleasures. I thought about how this evening started out uncomfortable, yet turned into an unforgettable night. It was near 3 AM before we arrived home, and we were feeling like old friends. The question of where Jim was going to sleep was now in front of me, but I wasn't nervous about it any more. I offered Jim a couple of options for sleeping arrangements.

As we drank one more beer from my refrigerator I asked, "Where do you want to sleep? I can take the couch, or you can take the couch, or you could take my bed or…"

He cut me off and said, "I would like to sleep wherever you sleep."

"That would be upstairs." I said.

We both retired to my bed and the fairy tale continued.

Sunday morning started late. Jim and I slept until nearly 10 AM. We went downstairs and made coffee. We talked about the wedding and we both felt glad we left early and went to the bar. Jim asked if there was someplace we could go to get some lunch and do something to enjoy the beautiful sunshine that was illuminating my house. I suggested we go back to town and get take-out and sit on the rocks by the lake. Jim agreed.

We had burgers and fries in our laps as we sat watching the ducks and gulls building their bravery to come closer in hopes of getting some of our lunch. Jim and I talked about what a great evening we had and laughed about some of the turn of events. The mood got a little more serious and we started talking about what time Jim would be leaving. We talked about what we might do next. The conversation centered on next weekend at his place or mine. We talked about knowing when the right person came along. We were both sure we knew it with our first spouses only to find out how wrong we were. We both felt there was something that felt right between us now. But we both knew we needed to give it some time and deal with circumstances to find out. Neither of us were in a hurry to tie a bad knot again.

Over the next few months we continued to see each other by taking turns at each other's places. Jim had met Dale and Bret and appeared to get along well with them. Bret had problems at school and was suspended. He changed schools and came to live with me.

Jim supported me more than I ever dreamed he would. He met my Dad and talked with him like he was a part of the family. Dad's cancer made it nearly impossible for him to put words together for any conversation, but Jim took it all in stride.

On Memorial Day, Mom had a family picnic with as many relatives attending as possible. Dad was looking forward to seeing everyone even though he was unable to stay up very long at one time. We had a backyard cookout with cousins, nieces, nephews and in-laws. Right after lunch Dad had to nap. I walked into the house with him to keep him from falling. He lay on the couch and tried to talk. Dad's ability to talk clearly disappeared a few months ago and he would struggle so much to say things and then get angry because he couldn't speak so any of us could understand. But today was different.

He paused, looked up at me and said, "Jim is nice guy?"

I smiled and said, "Yes, he is a very nice guy."

Dad, still looking at me, "He looks like a keeper?"

"Yes," I said, "I believe he's a keeper."

"Good, you're happy."

"Yes," I replied, "I'm happy."

The amazing thing about this conversation was that each word was spoken exactly correct. I got the feeling he needed to say these things and God gave him the ability one last time. I was glad he saw the things in Jim I had. I was glad to know that he too thought we were good together.

Over the 4th of July long weekend, I went to Jim's. His daughter, Heather was visiting him and I was meeting her for the first time. She was 11, soon to be 12 in September. She was very sweet and we all appeared to enjoy each other's company very much. We were able to spend time with all of Jim's family. We had a backyard picnic with Jim's parents, his grandmother, and Heather. By this time Jim and I had talked about moving in together and the reasonable option was for Jim to move into my house. I had a full-time job and he would have more opportunity to find a new job more suited to his background. We had decided to move his belongings at the end of the month and announced the move to the family. Even though they all said they would definitely miss him being around, they expressed sincere happiness at the change.

MOVING JIM AND GOODBYE DAD

J uly 30, was the day Jim would leave the town where he'd grown up. Except for a few years when he went to college and worked for a foundry, he had lived his life in this small town.

I arrived Friday night so Jim and I could pack. I drove my Dad's wood rack truck to load Jim's belongings and furniture. He lived in a nice apartment above a garage. Some of the furniture came with the apartment so there weren't many large pieces. I parked the truck at the apartment and Jim and I left to get something to eat before we started packing.

The local restaurants were bars so we had a few drinks first and met up with the local crowd of people. We socialized a lot longer than I thought we should, but this was Jim's move and I would wait until he was ready to start the process.

The packing process was completely ignored on Friday. Jim's friends wanted to party with him one last time. I understood that and we really had a great time. The group moved from the bar to Otis's (a long time friend of Jim's) trailer in the woods to have a campfire and do some serious reminiscing. We left to go back to the apartment about 4 AM. At the party everyone volunteered to help with the move. I felt better about that.

Jim didn't cook, so there weren't any "fixings" for coffee and I knew we would be starting late and slow. Jim was especially slow to get going because of his reactions to alcohol. Being allergic to most of the ingredients in beer gave him terrible hangovers. I don't think we actually started moving his belongings until noon.

The moving of Jim's belongings showed me a side of him I had not seen before which was his extreme attention to every minute detail. He wanted to cover every inch of his television so it wouldn't get scratched. He repositioned it on the truck at least a dozen times. The couch had to be covered and moved and changed and moved. I was getting panicky because the day was flying by and there was just he and I to load. The friends that promised to help were obviously hung over because they didn't show up. There was a storm predicted to hit somewhere between his house and mine. The forecasters called for severe conditions with thunder, lightening, wind, torrential rain and possible hail and tornado warnings were in effect.

Finally, around 6 PM we were packed and on our way. Jim said he would drive the truck and I should take his car. As we started out I realized there weren't any taillights or brake lights working on the truck. I got Jim's attention by flashing the headlights of his car and I told him the problem. We decided to drive close together so I could use the brake and tail lights of his car. I was very nervous about this whole trip, but we were on our way now and there was no turning back.

The clouds were moving faster than we were and it wouldn't be long before we would encounter the storm that was predicted. We were about thirty miles from my house. I had told Dale and Bret to meet us at the house about 6 PM, but now it was closer to 9 PM and the weather was looking dreadful. We kept driving as fast as we could. I prayed the boys were there and ready to help at least cover this load of furniture—and the television.

As we pulled into my driveway the boys were standing on the porch. I parked Jim's car in the lawn and jumped out. It was starting to sprinkle and the wind was blowing quite hard already. I told the boys to quickly move the cars (mine and Dale's) so we could back the truck into the garage. They both jumped to the task and I told Jim to turn the truck around and back it into the garage.

Everyone moved with the precision of professionals and just as we got the truck into the garage, the storm came with all its fury. The wind picked up so much we could not stand on the porch. The rain came down so hard we could not see the road. The thunder and lightening illuminated the fields around the house. All of us stood in the house and expressed how lucky we were to have gotten the truck in the garage just in time.

The storm traveled so fast that it was over in about 15 minutes. The sky was gray and the black clouds had passed to the east. We all talked about what our next plan of attack would be and we decided to get something to eat and unload tomorrow.

It didn't take long for Jim to adjust to his new surroundings. He was a neat freak and kept up with household chores while I was at work.

I would cook and we would do everything else together. He was very self conscious about not having a job, but I continued to remind him sometimes things take time. During that time Jim was around to help Mom with Dad on a few occasions and that made me feel good. Dad and Jim had very limited gesture type conversations. Dad was failing rapidly now and words came only one or two at a time and were difficult to understand. Jim told me he looked and acted peaceful on the days he was with him. The last two weeks of August his behavior was mostly unresponsive. On weekends I would help Mom change his diapers and dress his open sores. September 8, at 5 AM I received a call from Mom saying Dad had passed away in his sleep. I immediately went to her house. She called the rest of the family.

I walked into the family room where he lay on the couch. He looked like he was asleep. I reached down and touched his face. It was cold. I thought he must have died much earlier, but I didn't say anything.

Mom finished the immediate calls and now stood next to me.

"I'm glad it is over for him." I said.

"Yes, it's a blessing really." Mom replied. "He just wasn't able to be himself over the past few months."

"Well, his suffering is over and I'm thankful for that." I said solemnly and without tears, which surprised me.

I had never seen a dead body before except in funeral homes, where they had been prepared for showing, which I always hated. I knew it was more of a tradition to lay a deceased person out for friends and family to pay their last respects, but it wasn't like they were going to have eye contact to say goodbye. My thoughts were wandering.

"It was odd, really." Mom broke the silence and pulled me back to reality.

"What?"

Mom continued, "Well, last night when I went to check on him before I went to bed, he made sounds and gestures which I couldn't understand. But I had the feeling he was asking me to stay in the room with him. I asked if that was what he wanted and he gestured again and settled down. So I told him I would stay and sat near him in the recliner where he could see me. That was the last movement he made."

"He must have known he was going. They say dying people know," I comforted.

"Must be he did." Mom concluded.

Our solemn moment was broken by the sound of a car. It was Jim.

"Oh, I forgot to call the minister." Mom declared. "Would you call her for me? It looks like there is a sheriff pulling into the driveway."

"Sure." I answered, as she went to the door.

Within a few minutes there were more people arriving. Dick and Jane, Dad's sister and her husband, and at least two or three sheriff's officers were now filling the house.

I called the minister.

After the third ring, a sleepy voice questioned, "Hello?"

I started telling her who I was and when I got to the part when I had to say, "My father has just passed away," I started crying and couldn't talk. The minister had gotten enough information to know what was going on.

"I'll be right there, Laura." She assured me.

Mom was now busy tending to people and questions. When people die at home there are lots of procedures to follow. All the family members had been notified. Lyle and Trixie were on their way. The minister, Dad's sister, the ambulance people, coroner and sheriff deputies were all there for protocol and support. There were photos to take and official ruling out of foul play. After the investigation was complete, the coroner and officers loaded Dad's body into a black body bag (just like the ones on TV) and onto a gurney. They were maneuvering it through the sliding doors to go onto the open porch. It was then when Sophie, Dad's Bassett Hound, gave one long dog moaning cry. Everyone reacted to that sound. In seconds relatives were sobbing and the officials remarked in disbelief. Until that moment, she had been quietly observing the activities as she lay in her spot in front of the fireplace in full view of the couch where Dad had laid. During the procedures she was almost forgotten, but now she said her goodbye too.

The next few days were busy with all the typical arrangements for Dad's funeral. All of us kids were there to help Mom through this difficult time. This was the first funeral that we had to make decisions like selecting a casket, flowers, clothes for Dad to wear, closed casket or not. Mom had already purchased the grave plot and Dad had worked with the minister for his selections of songs and bible text for his service. Mom had Dad's only suit ready for him to be dressed in, but that didn't feel right to me. Dad hated wearing a suit and I thought of all he had been through, maybe he should go out in "his style". I talked to Trixie about it and she agreed when I suggested Dad be dressed in his bib overalls and his chambray shirt. Trixie called Dick and he also agreed. Then they told me to get mother to go along with the idea.

I walked into Mom's kitchen and she was sitting at the table.

"Hi. How are you doing?" I inquired.

"Oh, I'm fine." she replied. "How are you?"

"Good." I confirmed. "I talked to Trixie earlier and we wondered what clothes you were going to have Dad buried in."

"Well, I had his suit cleaned last month and was going to dress him in that." she declared. "Why?"

"Well we all knew how much he hated his suit and dreaded wearing it. We thought he should be dressed in the clothes he felt comfortable in."

"You're right. He did hate dressing up in a suit. What did you have in mind?" she asked.

"We thought he should be in his bib overalls and chambray shirt, like he wore every day. It just seems right to let him dress the way we all remembered him looking." I replied.

I watched Mom's expression. She was clearly pondering the idea. I was surprised she was taking so long to give me her answer.

"Have you talked to Lyle, Dick and Trixie about it?" She questioned.

"Yes. We all agreed we wanted him to wear his barn clothes. They just told me I had to convince you. I didn't think that would be a problem. Is it?" I held my breath for a moment waiting for her answer. She acted like I was taking control of a decision that was hers to control. I waited. She looked down at the table, expressionless, motionless. After a minute, maybe longer, she broke the silence.

"Well, I was going to have a closed casket service. But if everyone agrees, I don't see why we can't. I mean, after all, that is the way he dressed almost his whole life. He only wore the suit for you kids' weddings and whatever funerals we went to. I just bought him a pair of overalls last fall and he has one chambray shirt that is in good shape. I think we could do that." she answered.

I knew she was convincing herself as she spoke. But she agreed and together we looked for Dad's best bibs and shirt.

The funeral was the final goodbye. As painful as that was, my mother shed only a few tears at the service. We were all worried the final reality of Dad's passing would hit her sometime down the road. But it didn't. She went on with life. She was now able to do things she had been unable to do in the past either because of Dad's care or the farm.

***

Moving away from home was much more of a transition for Jim than I think either of us expected to deal with, but we were committed to being together. Jim had spent the last couple of years just existing. After the divorce, his ex-wife moved out of town with their daughter, and the loss of his job of 13 years left him pretty devastated. Jim was on his way to becoming something less than he could be. I saw his fear of leaving the only place he had known as home, yet he admitted he needed to start over. He reassured me, he knew in his gut this was right.

Now with a new location and many more job possibilities, life looked more promising. He had always been a very loving and caring man to me and we had a lot of interests we held in common, but he was a town kid and I was a farm girl. There were times we realized we had differences in our thinking and problem solving methods.

After three months of sobering up, learning to live in the country where it was so quiet you could hear ants walk in the grass, and dealing with a family death, Jim had been hired as an engineer in an electronics company. All in all I thought things were starting to fall into place and I was feeling that maybe we could have a normal life together.

JUST WHEN YOU THINK ALL IS WELL—IT USUALLY ISN'T! BEWARE!

Jim's mother called one Sunday evening in September. She asked "if they could come see where he was living". Jim was a little nervous about the visit, but he granted the request for the next Sunday. Suddenly I felt nervous about the meeting too.

I had always gotten the impression that Jim's parents thought I was a good person. They appeared to welcome me with open arms. Jim's father was talkative, but only in streaks. Sometimes he would just wander off with his pipe. I worried about that a little because now they would be at my house. The only wandering Don would be able to do would be down the road or up into the woods, and he just didn't impress me as the kind of person who would do that.

It was early afternoon when they arrived and we exchanged hugs, greetings, and introductions to Dale and Bret. As we settled into conversation, we heard the roar of a motorcycle. Bret looked out the living room window to see a motorcycle pulling into my driveway.

"Mom," Bret said, "Its Paul, what are you gonna do now?"

OH MY GOD, AFTER ALL THIS TIME HE HAS TO PICK TODAY!

My mind raced. What was I going to do? Jim knew about Paul and his habit of wandering in and out. He knew I had no way of telling him he couldn't come see me anymore until he showed up again. Too bad it had to happen on this day. I had to talk to him and that meant I would need to talk to him alone, right then. I wanted it to be out of the view of all the people in my house at the time.

I excused myself and assured them I would be back in a few minutes. I hoped Jim would be able to smooth things over and maybe keep the boys from giving their stories of Paul and me.

I met Paul in the driveway and asked him to walk with me up the lane towards the woods. As we walked I told him I had met someone and his parents were visiting. Paul expressed his happiness for me. He said he knew I needed more than he could give me. I thanked him for his kindness. He asked about coming over to see me and I told him he could if he wanted. I didn't get what he was implying until he asked if he should not come if the white and gray cars were in the driveway. I told him the white car was Jim's parent's car and the gray car was Jim's. He could visit if Jim was there. I thought it would be nice if he met him.

ARE YOU NUTS! HE IS ASKING YOU IF HE CAN COME SLEEP WITH YOU BEHIND JIM'S BACK!

The conversation fell off after that. I suddenly felt incredibly stupid, but chose not to say anymore. I walked back to his motorcycle with him and asked about Annabelle. He encouraged me to visit her because he had been quite busy and unable to see her very much. I told him I would.

He mounted his motorcycle and drove away. I took a deep breath and let out a sigh of relief. Now I had to face the group in the house.

YOU DON'T NEED TO GIVE THEM DETAILS! YOU JUST CUT THIS GUY OUT OF YOUR LIFE LIKE YOU SHOULD HAVE DONE A LONG TIME AGO. HE'S THE GOOF FOR SHOWING UP AFTER

*10 MONTHS, AND THERE WERE <u>FOUR</u> CARS IN THE YARD! HE
SHOULDN'T HAVE EVEN STOPPED!*

I smiled to myself, thinking, "Yeah, right."

YOU WANTED CLOSURE!

I entered the house and didn't explain anything to anyone. We had
refreshments and walked around the house. We went for a ride around
the neighborhood. Jim and I showed them where my mother lived and
the homestead where I grew up. The visit was pleasant and soon over as
they had to leave to drive the two and a half hours to get home.

That night, when Jim and I went to bed, we talked about Paul. I
told him I was glad it was over and assured him that I had not seen Paul
the entire time I was seeing him. Jim believed me and we both curled up
feeling glad this day was over and glad we were together.

Jim's job was just what he needed to feel good about his talent
as an engineer. He was making decent money and I had just changed
jobs to work as a marketing manager for a photographer, promoting
photographic art. Jim had been in contact with Heather and her mother
in Minnesota, so he could reestablish his child support, which he had not
been paying because of his lack of regular employment.

Heather had been going through some rough times with her preteen
growing stage. She and Jim called each other regularly, but they often
had emotional conversations where Jim would try to reason with her
about her problems at home. She kept telling him about how bad things
were. She was fighting with her mother and stepfather, and refused to
go to school. They had just moved to Minnesota from Connecticut and
Heather was not making the transition well. Jim received a call from
his ex-wife after Christmas saying Heather had run away. He found out
the root of Heather's problems involved drinking and smoking. She was
now in a shelter for runaway teens. It was only temporary housing for
runaways. It allowed the child to get help from counselors so she could
go back home.

Heather now insisted she come live with us. Jim and I talked at
great length about it and thought we could help. We could offer her a
stable environment closer to her original home and grandparents. She had
not lived with Jim since she was three and he felt guilty about his lack
of involvement while she was growing up. She had moved more than ten
times in twelve years and that didn't count the first three years of her life.

She never really settled anywhere. Jim and I made the decision to have Heather come live with us. Jim was very emphatic about rules in the house and insisted she go to school as soon as she arrived. She agreed. It was mid January when she came to live with us.

Jim and I soon realized we needed to set more rules and hire a babysitter to help enforce the rules Heather agreed to follow. But everything we tried to teach Heather about boundaries and responsibilities turned our world into a war zone.

The strongest thing Jim and I had together was our ability to talk things through. We had no idea our life together could get so complicated. Jim and I thought we could be good parents. Heather brought her cigarettes and preteen attitude and her talent for manipulating the adults in her life into our world. She and Bret had issues which negatively affected the living environment.

Bret would ask me "Why does she get away with smoking at twelve? How come she gets to stay up past 10 o'clock on school nights?"

That's when we learned about her cigarette stash. She blatantly smoked in front of Bret like that was her routine.

We started checking her bedroom. We found arrangements to go to basketball games that ended up going elsewhere with older boys in their car. It was a very difficult time. Through it all, Jim and I talked about everything and sometimes we agreed on things and sometimes not, but the one thing that was constant was our desire to stay together. We talked about marriage. We joked that if we got married it would be more difficult to split up. I guess we thought it would force us to stay together. So on July 21, 1989, Jim and I were married by a justice of the peace, arranged by my sister, in a ceremony that took place in a creek bed on their property.

The arrangements were kept from all our family members, including the children. We used the excuse of a family visit. It was Friday night near 8 PM before we delivered Heather to her great grandma's house. We went to the baseball field to find Trixie and Kyle before going to the creek. They had been celebrating for us most of the day. The justice arrived at the creek shortly after, while the clouds were moving in for a summer thunderstorm. (The paperwork was officiated as rain drops fell and lightening streaked, we said our "I dos.") We had a private party by the creek. Trixie brought champagne and cake. It was a sheet cake that said "This is your wedding cake". She didn't think to bring plates, forks, or a knife so we used our fingers to dig out a piece of cake, to later wash in the creek.

After several hours of celebrating at the creek and the bars downtown we drove to another town to get a motel room. Jim was so drunk he fell asleep in the car until morning. This makes for memories to laugh at the rest of our lives.

The next day we told Jim's family and they were happy for us. Jim and I took a few days in Niagara Falls to digest the plans for the future. We talked about telling my mother. Jim gave that honor to me alone.

The Monday after our vacation Jim returned to work and I drank two cups of courage before going to Mom's house. I walked into the kitchen. She was standing at the stove.

"Good morning. Do you have the tea kettle on?" I cheerfully remarked.

"Yes," She replied, "what's going on?"

Taking a deep breath first, I stated, "I wanted to tell you that you have a new son-in-law!"

Enthusiasm exploded out of her mouth with the words, "**I do... who?**"

My heart sank (again) and with somber disappointment in my voice I said, "Jim. We got married last weekend at Trixie's."

She realized her reaction was one of those "speak without thinking" comments.

"Trixie made arrangements with the Justice of the Peace in town. She and Kyle stood up for us. We just felt it was the best way to do it considering the problems with the kids and all. I'll pass on the cup of tea for now. I have to go to the bank and a few other places. I'll call you later when I get back."

YOU THOUGHT SHE WOULD HAVE KNOWN THAT ONE, HUH?

***

Bret had gotten his GED and a job, so I told him it was time for him to get his own place, which he did with a friend. Heather continued to be a challenge and we tried all the resources available to us to make it work, but it didn't. In a huge family argument I asked Jim and her to leave the house until they came to a decision.

Jim and Heather went for a walk. Jim told Heather he would not allow her to come between us. He told her he thought it best if she went back to Minnesota with her Mom. She had asked many times to do that in the past, but I kept objecting thinking we could get through the rough times. I was wrong. Jim agreed he didn't have the strength to continue this battle either, so on July 7 we flew Heather back to her mother and stepfather.

The week after Heather went back to live with her mother Jim was laid off at the electronics company. I had been laid off, but was working temp work in an accounting department of a large local company. The people I worked with were great and the work was low stress. I was relieved to live without the stress for a change. Jim and I were positive he would find another job and we would be fine.

JIM AND I MOVE

THIS IS GOING TO BE BETTER! BESIDES, YOU DON'T HAVE A CHOICE!

I sat on a box looking at my neighbor's house two tenths of a mile away, debating whether I should drive there to borrow a plastic spoon. The movers came today and boxed up all our belongings, including the plastic silverware.

DO YOU WANT TO EAT OR NOT! GO GET THE DAMN SPOON!

I got into my car and drove next door. Joanne came to the door.

"Could I borrow a plastic spoon?" I inquired. "The movers pack EVERYTHING, really!" Joanne laughed and said, "Sure. I saw the moving trucks at the house when I went to work. Are you ready to go?"

"Yes, I guess." I quietly responded. "The movers will pick up everything tomorrow. But I hadn't thought about them packing absolutely everything, including my plastic forks."

She laughed and said, "You can keep the fork. Do you want to stay for dinner? I'm just getting it ready and Archie will be home soon. It's no problem. You know me, I always make extra."

I smiled, "I'd love to, but Missi has been pacing the floor all day probably wondering what is going on, so I better go back to settle her down. Thank you though. I will call when I get there and my furniture is delivered." I paused for a moment then looked at Joanne, "I'm gonna miss you guys."

Joanne reached for me to hug. I fought back tears.

"Don't worry, we'll be down to see you guys and you'll always be invited to the 4th of July party."

I hugged her back, "Be sure to tell Archie "Hi and Bye" for me." I said.

We both laughed and she wished me luck as I went to my car to go home. Joanne was a good neighbor and lived with Archie. We had things in common—we all had been divorced. They always had a 4th of July party which we went to and had some great times. Whenever either of us needed anything, the other would be there. They were old fashioned country neighbors and I would miss them.

I went into the house and opened the can of Spaghetti O's with a pocket knife can opener. I heated the can on the stove (a trick I learned from Jim). Missi looked at me with fear and confusion in her eyes. I smiled and told her it would be okay. I assured her I wasn't leaving her this time. I thought about the past. I realized my life had become so unpredictable. I didn't think it was supposed to be perfect, but every time I think my life is good—something happens. I thought about the chain of events that brought me here sitting on a box, with Missi, looking out the window, eating my slightly warm Spaghetti O's with a borrowed plastic fork. I felt lost. Jim must have felt the same way the day before he moved.

***

Jim and I thought things would be calmer and more enjoyable after Heather went back to her mother. We hoped for boring, but that didn't happen. For several months Jim sent resumes and interviewed without luck. He sent a resume to an old customer he worked closely with, thinking his 13 years of experience in the passenger railcar business would be noticed. It was, finally, in late November. After a couple of interviews and job discussions, they offered him an engineering job. Jim accepted the job and was excited about working with trains again. But now it was my turn to move.

I was laid off from my temp job, just as we found out Jim would start working seventy miles from home. The company had a relocation package and would move us. The relocation process started and now I had to tell my mother about our move.

We hadn't gotten confirmation about the job until January 29th. That left us with very little time to find a place to live. Jim and I went down that weekend to find either a house or apartment that would allow pets. All day on Saturday we looked at apartments and found nothing that was to our liking. We called on one house that sounded promising, but didn't get an answer. Feeling discouraged, we ate dinner in our hotel room and looked at more ads. Sunday morning we made one last attempt to see the house where we didn't get an answer the day before. After the fourth ring, a man answered. He told us where the house was located and he could meet us there in about thirty minutes.

As we drove down a back road to the next town, we watched for the road we were to turn onto. When we found it we were shocked with what we saw. The road was one car wide with patches of black top in calico patterns up the road that disappeared into a large clump of pine trees. Two of the houses didn't look like anyone lived in them. We read the numbers on the four houses on the street and found the number we were looking for had to have been beyond the trees, or so we hoped. Slowly we continued up the road and as we emerged through the trees we saw a darling little house. One and a half stories with a separate garage, a back porch and yard completely circled with fence. It nestled in a glen between the bases of two mountains. There was a stream in the glen across the front of the slightly rolling yard. Mature pine trees encapsulated the yard.

The landlord pulled his truck in right behind us. He immediately got out and cheerfully greeted us. He was a tall thin man, older than us with glasses and very worn work boots. He had a country gait and manner to him. He was polite, friendly and had a very dry sense of humor. As we walked to the front door of the house I thought this location was perfect. Oddly enough, the siding on the house was identical to the house we were leaving. Right down to the color, medium green.

The front door opened into a 13 x 26' living room with three side windows that faced the glen. A very large picture window included side windows that just about filled the west wall of the room. The view overlooked the driveway with the silhouette of a large sugar maple tree cast into the window. There was a small room off the living room that faced the mountains and through the living room to the right were the kitchen and bathroom. The kitchen was long and narrow with 1950's cabinets and windows. The bathroom was large with space for washer, dryer, basement door and a staircase to the upstairs bedroom. Off the kitchen was a closed porch which was attached to a screen porch. The porches opened into a nice back yard that backed up to woods and a neighbor barely visible atop the hill behind.

We asked if we could rent it right away and the landlord with quirky smile said, "With a deposit and first month's rent, you could do anything you want."

"Could I do the painting and maybe wallpaper the downstairs bedroom to help the process along? Driving over three hours a day for work is hard and we want to move as soon as possible."

His facial expression changed, as if trying to hide a really big smile.

"You can do anything you want and charge the materials to my account at the local building store." he said.

This was a dream come true. I asked about pets and he didn't have a problem with the pets. I had Missi, Bret's cat, Kitty, and Hio who had come back to me because the co-worker that had him lost his house. Shellee had passed away in the summer of 1990. We were now one medium-sized happy family.

I handed the landlord, Ken, the check for the house and he gave me a key. We felt good about our new house "in the woods". We drove home thinking how lucky we were to have called back one last time. Now all we had to do was contact the movers and tell our families the news.

The next few days I spent working with the movers. The account rep came and assessed the contents of the house. She determined how many boxes it would take to pack it up. She called me back the next day to tell me the crew would pack on March 2nd; they would load everything onto the trucks March 3. They expected to unload the day after the drive to the new location. March 3 would be my last day in my grandmother's house.

In the past eighteen months Jim and I had been dealing not only with kid problems, but coping with a deteriorating house that we thought we were buying. Mom had developed a bit of an attitude toward Jim. She viewed him as a town kid from well-to-do parents. According to her, "those people don't know anything about country living". She didn't like many of his remodeling ideas for the house. There was a time her attorney drew up paperwork for us to buy the house with twenty acres of land. I signed the proposal, but mysteriously, the paperwork vanished. The subject was never brought up again. Now I had to tell her that we would be moving away. I wasn't sure how she would react. I would soon find out.

Thursday morning, after a strong cup of courage, I went to mom's house.

As I entered the kitchen, she remarked, "You're out early, want a cup of tea?"

"No," I said, "I just finished my coffee and I can't stay long. Jim just received confirmation on his job offer. He accepted the position."

"Oh." she replied. "What kind of work will he be doing?"

"The job is in the engineering department. I don't know much about what he will be doing, but he can tell you. He'll be engineering something on passenger railcars."

She fell silent.

Feeling awkward with the length of the silence, I continued. "The company is seventy miles away and it takes a little over an hour and a half to drive, so we will be moving closer to his work. The company has a relocation package and will move us. We went down last weekend and found a small house to rent. The movers are coming March 2nd to pack everything and then move us on the 3rd.

The dreaded silence returned.

MAYBE SHE THOUGHT ABOUT THE LAST TIME SHE BLURTED SOMETHING OUT BEFORE THINKING ABOUT HER CHOICE OF WORDS!

I didn't know what more to say. I thought maybe I should try to further explain the situation to see if that helped.

"I..." I started.

"I need a month's notice for the rent ya know." She retorted.

Her tone was curt and emphatic, laced with anger. Her tone and facial expression made me feel like I was the tenant from hell and she was not happy that my notice was four days short of a month.

I looked at her. She was looking down at the table. Her facial expression was taut and angry. She repositioned herself in her chair as if to sit taller than me.

ARE YOU SERIOUS? THIS IS HER DAUGHTER! THE ONE WHO HAS LIVED IN THIS HOUSE FOR FIVE YEARS, REMODELED AND MAINTAINED IT AND THE BARNS ACROSS THE ROAD, PAYING FOR MOST OF THE UPGRADES OUT OF HER OWN POCKET! YOU WANT A FULL MONTH'S RENT BECAUSE THE NOTICE IS FOUR DAYS SHORT?

I took a deep breath and said, "I understand. I will give you the next months rent before I leave on the third."

At that I turned and walked out the kitchen to my car. I left as quickly as possible and went home to cry. The tears started before I got out of her driveway and by the time I got back to the house I could hardly see through the tears. I sat on the porch and cried while Missi quivered in fear by my side.

That weekend Jim told his parents. They were happier about the announcement than mom. It would cut off an hour of driving time for them to visit. Next we called some friends, Dale, and Bret and asked them to meet us for drinks at a favorite hang out. We told everyone about Jim's new job and that we would be moving by March third. Bret was very upset. He and I talked about us moving away and he eventually realized it was something Jim and I had to do. Dale was fine with the move and we all spoke of future fun-filled visits to a new place.

***

I finished my Spaghetti O's and thought about going to bed on a mattress without sheets. I gathered my notepad of tasks for tomorrow and looked around to see what I had to put in my car. I would have to find some way to put two dogs and the cat in the car without them fighting. Thank you, Dad, for those potato crates you made.

I had things the movers wouldn't take that had to go into my car. I planned to stack things to have just enough space for Hio in the back seat to lie down. Missi could lie on the front passenger seat. Kitty, well she would have to go in the trunk under a potato crate with everything else that had to go in the trunk. I thought I was all set. The movers arrived around 8 AM. I was ready to go and anxious to start settling my new house. There were a few moments of concern when the movers told me they couldn't take the motorcycles with the gas tanks full. I was horrified and the head guy said they would stick them on the back end of the smaller truck and pretend they didn't know. I promised I wouldn't tell a soul. By 3 PM they had finished loading everything. I quickly swept the floors, took one last look and locked the back door. I put Hio in my car, Kitty under the crate and Missi in the front seat on top of the pillow and blanket I slept on the night before. Then I drove to Mom's house.

I walked into the kitchen and found her sitting at the table as usual.

"Hi." I said with forced cheerfulness.

"Hi." she repeated back with the same.

"The movers just finished loading. I swept the floors in the dining room and kitchen, but didn't vacuum the rugs in the living room or upstairs. They had already loaded the vacuum cleaner. The doors are locked and here are the keys to the front and back doors."

I placed the keys on the table and reached in my purse to get my checkbook.

"I have the month's rent for you." I said.

She didn't look at me. She just said, "Oh, don't worry about that. You don't have to give me that."

"Are you sure?" I asked, "Because I can give you the rent." I wanted to give her the rent just to comply with her earlier demand.

"No, I'm sure." She replied. "You don't have to do that." Her voice was soft and slow. She sat motionless staring into her tea cup.

"Thank you," I said, and paused. There was that silence again. *WHAT IS THERE LEFT TO SAY? SHE'S NOT TALKING! JUST LEAVE!*

"I have to go." I said. "I want to get back before the movers leave, in case they need me for anything else."

She didn't get up from her chair and she didn't look at me. I just turned and walked out the door to my car and drove away. For an instant it felt like the last time I left home when Dick told me to get out, but I quickly cast the thought out of my head. I couldn't cry now. It would be too hard to explain to the movers. I didn't want them to wonder why I was crying, so I fought back the tears for the mile drive back to the house.

As I drove into the driveway, the movers were just closing the doors of the smaller truck.

"Are you guys all set?" I inquired.

"Yes, I believe we are." the crew supervisor replied.

"Are you guys okay with the directions to the other house?" I asked.

"Yeah. We have been talking about it and getting loaded this earlier, we can deliver this tonight. We know the area and we all live closer to there than here. We should be done unloading by 9 o'clock if you want."

"I would love that!" I exclaimed. "If you are set to leave, I'll head out and will get the animals settled before you arrive. Back up to the front door to unload."

"That sounds just fine with us." The supervisor confirmed.

"I'll see you there."

I got into my car, gave comforting words to the dogs and started driving south. As I pulled away from my house, my grandmother's house, I could see the movers pulled out right behind me from my rear view mirror.

I looked at Missi, and said, "We can never go back, but it will be okay."

I petted her head to try to ease her stress.

I was excited about getting to the house. I dismissed thoughts of my mother and my grandmother's house. Kitty would remind me at every traffic light and stop sign that she was scared and not happy. She would yowl at the top of her cat voice to convey the message. The people at the crossings would look around with puzzled expressions, looking, trying to find the cat in distress.

It was about 5:30 PM when I arrived at our new residence. I quickly unloaded Hio and Missi and put them in the screen porch. Then I put Kitty in the house. She found the basement door ajar and sought refuge there. I was glad for that. I barely got the animals settled before the phone rang. It was Jim.

"Hi! You're there already." He exclaimed

"Yeah, the movers finished the loading sooner than they expected, so I was able to leave earlier."

"Did you have any trouble driving down?" He asked.

"No, not at all and the movers left right behind me. They said they would unload us tonight. What time can you come home?" I asked.

"In a few minutes." he said. "I'll stop and pick up something to eat."

"Great!" I resounded, "I'd forgotten about dinner. That'll be perfect."

I grabbed the dog food from the car and fed the dogs. I was unloading things from my car when Jim arrived. He petted the dogs and asked how they handled the ride. He laughed when I told him about Kitty and that she was seeking shelter in the basement. As I asked about his day, we ate submarine sandwiches on the steps of the screen porch.

Within an hour the trucks were coming up the dead-end street to our house. The big truck with all the household stuff backed up to the front door. We all started the parade of boxes until they could get to the furniture. Sixty four boxes in the closed porch made it near impossible to walk through. They brought in the couch, chairs, bed, guest bed, washer and dryer, kitchen table and chairs, then hooked up and assembled anything that needed to be. By 11 PM the trucks left and I made the bed. Jim and I sat on the couch with a beer to unwind. We looked at our new house and talked about how things would be okay.

I had a better understanding of how difficult it must have been for Jim to leave home like he did. I felt the uncertainty of change now too. But this little house was perfect for us. We found the best place for all of us. The fenced yard completely surrounded with trees made it the paradise built for Jim, me, Missi, Kitty and Hio.

The next day I started to settle the stack of boxes. I would occasionally take breaks in the yard with the dogs. Kitty came out of the basement the next day seeking food. After a few days she would wander onto the porch then around the perimeter of the house. After a couple of weeks, she acted more comfortable with her new residence. Missi and Hio were enjoying the freedom they had to run free in the yard and play with each other every day.

I was able to paint the living room and wallpaper the downstairs bedroom in the two weeks before the move. Now I could put our personal touches in the house. With spring just around the corner, I planned to plant flowers, just like at Grandma's house. As the days and weeks went by I had a new outlook on my life. I was eligible for unemployment insurance and wanted to go back to college for my bachelor's degree. After a little investigating I enrolled in college and my classes started in April. I was amazed how everything fell in place so perfectly.

I had left friends and family, yet I was in a new place making new friends from college and Jim's work. We were actually socializing more after the move than before. Dale and Bret now shared an apartment and would come down to visit and sometimes stay overnight. They seemed to enjoy a weekend away from home. I got to see my sister more often and that was wonderful. Jim would call Heather to see how she was doing. For a while her anger was very apparent in their conversations. Slowly the anger began to fade and their father-daughter talks improved. They always seemed to demand the same things from each other yet unable to give until the other person gave first. They say time is the healer of all. I hoped that was true.

The spring and summer were very busy for me, but I was having a great time. Many times I thought of the chain of events that brought me to this place. There was always one unsettling thought that wouldn't go away. Since the day I left my grandmother's house and dropped off the keys to mom, I'd not heard from her. I received a birthday card and it was just signed, "Happy Birthday, Mother." She used to sign them with "Mom" and at the time it felt very cold. I thought back about it. It still felt cold and hurtful. I tried to figure out what I had done wrong. I just didn't understand why I was treated like I didn't belong in this family.

By the end of September the thoughts of my mother's absence had gnawed at me until I got the impulse to do something about it. I had to put the nagging questions away. What did I do to make her angry with me? Was she so angry that she couldn't call to see how we were doing? I was afraid to call her, thinking we would get into a shouting match. I didn't want that to happen, so I decided to write her a letter asking why. After rereading the letter about thirty times I placed it into an envelope and sent it, wondering and worrying of her reaction.

Three days later I found out. It was afternoon when the phone rang.

"Hello." I answered.

"Well, hello!" she replied.

I realized it was mom (Mother) and was a little unsure of what to say. I paused, waiting for her to say more.

"I got your letter," she paused, "and to be honest with you, I'm completely dumbfounded by it. Where did you get the idea I was mad at you?" She questioned.

Much to my surprise and disappointment her voice was too friendly, almost dripping with sweetness. She spoke as if there was nothing wrong. She talked as if I left just yesterday.

"Why would you think I was mad at you?" She asked.

"Well, you seemed upset when I gave you the keys to the house."

"No, I wasn't upset." she said in an odd bubbly comforting reply.

"I didn't hear from you since I moved and I was afraid to call thinking I had really made you angry." I admitted while holding my breath for her reaction.

"Oh, no I wasn't angry. I just thought you would be busy settling into your new place."

FOR SEVEN MONTHS?

I immediately felt angry.

"Did you think I would be so busy that I couldn't answer the phone for seven months?"

She paused. I heard her exhale into the phone. She took another deep breath.

"No." she sheepishly uttered with a hint of her sarcasm.

"If I have done something wrong," I continued, "I really need to know what it is. I feel completely disconnected from you. I have been racking my brain to figure what I did to cause this separation. Now, you're telling me there is nothing wrong? I haven't heard a word from you for seven months. What else am I supposed to think?"

There was that dreaded silence again. After what seemed to be several minutes, she answered.

"Maybe I could come down to your house for a visit and we can talk."

"I would love to have you come down and see where Jim and I live." I said. "Maybe we could do lunch and talk for a while."

"Okay." She said with an almost defeated tone in her voice. "How is Friday?"

"Friday is just fine. I am up by 7, so any time is alright." I answered and continued giving her directions to our house.

We gave our goodbyes and I hung up the phone. I stood by the phone looking out the window. I felt drained. I didn't feel excited about her visit. I didn't know what I felt, but I knew I didn't feel any better about our relationship.

***

SHE'S HERE!

It was about 9 AM on Friday when she arrived. I greeted her at the porch door as she walked up the sidewalk. I was nervous, but glad she came. We exchanged greetings at the porch door and we walked around the house and yard as she commented with flower planting ideas. We both laughed about the house being the same color green as grandma's house. We went inside and I gave her the tour. She gave positive comments as we walked from room to room.

We went back to the kitchen for coffeecake and tea at the kitchen table. The conversations were simple in the beginning; weather, Jim's work and my college. This was the first time she heard about my attending college again and she seemed pleased. The conversation started to wane and I thought it might be time to bring up my letter.

"I know this is a tough subject, but I have to talk to you about my letter. I wanted you to understand the hurt I felt. When I told you Jim accepted the job offer and that we would be moving, you barely spoke to me. You didn't say ten words to me when I dropped off the keys. That made me think I must have made you angry for some reason. I was afraid to call because I didn't want to get yelling at each other over the phone. I just want us to talk about this."

The dreaded silence again. She looked down at her plate and tea cup. I looked at her and decided I would wait until she answered. After all, I had all day to wait for an answer. I had waited for seven months to know what I had done wrong.

"I don't know what you are talking about." She said, breaking the silence. "I don't know why you're upset. I don't know why you think I'm mad at you because I'm not."

SHE'S IN DENIAL! SHE ISN'T GOING TO TELL YOU! YOU DIDN'T DO ANYTHING WRONG—SHE DID AND SHE WON'T ADMIT IT! SHE WILL JUST STUMBLE THROUGH THIS CONVERSATION UNTIL IT'S OVER! WATCH AND SEE!

"When I dropped the keys, you didn't even look up from your cup of tea. I made sure you had my new phone number and yet I didn't get a call from you for seven months. What else was I supposed to think. Why did you do that to me?"

"Are you saying I am a bad mother?" She retorted.

"What? I didn't say any such thing. Where do you come up with that in what I just said?" I angrily responded.

"I tried to do everything I could for you, and this is the thanks I get." She said with cracked voice while tears formed in her eyes.

She was now fishing for a tissue from her purse. I felt panic as she took my questions and drove them to another planet. I tried several different ways to get an answer that fit my questions.

"How did I upset <u>you</u>? What did <u>I</u> do wrong?" I asked, pleadingly.

Each time, each way, her response was the same. She didn't know what I was talking about or I was saying she was a bad mother. I felt frustration first, then anger, hurt and finally defeat. She wouldn't tell me why she hadn't called me all those months, or if I had made her mad for something I did or did not do. Our conversations lasted all day with tears, tissues and angry comments. I think we both were tired when I finally gave up the mission. We both looked down at the table and the words came very slowly now. Our emotions were used up. There was no energy left to bring our buried feelings to the surface. I knew I had to lie to her to get out of this situation. I finally apologized for upsetting her, explaining I didn't mean to. I just thought she was mad at me. I wanted to know why. I couldn't look at her when I said it. When I did look up, she wasn't looking at me either. I said I felt better and thanked her for driving down. It was over. We said goodbye and we promised to call each other more often. She got into her car and drove away. As I waved to her I could hear...

I TOLD YA SO!

I went back into the house feeling exhausted. It was near 4 PM as I thought about the day. Sometimes things enter my head that make me laugh when a situation is this stressing. I thought, we didn't eat lunch and neither one of us used the bathroom after drinking a whole teakettle of tea! I smiled and went to the bathroom.

***

As time passed my emotional wounds healed to scars and my thoughts of past events became less and less vivid. I graduated with my Bachelor of Science in October the next year and was hired as a cost accounting clerk with the company where Jim worked.

I met another group of new friends, co-workers, and was having a really good time. The best times were at birthdays. The cost accounting department consisted of four people: the boss who gave our evaluations and raises, the second in charge with whom I worked directly (both named Dave) and a girl, Nancy, who handled phones and paper shuffle for all the reports. All of us had a strong sense of humor and would often play games on each other for entertainment. Birthdays however, got to be a competition—who could out do the last stunt?

One stunt I played on my counterpart for his birthday was my all time best. I went into the office about 10 PM with his best friend and Nancy. We filled his office about half full with balloons. We taped balloons to the tiny window from floor to ceiling leaving the illusion the room was full of balloons. Nancy helped me collect shredded paper to put in his desk drawers, filing cabinets and around the balloons. We all showed up at work by 7 AM so we could watch his reaction. He was surprised, to say the least! After the pranks we had gifts and cake.

On my birthday, I found a huge balloon filled with all kinds of little gifts and collectables (plus confetti so when I broke the balloon it would make a huge mess). They tied cans to my car bumper and then asked me to drive to the other plant. Of course I didn't know they were there until I went rattling off down the street. That was a riot! I had gifts and little cards from people in other departments and it was like my vision of the perfect birthday celebration I dreamed of when I was younger. I remembered thinking wishes do come true, eventually. I wished for a birthday celebration like this and now I had one. It was a time I would cherish forever.

My sister and I had been getting together more often (sometimes with our mother) and enjoyed days of shopping at nurseries for plants, Amish crafts, for homemade gifts and at the mall for "pig out lunches." Sometimes we even helped each other with landscaping and remodeling. One time during one of our morning coffee chats we (Trixie, Mom, and I) told stories of when we were kids. My sister told of the day I got in trouble for breaking the silver bank.

I started defending my position and she began laughing and said, "Yeah, I know. I broke it and took the money and you got the blame, ha, ha, ha, ha."

I was stunned she admitted it and mother sat there laughing along with her for a moment and then made the comment that she really liked that bank because it came from a dear friend of hers.

Trixie continued her confession in repartee asking "Do you remember that $10.00 bill you had? I took that, too!"

We were all laughing, but my enjoyment in this confession session just came to an abrupt end. She had no conscience about stealing the money and now, years after the fact, thought it was a huge joke! Obviously, she didn't have any concept of how her actions had hurt me (and mother) and this confession was becoming too much fun for her. I felt a revival of the anguish I felt all those years thinking I had been careless. I quickly changed the subject, asking what we had planned for the day. She and Mom followed suit spewing out suggestions of places to go for lunch. I tried to bury the past. But I took comfort in the confession. It proved I had not been the guilty person breaking the bank. Nor was I careless and lost my $10.00. I wasn't surprised to watch mom take this all in stride passing it off with little reaction.

I had "proper" conversations with my mother. I often thought she didn't realize her statements and actions came across as hurtful to me. She often reminded me that I was too sensitive and I shouldn't let things bother me. She forgot that she was the one that taught me the standards I lived by. She profoundly stated on several occasions that her relationship with her tenants was business. I thought, as her daughter, I'd be the exception. I wasn't. I know she will never tell me what she was thinking during that time and in a few years she won't remember it happened.

Trixie and I tried to be close. We tried to be sisters. It worked for a while and we enjoyed some fun times. But as the years drew on, and our lives changed, so did our relationship. Our visits became fewer and farther apart even though we lived closer now.

The fall brought us one of nature's most precious gifts. The leaves on the maple tree in our front yard turned the most incredible deep golden color I had ever seen. The sun would reflect so much color it would make the whole yard appear golden. Jim and I loved fall colors and this tree was like a pot of gold in our front yard just for us to enjoy. As the leaves fell to the ground, they became a golden carpet that we would run through with the dogs in playful dance to the music of leaves rustling, while dogs barked and nipped at our heels. We took pictures of us under the golden tree and sent them to our kids. Jim and I were having a wonderful time in our life. We were grateful that fate pushed our paths together and then on down the road.

***

Change is usually for the better. I just need to trust and believe that everything will work out. That old phrase, *"Things happen for reasons we don't understand"* seems to have deeper meaning to me now. Moving away from home made this come true. When I look back far enough I can see things that happened to me that now make sense. I realize that my brother, Dick, did me a favor by tossing me into the street!

Many times I've thought of the path my life has taken. Events of my past are now floats of memories trailing off in the distance. Yet I see new faces of unfamiliar people waving in the road ahead. Another phrase often spoken: *"There is nothing to fear but fear itself"*. I now realize just how true that is.

I know the changes in my life will take yet another turn down a foggy road, up a steep hill or around a sharp curve where I can't see what lies ahead. There will probably be ruts and potholes, rain and snow, but I know there will also be green grass, sunshine and flowers if I just keep going. But for now my life is great, perfect actually and I love it. I didn't need a trip to Willard to fix it.

DO YOU REMEMBER? JUST WHEN YOU THINK ALL IS WELL...

Made in the USA